The Truants

The Truants

Adventures Among the Intellectuals

WILLIAM BARRETT

ANCHOR PRESS/DOUBLEDAY, Garden City, New York   1982

Library of Congress Cataloging in Publication Data

Barrett, William, 1913–
    The truants: adventures among the intellectuals.

    1. New York (N.Y.)—Intellectual life.   2. Barrett,
William, 1913–   . I. Title.
F128.52.B37   1982   974.7'1043
ISBN 0-385-15966-8 AACR2
Library of Congress Catalog Card Number: 81-43141

Copyright © 1982 by William Barrett

For Delmore and Philip,
restless shades

Contents

The Truants

Prologue

A Mass for the Dead

I.

It was raining in my part of the country on February 17, 1974. The reason I remember lies before me now on my desk: a copy of the New York *Times Book Review* for that date. On its first page is a picture of Philip Rahv, dark and faintly menacing as in life. The gaze is heavy-lidded, exotic; he might be a diamond merchant in Antwerp or a mysterious agent on the old Orient Express. Only the manuscript in his hand and the books at his elbow convey that his business had been with literature. He had died more than a month earlier, and the *Times* had then given him a respectable obituary. It might have seemed that that would be it, that a great newspaper, busy with all the large and small affairs of the world, having now done its duty by him, would have passed on. But there suddenly he was; and when I opened the paper that morning, I jumped with surprise, as if Rahv himself had entered the room. I knew there would be no surcease of memories that day. Well then, let the ghosts come as they would, wreak their

1

havoc or grant their blessing as they chose, and maybe be a little exorcised in the process. A gray rainy Sunday is a good time for conducting one's own private Mass for the Dead.

But who was Philip Rahv, I imagine an impatient reader asking at this point. And why is he worth remembering at all? For anyone who knew him this last question would seem idle: even his enemies, though they might say he was not worth remembering, would find it impossible to forget him. Still, the question has its point. When one gives way to memories in public, the reader or listener would like to be reassured that their subject is worth remembering in the first place, otherwise reminiscence seems mere self-indulgence. Had Rahv been a more public figure, a celebrity of some sort, movie star or politician, or even editor of a great popular magazine like *The New Yorker,* as Harold Ross was, no preliminary apology for remembering him would be necessary. But he was none of these, so the identification has to be made. Perhaps we should let the *Times* itself give answer here, as if to justify the featured space it had allotted him. Rahv had been a literary critic, we are told, an influential New York intellectual, whose principal channel of influence came through his editing of *Partisan Review,* a magazine of which he had been one of the two founders in the 1930s and whose fortunes he had continued to guide through several decades thereafter. During those decades, the *Times* goes on to say, *Partisan Review* had been "the best literary magazine in America," and further, "it would be hard to overestimate the cultural importance" of what the magazine represented and achieved.

The *Times* had certainly put itself on the line here, and that in itself was a little bit unusual. What we prize in this newspaper is its measured and unexcitable tone, the judicious reasonableness that avoids extremes and seeks to strike the moderate balance. Its enthusiasm here must therefore carry all the more authority. Philip Rahv would have been pleased, even more pleased that this judgment appeared on the first page of the *Book Review* section. He thought about death a good deal, about his own death particularly and the mark he might leave, and in his more irritable moments he used to grumble that the *Times* probably wouldn't even give him an obit. It would be nice if he knew that the *Times* had come through with even more than that.

He would have been pleased—but not satisfied for long. Satisfaction was never a lasting mood with him. Whatever pleasant item the Fates might serve on his dish got turned over, questioned, dissected, and

2

ground down in the somber machinery of his mind. And I could imagine now his restless shade carrying on this same habit into the great Beyond. The *Times* had given him star billing, no doubt of that. What was the Sunday circulation of this newspaper? How many people would it reach? How many millions, in fact, might be looking at his picture now as I was? The sheer numbers of this possible readership would have given Rahv pause, for he had dealt always with a small audience and his life had moved within a rather narrow circle of intellectuals. But here his caustic mind would go to work. What did the book section of a newspaper represent as far as serious criticism was concerned? It was, after all, only a kind of trade journal for the publishing industry, as the financial section was an organ for Wall Street. Still, it was hard to imagine how the *Times* could have done better by him. Perhaps only by printing the notice on the first page of the whole newspaper. But that happened only on rare cases where cultural figures were concerned: Joyce, Eliot, Matisse, Heidegger. Rahv had enough critical sense of proportion not to try to elbow his way into that group. A year later, however, Lionel Trilling died, and the *Times* did give the notice of his death on the first page. Had Rahv been around, he would not have failed to make the comparison. Trilling had been his contemporary; they had dealt with similar themes and issues in their criticism; and Trilling had frequently used the pages of *Partisan Review* as a principal platform. How come, then, that he should rate the first page over Philip Rahv? The literary life is a trying one, even beyond this mortal pale.

I had been out of New York intellectual circles now for a long time, and I was never adept in their ways even when I was part of one. But on this rainy afternoon Rahv's ghost seemed to have taken possession of me and I was drifting back into his ways of thinking. What was the machinery behind this prominent notice in the *Times?* Who had pulled what strings? The editor of the *Book Review* must have made the decision. I didn't know him personally, but I knew some of his writing and I could guess his affiliations—that peculiar linkage of tastes, political orientations, and personal connections that operate to form literary groups. The sense of these things is hardly communicable to anyone who has not gone through the mill himself. Then too, there was the fact that the notice by the *Times* was accompanied by a loving and adulatory memoir by Mary McCarthy. Had she initiated the whole idea, or had she simply been invited to contribute her eulogy? Were she and the editor friends? From their literary personalities I could imagine them at least as having mutual friends in a particular circle. I don't want to give the impression of any exceptional or even objectionable intrigue at work here. Human beings naturally form groups; and the literary life has never been carried on without the formation of circles and coteries. It was second nature for Philip Rahv to think in those terms, and he would have wondered about them now.

But however his restless shade might be chafing in the great Beyond, he could not have found fault with Mary McCarthy's accompanying memoir. Her pen, usually dipped in acid, here dripped with honey. Her tribute was a lovely gesture, graceful but making its serious points, sentimental without being mawkish. True, the rough edges of Rahv's personality were bathed in a rather rosy light, but under the circumstances this was understandable. Under these circumstances too it was understandable that a certain exaggeration might be in order. Rahv emerged from Miss McCarthy's glowing account as something of a Diaghilev and Alexander Herzen: the promoter and discoverer of new talent on the one hand; and on the other, the free spirit, the searching and dissident critic of his time and place. Nevertheless, all exaggeration aside, Rahv might claim some credits under both headings.

It was appropriate, given the personal history between them, that Mary McCarthy should be the one to deliver this final tribute. For me personally there was even a certain symmetry about it, since I had first met Rahv in her company. Now on this rainy Sunday, when I seemed to be drawn into my own private rite, it was meet and proper that she should appear to deliver the funeral eulogy. As I stared at the rain pouring down over the window, the whole of that original scene washed back over my memory.

II.

It was the winter of 1937–38. *Partisan Review* had just been launched that fall. Actually, this was a kind of rebirth, since the magazine had been started a few years earlier by William Phillips and Philip Rahv under the auspices of the Communist Party. But its publication had ceased when doctrinal differences developed between the editors and the Party, and for several years it languished in limbo. Now, in 1937, it

4

had really begun its own career, with its own independent and proper identity. In the process it had now acquired a few more editors: Dwight Macdonald, Mary McCarthy, Fred Dupee, and George L. K. Morris. In numbers there is strength, and they needed whatever strength they could muster against the hostile climate they faced. This particular evening they were gathered at William Phillips's apartment. It was not exactly an editorial meeting and yet it was too restrained to be a party. The tired quality of the season hung over everything, that fag-end of the year between Christmas and New Year's Eve.

Delmore Schwartz was the friend who took me there. I was an outsider and did not belong, and I told Delmore that, but he had the habit of bringing me along with him everywhere, as if my presence provided some invisible means of support for him; but perhaps most of all that I might be company in the post mortem afterward and the long, desolate journey home.

In the past few years Delmore Schwartz has made a sensational posthumous return to public fame. Two books about him have attracted considerable attention: a novel by Saul Bellow, *Humboldt's Gift*, in which Delmore is clearly the protagonist, and a remarkably sensitive biography by James Atlas. In this particular novel Bellow is in his more fantastic and myth-making mood, and the portrait he draws of Humboldt (Delmore) is larger than life size: a madcap and a zany, tormented and pathological yet somehow still brilliant and inspiring. Atlas's portrait is drawn along more factual and less sweeping lines, but something of the same figure emerges. For the younger generation particularly his book seems to have given new life to the figure of Delmore as an archtype and symbol: the tragic figure of the doomed poet.

Yet when Delmore Schwartz died in 1966, he was on his way to becoming a forgotten man in literary circles. He had actually disappeared from the scene, hiding out from the last few friends he had kept. Thirty years before, after his first book, *In Dreams Begin Responsibilities* (1938), he had been proclaimed the bright new star in American letters. Principally a poet, he had shown himself also brilliant in fiction and prose—there seemed nothing he couldn't do, and do successfully. His second book, *Genesis*, in 1943 was something of a setback, but thereafter as an editor of *Partisan Review* he still remained prominent as critic, commentator, and general man of letters. His declining reputation as a poet was given a lift again by the Bollingen

Prize in 1960 for his *Selected Poems*, though the award was largely commemorative of past performance. Thereafter he went to pieces rapidly, and at the end of his life was scarcely sane. The lines from Wordsworth he particularly loved to quote became prophetic in his case:

> *We poets in our youth begin in gladness,*
> *But thereof come in the end despondency and madness.*

Those who mourned his death at the time hardly suspected that his fame would ever be resurrected. The stockmarket of American success can be as unpredictable as Wall Street.

But no shadows of this dark fate were visibly hanging over Delmore on this evening in 1937. He had just published his first, and as it turned out, his best story, "In Dreams Begin Responsibilities," in *Partisan Review,* and it had aroused widespread and favorable attention. He was the young prodigy the magazine was in the process of discovering. Now he was meeting the editors in a body, and it was important to make a good impression. His manner accordingly was quiet and self-effacing, almost diffident. Rahv was quizzing him, in the tone of an elder, about his age and background. What impressed me, as I remember it now, was the tone of quiet authority and maturity Rahv assumed, as if he were somehow the one in charge here. He did this without any bluster, without getting up and pacing about in some sudden fit of oratory, as was later to be his habit. That evening, in fact, there was no shouting and arguing, and that in itself was remarkable when this group assembled. Dwight Macdonald had to leave early, or perhaps the quiet might have been shattered. Macdonald had some kind of galvanizing power, either generating arguments of his own or attracting them down on his own head, so that when he was present disputes seemed to go off like small firecrackers all over the place. But not on this night.

Rahv sat on the sofa beside Mary McCarthy. They were lovers, and they were living together. That was a daring thing at the time, or at least to the youthful minds of Delmore and myself, and in our eyes it cast a certain aura about her. Not that Miss McCarthy had need of any additional aura beyond what nature had furnished her with. How describe her? She was not quite beautiful, and too good-looking to be called pretty; and "handsome woman" sounds too stiff and complacent for her vivid good looks. She was much younger then, of course, and somehow darker; altogether, there was something wayward and even *gamine* about her. She did not seem to worry about her clothes or appearance generally, and I noticed—an odd detail to remember now!—that her legs were unshaved. Probably it was no affectation, she had simply been too busy to attend to her toilette; but it reinforced the touch of the gamine about her. Nobody seeing her for the first time would have surmised that this striking and vivid girl would prove to be one of the most brilliant women and formidable intellectuals of her time.

As she sat beside him, she listened intently to whatever Rahv said, and her hand rested on his knee affectionately now and then. Later, when we had left, Delmore grumbled to me, "Did you see Mary McCarthy giving Rahv a feel?" I was amazed at his remark, for her gesture seemed to me to have been proper and affectionate. It was one of the first intimations of how deep the puritan, and even prudish, streak ran in Delmore. This was a fact of his being, however, that he never seemed to accept; and his various escapades into sex were like so many deliberate acts of war upon this part of his nature. He seemed, generally, to do everything to intensify his own conflicts.

But it is not for their separate eminence as individuals that I now justify these memories of them. Besides, that eminence was still in the future, and hidden to me. The awe and admiration I felt was for them as a group, and what as a group they represented. To my youthful eyes they belonged to the great world outside the walls of academy where I was still drudging for a degree. Theirs was the world of bohemia and the arts, of political movements and countermovements, bold and sweeping ideologies; and they were the intrepid spirits who bravely walked within that world. They were therefore beings invested in my eyes with a strange and mysterious glamour; and I felt tongue-tied and stupid in their presence. It seems strange to recall these feelings now, like meeting a woman one had been in love with years before and finding her a stranger; everything is changed, but somehow the old sentiments still shine through, yet at a very great distance, like a winter sun. I was young and ready for hero-worship.

Yet, as a group, they deserved this admiration too. It took a lot of courage to be setting out on the course they were taking, for they were in fact swimming against the general current of the time. They were dissident Marxists, Trotskyist in their sympathies, fighting the

7

Stalinist tide that had taken over both the Left and the Liberals in this country. These might look like intramural squabbles, but the reader has to remember the atmosphere of the time. The year was 1937, and the last of Stalin's purges, featuring the great circus of the Moscow Trials, had claimed the attention of the world. By Western standards these trials were questionable enough, and intellectuals throughout the world were in confusion about them. From his exile in Mexico, Trotsky—who was really the absent defendant throughout the Moscow procedures—issued a stream of rebuttals and denials. What was the truth? The world had a right to know, and a commission of inquiry was formed with the American philosopher John Dewey at its head. The response of the Left and the Liberal Left was almost immediate: a manifesto was published, signed by a considerable number of prominent American intellectuals, warning all men of good will against assisting the commission and declaring that critics of the Moscow Trials were slandering the Soviet Union and "dealing a blow to the forces of progress." Among other things, the manifesto sought to justify the awful purges that had been going on in the Soviet Union and spoke of the "integrity" of Stalin. It was an extraordinary document, as we look back on it now, but in the 1930s it was a perfectly ordinary expression of the political atmosphere of the time. And it was this prevailing atmosphere that this group was engaged in resisting, like the legendary hero fighting the tide with his sword.

That took courage, lots of it, but it wasn't only or even mainly for their courage that I admired them. Something more ideal glimmered about them and beckoned. Had they criticized the Soviet Union from the point of view of the Right or even the Center, I, like most of the radical youth of my time, would have turned my back on them. But these intellectuals of the new *Partisan Review* were attacking Stalin and the Soviet Union from the point of view of a purer Marxism, and it was above all the purity of their radicalism that lured me on. Youth, intellectual youth, wants to be right; it is impatient for the truth, and the surest way to get at the truth seems to lie in adopting the radical position of greatest purity. In any case, one is assured of the purity of one's own motives: one's heart is in the right place. And this hankering after self-righteousness lies secretly behind a good many of the positions we take. Hence too the great attraction of the avant-garde for youth.

Moreover, this radical and avant-garde attitude was not to be confined only to politics; it was to embrace literature and the arts as well. The magazine that Rahv and his friends were launching had bravely announced that in its future course it would be guided by a twofold policy: (1) it would follow a radical line in politics, a line not dictated by a party but freely chosen by itself; (2) and it would seek to advance the cause of Modernism in art. Put in this general form, these prescripts may look bland and rather unobjectionable; in the actual situation of the time they were anything but that. I have already indicated that it was to battle the prevailing tide to try to be of the independent Left; it was almost equally a battle to champion the cause of modern literature and art amid the atmosphere that then attended the politics of intellectuals. The Communist Party and its Fellow Travelers had brought with them a cultural doctrine of social realism and proletarian literature: art should serve the interests of the masses and be understandable to the masses. Modern writers were difficult and complex, and they dealt with rarefied states of consciousness that seemed to have no bearing upon the social struggles of the day; and they were therefore disparaged. Steinbeck was to be preferred to Joyce, and the populist writers of the nineteenth century to Henry James. In this situation it was a bracing challenge to be on the side of the difficult and rare, and to defend the artist's freedom to be as complex as he wishes within the boundaries of his talent and his medium.

Perhaps the reader today does not appreciate the peculiar fascination of avant-garde art for some of the young in those days. We grew up with Eliot and Joyce as sacred texts; they were a kind of secret conspiracy among ourselves against our teachers. We were not old enough to have experienced the startling impact of these writers in the 1920s, but something of their strangeness and novelty still persisted in the 1930s. A few of my English professors, for example, thought *The Waste Land* was a spoof. I first read *Ulysses* in a borrowed contraband copy while the book was still legally banned. Only two or three of my professors had read it or even looked at it, and on only one of them, so far as I could tell, had it made any powerful impact. Nowadays these authors come neatly prepackaged in survey courses, and the young have absorbed the "explanations" of them without any shock or groping with the texts. This is an advance in general knowledgeability, no doubt, but it may be questioned whether it is not a dulling of aesthetic response, which requires the primary shock when it encounters a really new great writer. We grew up dis-

9

covering Picasso for ourselves and trying to explain him to some of our friends. The Museum of Modern Art had not yet become the institution, not to say industry, that it has since become. I was hardly more than a boy when I saw my first Matisse show at this museum, which was then only a few rooms in a building on Fifty-seventh Street. For New Yorkers who grew up with MOMA, as it has come to be called, the development of this institution represents a whole chapter in the history of modern culture. And that chapter is of central significance for anyone who would understand this history: it is nothing less than the academization and institutionalization of the avant-garde. The avant-garde, or what still calls itself that, hasn't died, it has simply found its place.

The German sociologist Max Weber described the great movement within modern history as one toward the rational organization of life. Society becomes larger and more complex, more hierarchical, more rationally planned. We as individuals become more departmentalized, tagged, and labeled; we find our niche in the great interlocking mechanism of society. At the same time the open and uncharted areas of social life become encroached upon, fenced off, departmentalized. Even the once rebellious avant-garde cannot resist this all-devouring process, and enters the academy or the museum. The magazine that Rahv and his co-editors were now launching was to prove no exception. It was a "little" magazine, which meant that it was non-commercial and therefore with no strings attached to any publishing institution. It was equally free of any ties to the academy; none of its editors or the people directly concerned with it were academics. In fact, on that evening in 1937 when I first entered their presence I felt a secret sense of shame that I was an "academic," since I was completing a degree that would enable me eventually to teach. Somehow in the loose-jointed society of America during the Great Depression there was enough open space so that a little magazine could be launched, without institutional ties or backing, and manage somehow to stumble along financially on a shoestring from issue to issue. But, alas, times change and the great jaws of Weber's Leviathan were to close upon it. Years later it would find academic support, and eventually be published under the auspices of a university, in the course of which it has become a different magazine. But on that evening in 1937 no one in the group could have foreseen that academic fate; and if it had been prophesied to them, they would have scoffed indignantly.

The two M's then—Marxism in politics and Modernism in art—were the slogans that this group carried on its banner before the world. They were enough to enlist my youthful enthusiasm in any case, for they named two regions of the spirit where my loyalties already lay. Whether the two parts of this program—a radical Marxism in politics, and a radical championship of the avant-garde in art—were really consistent with each other, did not particularly disturb us at the time. A few years later Lionel Trilling, with his searching and tactful intelligence, began to probe at this question. The great modern writers whom we admired, Trilling pointed out, did not subscribe to the ideals of socialism and progress to which our political thinking was loyal. More important still, the work of these writers did not seem to support those ideals but in fact to move in a contrary direction. Trilling was to worry about this question for the rest of his life, and in effect to leave it unsolved beyond the recommendation that we cultivate enough flexibility of mind to live with these opposites. But at this early time his difficulty did not seem to trouble anybody else in the circle. We were ready to juggle our accounts, though it never looked like that to us. We were untroubled by Trilling's question, I think, mainly because we did not look too closely at our own Marxism and what it entailed.

These were suddenly stabbing thoughts in the midst of my reverie on this rainy Sunday. It was as if my private ritual for the dead were now punctuated with heretical ideas. But memory inevitably leads to reflection, and the stuff of these memories had to do with intellectuals and their ideas, and thus led even more abruptly that way. Moreover, these ideas seemed to cluster about a theme, and the theme became like an antiphon that took over my little mass for the dead. Perhaps that was the significance of my remembering after all. On the face of it, what did I have to hold to? A few memories of a handful of intellectuals in the milieu of New York City years ago. It did not seem much to interest any possible reader. It's a small world, as they say; and this one was a tiny bubble within the larger currents of American society. Yet, marginal as its existence might seem, it might not be without some significance. The microcosm reflects the macrocosm; the smaller world is a mirror of the larger one. And smallness here may have the advantage that within a narrower compass one may perhaps see more sharply defined the issues that are crucial to the larger life of the time.

III.

The rain did not cease all day. But toward evening it began to let up, and blew now only in sudden random gusts. My memories too seemed to come now in sudden gusts.

Later a friend dropped by on a casual visit. He had read the newspaper and wanted to talk about it. In our secular world the Sunday *Times* does for a sacrament, and a particular issue may color a whole Sunday, as going to church once set apart the day for more pious folk. This friend had known Rahv very slightly, and at a distance, so that he too had been drawn by the prominent notice in the paper. From his own brief acquaintance with Rahv, he had wondered about Mary McCarthy's portrait of him, which sounded a little too good to be true, and he wanted to draw me out. "No, that wasn't exactly the way I remember it," I yielded; and proceeded to tell a few things out of school to add to her account. My friend was interested. "Maybe you should tell your own version of it," he advised. He thought there was a story in it.

When he had left, I thought for a long time about what he had said, and then I had my last visitation that day from the ghost of Philip Rahv. It was sometime late in the 1950s, on a weekend summer evening in New York, when the city was so quiet it seemed deserted. We had run into each other by chance, and being at loose ends spent the rest of the evening walking about and talking. This time we were strolling far off our usual beat, as I recall, around Gramercy Park and Stuyvesant Place, through very quiet streets. Rahv was in a reminiscent mood. He had just returned from Boston, where he was in the process of preparing to move to Brandeis University. It was strange to think of him entering into the professorial world, stranger still to think of him being extricated from the milieu of these New York streets where he seemed so eminently to belong. He did not want to dwell on that prospect, and his conversation turned now to the past that we had known together. He told me he had often thought of writing a novel about the people we knew, and if he did, he would call it *The Truants*. It's a pity he never got around to writing it; even if it were not a good novel, it would have been an unusual book, for in his position a large and interesting chunk of life had passed before his eyes.

The point of his title, he explained, was that during all those years the people who had come and gone in connection with the magazine had been playing truant, escaping for a while from the harshness of whatever practical reality would claim them again. And he began ticking off one by one some of the people we had known and their initial hopes, ending always with the refrain, "It wasn't in the cards." But this time he wasn't in one of those black destructive moods I knew so well from the past. Reflective and sad, his voice seemed to speak gently out of the vacant summer evening. It was the last long talk I had with him alone, though I continued to run into him socially from time to time.

I thought again about my friend's advice, that there might be a story in all of this. Since Rahv would never get around now to using his title, he might not mind my borrowing it. Besides, I seemed to see a further meaning in it than he did. He was thinking of all the young literary aspirants who had come and gone during his years as an editor. They were escaping for a few years into bohemia, playing truant from the ordinary ways of life, hoping to spread their wings and soar for a while. In most cases the flights would be short-lived, and the old life would quickly claim them again. Even those who might make it, as the world viewed success, would be uneasy at the discrepancy between what they achieved and the great literary models that haunted their dreams. The literary life is a hard one. Many are called, few are chosen.

But there are different ways to play truant. The young man flees from Dubuque, or from his job in the ad agency on Madison Avenue, and holes up in Greenwich Village to write the great novel. This was the kind of personal escape Rahv had in mind. But the intellectual is tempted into a more subtle form of truancy. He has only to turn his mind in a certain direction and some unpleasant realities can disappear. He goes in search of original and sweeping ideas, and in the process may conveniently forget the humbling conditions of his own existence. In politics, for example, that his own continued existence as a dissenter depends on the survival of the United States as a free nation in a world going increasingly totalitarian. If his thinking deliberately operates outside the paths of our common life, he complains that he has been alienated. In fact, in no age of history has the intellectual been more influential upon human affairs than in the modern world. Consider the intellectuals of the French Revolution: they have shaped the world we live in, and they were certainly truants, if we may believe Edmund Burke. Never mind Burke's own politics, consider him

13

for the moment only as an observer. He happened to be an uncommonly sharp one, and he was in a privileged position to notice the advent of this new breed of mankind—the modern intellectual. These Frenchmen whom he observes were literary intellectuals and they loved large and sweeping abstractions, often without regard to the complex interworking of the very prosaic details that make social life at all possible. They spoke, for example, of something they called The People. My God, how they loved The People! But Burke, as an experienced parliamentarian who had been active on many bills of legislation, knew there was no such thing at all as The People: there was only a multitude of concrete groups, farriers, weavers, farmers, merchants, with sometimes quite conflicting interests, which had to be balanced and reconciled somehow or other into the actual working of society. As soon as you have replaced this concrete plurality by the abstraction of The People, you have homogenized it into the Mass—a plastic and passive dough to be kneaded at will by the Dictator. You have taken the first step toward Gulag.

Disturbing thoughts on a rainy Sunday. This history of the modern intellectual was too tangled and vast a theme for me ever to attempt. I might, however, nibble at its edges simply by reporting on the small group of intellectuals whose fortunes I shared for some years. Trivial as these memories may appear, they might shed a tiny light on that larger theme.

In any case, it seemed an idea worth exploring. There might even be—as my friend had suggested on that rainy Sunday—a story in all this. I have waited, as an omen now for another rainy day to begin. Here it is.

Part I

Arrival

Chapter One

"1919! 1919!"

I.

There is nothing quite like the shock of reaching thirty.

This sentence once seemed to me to have a fine Fitzgerald ring to it, like one of his sad young heroes mourning his vanished youth; and I used to turn the words over in my mind from time to time for whatever preparatory solace they could provide. Our youth is usually a more somber affair than we like to imagine. Beneath the surface the invisible clock keeps ticking off each year of our twenties as we approach nearer and nearer turning the dread corner of thirty, when we have to face the questions what we have done with our life, where we stand and who we are. Of course, there are always excuses one can make to oneself; and for my generation there were the very great excuses of the Depression and the coming War that had claimed our youth. How often have I heard my contemporaries lament these two great accidents of their fate—"We went from the Depression right into the War"! I have used the same excuses myself; but secretly I was never convinced that I might have done better under other historical circumstances. But now the War was coming to an end more speedily than we had ever imagined, and surely this must mark the beginning of a new life and a new era. Being thirty under those conditions might not then be so old after all. One could really begin again.

In any case, when the dire moment struck and I had turned the corner, there was no chance for any elaborate ritual of reflection. I was waking to one more day in the general disorder while waiting for the Second World War to grind down and the authorities to ship me home from Italy. In the fashion of my generation I may have grumbled that this was typical of the experience that had been inflicted upon us: the forces that had taken away our youth did not even allow us the private and proper leisure to lament its passing.

There were a few moments for reflection on the long flight back home. But one could not do much concentrated thinking while struggling for whatever comfort one could manage on a bucket seat, and now and then snatching a few moments of fitful sleep. There was one lucid and happy interval on the trip, but it was so calmly and fully immersed in the sunlight of the present that I had no impulse to turn inward and brood on past fortunes or future prospects. I chose, instead, to play the truant.

There was a change of planes and a long layover in Naples. An enterprising friend from the State Department who was making the trip with me, and who was a master of the *bon vivant* strategies in which minor diplomats become expert, managed somehow to get hold of an official car and we drove out to Posillipo. There we spent the long afternoon lunching in a garden restaurant that overlooked the Bay of Naples. Across the blue water Vesuvius loomed, unchanged by the centuries, while we consumed mussels and drank wine, submerged in the delicious and timeless pause of the afternoon. There were few people besides ourselves; and then, as our lunch went on and on, there were none but ourselves and the friendly proprietor who mostly left us alone. We had the garden and that marvelous bay to ourselves. A timeless hiatus between the War, which for the moment had vanished like a puff of vapor, and the future whose possible troubles were banished from this calm. It was the pure fullness of the present moment, which the French poet Paul Valéry celebrates in his *Cimetière Marin:* the afternoon like a "pure diamond," and the Mediterranean immobilized beyond time.

The Bay of Naples inevitably recalls the Greek colonists who held this area long before the Romans took over. Cultivated Neapolitans always insist with pride upon this Hellenic origin of their city: Nea Polis, the new city, as those early Greek colonists called it with a great surge of hope that they must have felt when they entered this beautiful harbor. A few miles south had been the home of the sage Parmenides, who, looking out perhaps on some such view of the sea as this was caught up in his vision of the fullness of Being, motionless and radiant beyond all the petty turmoils of humans. Here one could enter again the immemorial world of the early Greek philosophers. Ironically enough, this was the last glimpse of war-torn Europe I can remember, but there were no traces of War, nor even of modern history, in what I saw. The War was behind me, and never further away than at this moment. I seemed, for a few short hours, to be suspended beyond time.

When I awoke to the present again, it was night on a plane over the Atlantic. This was my first air crossing, and I should have been excited at the thought that the ocean was there, somewhere in the night, spinning by beneath us. But in the dark and crowded belly of the plane, the ocean outside somehow remained only an abstract idea. Our sense of geography becomes more relative and abstract in the space age. We lose the felt sense, the physical presence, of earth and ocean. I gave up at last struggling with this thought; at the moment my effort to make peace with my bucket seat seemed to take over my consciousness more and more. The bucket seat became something of a cherished institution in those days. For thousands and thousands of Americans it was a kind of life raft of deliverance that was bringing them back home. I imagined them in the dark like me alternately squirming or listless, slumping or sitting bolt upright, but through it all each one hugging that scooplike seat in sheer bliss, for it meant that he was alive and coming home.

Sometime in the middle of the night the plane had grounded, and there was a commotion of trucks and voices outside. I remember dimly being told this was the Azores, where we had landed in order to refuel. In those days the Air Force pressed every usable crate into its shuttling service, and very few of those old planes could have crossed the ocean non-stop. I did not come broad awake until we were in the gray fog over Newfoundland, where the plane had to make a radar descent and, suddenly swooping down, came to rest on a runway, like

19

a panting bird, ready again to refuel. The rest of the trip then seemed to speed by more and more rapidly until journey's end in Washington; and there for a day or two I was absorbed into the maze of the State and its officialdom until the proper rites and forms had been complied with, and I was spewed back again into the private sector in order to resume my own personal life.

To resume one's own life! It seemed a small and humdrum thing to be asking for, and yet most of us believed it would not be the same old life again. Hitler and the Nazis were gone, the whole face of the world seemed changed, and a long period of peace and promise must surely lie ahead. One felt a new world was opening up before one. Even those, like myself, who had thought their youth was gone were now granted a reprieve.

It was a feeling I was sharing with millions of other Americans. A little later on, the movie *The Best Years of Our Lives* tried to capture something of that feeling, which each of us knew in his or her own private way: the sense that in taking up our lives again, we were not in for some dull continuance of the past but a real renewal. But Hollywood chose to go "serious" in that movie; and as usually happens when it so chooses, it missed. It presented a number of troubling case histories, but it missed the heady and almost intoxicated sense of release from war that now gripped the nation. Of course, there was the tawdrier side. On the train back from Washington, a lawyer with whom I had struck up conversation told me he was transferring his practice to divorce cases. "There's gonna be a lot of money to be made there," he said. "All those 'Dear John' letters. The boys coming back may be in for some surprises." Still, despite some painful shocks of readjustment, the pervasive mood of euphoria bubbled and simmered.

Perhaps it was not the best mood for Americans to be in as they entered an absolutely new chapter in their history. The War had catapulted this nation into the position of a world power from which it could never escape into isolationism again. But it was hard for us to think of this new position and the responsibilities that must now go with it while we were clamoring to get the boys back as soon as possible. It was understandable and altogether moving that Americans should want their sons home again; but the mood that accompanied this—the sense of overwhelming relief at something over and done with—might have brought some forebodings. We had got through the War, and now our job in Europe was finished. It took us some time and much turmoil to learn that we were not finished in Europe; that, indeed, the War had left nothing finished.

At the moment, however, for me like so many other Americans, my own world seemed to lie open before me. Yet I was shortly to enter a little world of its own, which, exciting and stimulating as it would be in so many ways, was nevertheless as closed and inbred as a conventicle of monks.

II.

And, like many other Americans at the time, I was without a place to live. So for a few days I descended upon my mother's home in Queens. I was in the right place for my purpose: back at my beginning in order to begin again. I had no plans except, after a few days of this family visit, to find a cheap place to live in Manhattan. There I would hole up, collect myself, and wait to see what would turn up. I had already decided to cut myself off from the academic world in the provinces, where I had been a teacher for a few years before the War. Meanwhile, reflecting in the familial home, my imagination could look across the waters of the East River toward the city that was both the home of my spirit and its persistent challenge.

Native New Yorkers who have grown up in the outlying boroughs have a very different vision of New York from that of Manhattanites. When we speak of going to "the City," we mean going to Manhattan and usually by subway. Thus New York has always seemed to me like an immense octopus whose tentacles reach out into the outlying boroughs. Daily, morning and evening, the tides of life are sucked into the heart and at nightfall flow back into the members—contraction and expansion, systole and diastole. Millions of New Yorkers live with that vision of the city always against the prospect of the daily trip back and forth into it. Those who have grown up in Manhattan, or the outlanders who have come to settle there, have a different spiritual topography of the place.

The subway—the crossing into Manhattan—had another special significance for me. If I try to remember when I first became a Marxist, I would have to fix on the time when, as a teenager, I took the subway regularly five times a week, twice a day, to attend City College. Not that the two things—my dawning Marxism and the subway rides—had any intrinsic rational connection in my mind. They simply happened to coincide in time. If I had reasoned about the sub-way as a case of public ownership, it would have been a poor argu-ment for socialism, for it was as badly run then as now. But one seemed to need no arguments then. The Great Depression hung over our heads, and socialism seemed the simple and inevitable answer. I have to think now, however, that the same reasonably intelligent and alert youth I then was would have every reason today to be wary of socialism. The whole experience of our century weighs heavily against it; and if we are not going to learn from that history, our position is in-deed desperate. But all of these chastening lessons lay in the future and were hidden from us then; and I remember only hugging my socialist thoughts, aggressively but cheerfully, to myself amid the crush of bodies in the subway as I rode back and forth to school. Still, to have breathed the Marxist air so young gave one an intimate and human insight into it that is lacking to those who know it only from a distance. Which may be why Liberals seem never able to understand the Soviet Union.

The Marxist activities at City College during the 1930s have been much exaggerated, in my opinion. The bulk of the students, who were poor, were strenuously engaged in getting an education, posting good marks, and generally preparing themselves for getting on in the world. They may have had radical and Marxist sympathies, but they did not have much time to be activists. The competition for marks in the classroom was sometimes unpleasantly strident. Indeed, one's physical memories of City College were a combination of noise, crowding, and dirt that nostalgia cannot possibly glamorize. (But even there we may have had the psychological advantage that we were not tempted afterward, like some alumni of the Ivy League, to let sentimentality hover forever around our college days and so remain chained to an idealized adolescence.) And yet through all its clamor and dinginess there was a redeeming gleam of mind—a certain intel-lectual dedication that shone here and there among the students and some of the faculty. The life of the mind, if only dimly glimpsed from time to time, did have a meaning in that otherwise shabby institution. And at that particular time the students, though in their own grubby and ill-mannered way, were probably the most dedicated body of un-dergraduates in the country.

Also, these students were mostly Jewish. The unofficial statistic ru-mored about was 98 percent, but this was probably a gross exaggeration; the more likely figure would have been somewhere around 95 percent. In any case, it was something of a shock for me at first to be thrown into an almost completely Jewish environment. At that time the borough of Queens, where I grew up, had a very different demographic constitution from what it has since acquired; there had been very few Jews in the high school I attended, and in the successive neighborhoods to which my family moved, Jews were a very small minority. Now I was suddenly thrown, like Daniel in the den of lions, into a swarm of intense, squabbling, and noisy young Jews. Nevertheless, I seem to have acclimatized myself quickly: I disappeared into the throng—I "passed." There was nothing planned or self-conscious about this identification of myself with Jews: it simply happened, I became assimilated.

Having a New York accent, and some of the mannerisms that go with it, must have helped, of course. Years later, Sidney Hook suddenly surprised me one day by telling me I had more of a New York Jewish intonation than he. Of course, I thought, he cannot hear his own voice—but then, I had to reflect, neither can I hear my own. He might be right. Still, my amazement was somewhat on the order of Delmore Schwartz's when Diana Trilling came up to him at a party and said, "Don't you think we look alike?" Delmore could only stammer that he had not given the matter much thought, but he wasn't sure who should feel complimented—a remark that did not further endear him to the Trillings. But whatever natural assets may have helped me, my original assimilation had seemed to happen of itself, spontaneous and unplanned.

Very shortly, however, this self-identification with Jews became reflective and deliberate: yes, I was pro-Jewish because the Jews seemed to me the people of the mind. When I visited at the home of some of my college friends, and observed that they could bring into the midst of their family, and as noisily as they liked, their own radical ideas or the intellectual themes of the classroom, I found this a startling and wonderful thing. Nothing like that happened where I came from. So far as my family was concerned, whatever paths of the mind I followed, I strayed there alone and lonely, and secretly felt guilty at harboring thoughts I dared not divulge. I envied those friends who did not have to feel, so it seemed to me, like intellectual aliens at home.

I do not bring up these matters for any autobiographical interest they may have. In this memoir, I must warn the reader, I am not a walker in the city seeking narcissistically to capture myself. The "I" here is not the subject of these pages but only an observer; and if some personal facts are brought forward they are intended merely to convey the mood of the occasion or the point of view of the perceiver. The fact is that in the New York intellectual circle in which I was to move, the background was subtly but nonetheless pervasively Jewish. After a while one became so used to this atmosphere that one ceased to notice it until one stepped outside of it. I have therefore indicated the foregoing bit of personal history of how I myself became acclimatized very early on.

Indeed, since the question of Jewishness plays some part in the events that follow, I think it worthwhile to venture on one further personal statement here at the beginning. After many years and much thought on the subject, I have no new or original theory of what it means to be a Jew. Sartre, in his sweeping and facile way, declares that it is all merely a matter of thought: a Jew is someone who thinks of himself as a Jew. I think not. On a few occasions in my life I have had the abrupt shock of discovering for myself that I was not a Jew after all. Some of those painful experiences occurred during the years I moved in the *Partisan Review* circle, when I had at last to retrieve some other more commonplace and neglected portions of my own inheritance. If you are not a Jew, you are not a Jew—and the abyss yawns between yourself and that idealized image you have constructed, no matter how close you seem to approximate. Being a Jew is really being a Jew, and merely thinking cannot make it otherwise. I might add, however, that enough of the old identification still persists so that I still feel most at home in the company of a few Jews to whom I feel close. And if, in the pages that follow, some irony may appear from time to time on Jews and things Jewish, I consider myself a participant and fall under its shadow.

III.

As this particular fall hovered near, however, the old and familiar trip into the city would be a very different one for me. I would not be setting out to school. The academic calendar would not measure out my days this year; I existed already in the timeless haze of the unemployed. But there was one trip clearly marked on the calendar of duty:

as soon as possible I would have to look up my friend Delmore Schwartz. It was necessary to establish this link again with the past. Our friendship had been left dangling by the War, and I would have to see where we now stood.

And with that visit my narrative should properly begin.

Delmore was on leave from Harvard for the year, and he was now living in a cold-water flat on Bedford Street in west Greenwich Village. I got this information by calling the *Partisan Review* office. But he had no telephone, the girl told me; when they wanted to reach him for any urgent reason, there was nothing to do but walk around to his place and leave a note. It was typical of Delmore that, at the cost of great inconvenience he should nevertheless choose to protect his privacy against the aggression of the telephone. When he was in New York, his life was likely to expand into a whirl of intense and haphazard socializing, but he needed always his cave of solitude into which he could dive back again.

He was divorced from his first wife, and he was now living alone. How would that divorce have changed him? What was he up to now? Where did he stand in the trajectory of his literary career? His second book had been something of a setback, but I imagined this as only a momentary *contretemps*, and that the prodigious energy which had always been his must now be turned on some new and ambitious work. The questions buzzed in my head.

I went around in the evening and rang his bell. There was no answer—he was either out or incommunicado for the evening. As I came out from the clean but dingy hallway, I caught sight of a figure on the near corner scurrying back into the shadow. I was walking in that direction anyway, and when I came under the lamplight, the mysterious figure came out and saluted me. It was Delmore all right.

After our first greetings he explained the reason for his peculiar vigil on the street. He had just turned the corner on his way home when he saw someone enter the hall. "I thought you might be John Berryman," he explained.

Without realizing it at the time, I had suddenly entered a new world of complicated personalities, with its peculiar theater of entrances and exits, cues and signals. John Berryman has left his mark as a poet, and probably needs no introduction to the reader. But there was a side to his character in those early days that is not generally known. Contrary to the later public image, which *Life* magazine was to celebrate in an article, of Berryman as the genial and expansive Dionysian who drank a quart of whiskey a day, he was in these days a rather sharp, fussy, and precise person, who could sometimes be quite tiresome. It was not at all that he and Delmore were enemies at the moment; on the contrary, they were poetic allies and good friends; but even with friends Delmore often found himself involved in complicated strategies. The simple fact was that he found Berryman boring in large doses, and at certain times preferred to be spared his company.

Berryman's attitude toward Delmore, on the other hand, was almost pure adulation—and apparently never ceased to be such even during the years of Delmore's decline. Delmore, of course, was flattered by this veneration of him as *cher maître;* but he was also sometimes embarrassed by it, since Berryman had a very point-blank and overemphatic manner of making his attitudes known. One of Delmore's poems had begun with the beautifully simple line:

> *"Tired and unhappy you think of houses;"*

whereupon Berryman opened one of his poems with:

> *"Exasperated, worn, you conjure up a mansion."*

At least, the imitation here makes no particular effort at concealing itself. Delmore's remark about it was: "Berryman always has to outdo me. I think of a house, he has to have a mansion—a house isn't good enough for him." Yet Delmore never abated in his good will toward Berryman, helping him first to get published and to find a job at Harvard for a while.

Delmore was genuinely puzzled by the fact that Berryman, who was a good poet, seemed stupid. "It's an ontological contradiction," Delmore used to insist—not a contradiction in logic but in the very being of the man. How could anyone that stupid write good poetry? Whether Berryman was really stupid or not, I cannot say with any certainty; but he seemed to do his best to make one think that he was. Partly, this came out of a certain insistence on reiterating for emphasis something that had already appeared in the course of the conversation. He could take the words you had just said and, repeating them with more emphasis, give them back to you sounding hollow. Indeed,

I always felt there was something of a hollow man behind Berryman's persona. The impression was confirmed by a woman whom he had tried to court, though the affair never came off: Berryman rather frightened her, she said, because he seemed like a mask, and behind that mask she might have found just emptiness. I suspect what she would have found would have been nothing but the clamorous, panting, plodding desire to write verse.

In later years, when Berryman put on his other persona, he was to grow a beard and dress casually. In the late 1940s, however, he was carefully clean-shaven, and affected a considerable preciseness in dress and speech. Having been to England on a fellowship, he carried away a number of British echoes and mannerisms. The popular song, "There'll always be an England," had helped carry the British through some of the darker years of the War. Delmore applied it now to Berryman: "There'll always be an England—so long as John is around."

Perhaps, however, it was the sheer insistent persistence of Berryman's mind—boring as it could be in ordinary intercourse—that enabled him eventually to triumph as a poet. His mind was perpetually on the poem he had written, was writing, or just about to write; and this inner absorption on his muse left him little attention for the agilities of conversation. Robert Lowell struck me as having something of the same quality. Delmore used also to complain about Lowell as "dumb"—not "stupid," that was reserved for Berryman. Delmore had in mind particularly what he thought were Lowell's naïveté and gullibility on political ideas. Lowell did seem to move slowly in intellectual conversation, as if he had to assimilate each point at the deliberate pace of his own more solemn pentameters. He could think only as fast as you intone one of his poems. Delmore's mind was not chained to the poet in him; it darted nimbly and agilely about, and he liked talking with someone who could follow his sudden swoops and flights. Thus, except for Auden, who had a similar nimbleness in conversation, Delmore was likely to find the company of other poets a little narrow and dull.

So on this first evening, in this odd meeting on a street corner, I was already involved in the intricate web of literary personalities. To be a friend of Delmore's was inevitably to be drawn into the web of some small intrigue or other. Thus the apartment I got, a few days later, came through a bit of maneuvering on his part: I took it over from one of his girl friends on the condition of my buying the furni-

27

ture she was leaving behind her. The furniture was not worth the money, but apartments were scarce and I thought I was lucky to get this one. It was a dismal little cold-water flat on West Third Street, but I sat contentedly in it as if at last I had come home to the place from which I could now begin all over again.

Greenwich Village, like the post-War world in general, was open and humming. Not all the troops had been demobilized; there were still uniforms around—soldiers and sailors on dates or hunting for girls —that lent a certain randy excitement to the streets and bars. Delmore himself was in one of his manic and exhilarated phases; and New York and the Village, in their present mood, seemed almost electric after Cambridge and Harvard. He was carrying on with two girls, but he had a place for me as the indispensable male companion, and I tagged along. Our friendship seemed to resume as it had always been, as if there had been no interruption by the years of the War.

For the moment, too, I seemed to carry a new aura in his eyes: I had been to Europe, and no matter that it had been under the conditions of war and devastation, I had trod some of the sacred places of his imagination. He pressed me for what stories I could tell him, but almost immediately he would be matching them with stories of his own about the things I had missed while I was away. The day of the Japanese surrender, V-J Day, the day the War officially and publicly ended, was only a few short weeks back, and the memory of it still excited him. He had made a point of going to Times Square to see the celebration. It was history, he felt, before his eyes, and he would not have wanted to miss it. The mood of the crowd, as he described it, had been bacchanalian, most of all in some of the smaller side streets leading off Times Square. "If I had a uniform on," he said, "I felt I could have laid any woman on those streets." All that energy, that frenzy of deliverance from the War, would surely turn in a more positive direction, he thought, and an extraordinary decade was going to open up for all of us.

Quite casually, almost as if to pass the time, I sat down in my shabby flat and wrote a brief piece about my last impressions of Italy at the end of the War. I brought it to the *Partisan Review* office and they liked it. Then a few days later Delmore dropped in to tell me that I was now on the staff of *Partisan Review*. The news was altogether a surprise to me; we had said nothing between ourselves on the subject, and the possibility had never entered my mind. But now Delmore, having made the announcement as of something already signed and delivered, was grinning gleefully from ear to ear. He would have his ally in any editorial squabbles and that would add to the excitement.

The new arrangement would be that he and I were to be Associate Editors, while Philip Rahv and William Phillips would be listed as Editors. The difference in rank was meant to register the fact that Rahv and Phillips, who had founded the magazine and were its legal owners, kept that status; but so far as strictly editorial participation and influence on the content of the magazine were concerned, we were all to be on an equal footing. In fact, as I was to find out, this putative equality was mostly mythical. One person took to himself the preponderant power in shaping the magazine, and that was Philip Rahv. He did so by sheer self-assertion; by the power and force, and at times the sheer rudeness of his personality. He thought more about the magazine, concocted more plots around it, and generally gave it more of his energies. It was an extension of his personality—one might almost say, of his body; and his personality was not a shrinking one. To have attempted to cut in on his influence would mean that one would have to spend as much time as he on calculating, and be ready for the unpleasant abrasions of personal confrontation over large and petty matters at once. Delmore used to remark that it was a peculiar coincidence that the initials PR, which is how many people referred to the magazine, were also those of Philip Rahv; and Rahv himself had undoubtedly made the identification. On the whole, however, his peculiar leadership was accepted because we all shared the same general ideas about what the magazine stood for. The conflicts, when they came, were to be of a peculiar personal kind.

Perhaps it was due to the expansive spirit of the post-War, as I have tried to sketch it here, that I was taken into the magazine. The world was now opening up again; and for those Americans interested in matters of culture, Europe would be a chief topic of interest once more. What was going on there? What new writers or new movements in the arts and philosophy awaited our discovery? I had just come from Europe, I read the languages, and perhaps I could help out in this area. (I was later to become the magazine's man on the subject of Existentialism, which was then still unknown to Americans.) Whatever the editors' reasons, I was not to know the particular machinery of persuasion by which I was accepted to the staff. Philip Rahv may have had no objection to taking on a particular friend of Delmore's at that time because the personal divisions between the editors had not yet broken above the surface and he felt secure in his position.

In any case, I was glad to become part of the group. In the last few days I had been happy in the solitude of my flat, enjoying a tranquillity of reflection that the years of the War had taken away from me. But now I had a center of activity to turn toward, and yet it would not chain me down like a regular job. And I was ready to throw myself with enthusiasm into all its causes and battles.

IV.

Our glimpse of large-scale historic movements is always miserably finite and personal. We speak of the vast commotions of history—the War and the post-War; but looking back in memory, we meet only ourselves in some small corner or other, able to fix those great changes only in a few tiny incidents that happen to mean much to us for reasons that will seem trivial to the stranger who was not there. From the fall of 1945 two small episodes come back to me now and seem to sum up our world at the time:

The first was in a Village bar with Delmore. The Village and its bars were very different then from what they were later to become. The people who lived in that part of the city worked, or tried to work, and were known to read books; and when they dropped in on a neighborhood bar, it was for the respite of a drink or maybe some conversation with friends. The Beats of the 1950s and the Hippies of the 1960s had yet to decimate the region and turn its bars into galleries of human grotesques and infantile *poseurs*. This bar, for example, on this particular night, was alive and humming—but the sound was the human one of voices in animated conversation. Television had not yet made its public appearance on the scene; and if there was a jukebox or radio in the place, it remained hidden and unheard. Instead, people talked; and as they talked, they sometimes moved from table to table to share other friends and other conversations.

We had come alone, but were soon at a table with other people. One of them was David Diamond, the composer, an old friend of Delmore's from before the War. Diamond had been something of a musical prodigy, and at a quite early age had been sent on a fellowship to study in Paris. When he returned among us, he had thus already be-

30

come a legendary presence. While we youths of the Depression had been wearing ourselves out back and forth on the subway, Diamond had been strolling through the City of Light and haunting the fabled places of the great. Whether Diamond composed any music while in Paris, I do not know; but in our youthful eyes, he had spent his time there well. He had found out where James Joyce lived, had waited outside, and then at a discreet distance had followed the great man on his daily walk. He had visited the cafes that had been Hemingway's haunts in the 1920s, and even was supposed to have tracked down the particular cafe that Hemingway and Miro had favored when they were drinking companions. Whenever he was among us, Diamond somehow quickened our imagination of Europe, and that last shining decade of European creativity, the 1920s.

What had it been like in those days right after the end of that first war? Were not the cafes of Montmartre buzzing with the same kind of excitement as here in this bar, the same overwhelming sense of release from the war and of energy waiting to find its own creative channels? Need we go to Paris now to find it? Why not here? We could move Paris to New York and begin it all over again here.

No one I have ever known has been able to catch the excitement around him and concentrate it into such electric concentration in himself as Delmore could. He turned to me with excited and gleaming eyes: "1919! 1919!" he kept repeating, "It's 1919 over again."

The year 1919 had been the first after the Armistice that ended World War I. It had thus been the first step into that fabulous decade of the 1920s, which had given us *The Waste Land, Ulysses,* and the great painters of the School of Paris. History never repeats itself, they say, but in this case, in this new post-War of ours, it might repeat the pattern if not the detail. Surely some splendid and flourishing period lay before us even if we could not foresee what it would be like.

The second episode had a quieter exuberance about it, and a more sobering aftermath: One of my first duty visits would be to bring news of his family to Nicola Chiaromonte, the Italian writer and journalist, who had been a refugee in New York since 1941. Years before that, he had been a youthful rebel against Mussolini and Fascism, and had had to flee Italy. He had not seen his family since; and like all Italians, he had a strong familial sense. During the last years of the War, I had been the means of bringing some messages between them, and in the course of this had become a good friend of the family. Now Chiaromonte would be glad to hear that they were alive and well, and that in this new period of freedom, they looked forward to seeing him again at long last.

When I arrived at Chiaromonte's apartment I found myself in the midst of a very lively and jolly little gathering. Saul Steinberg, the artist and cartoonist, was one of the surprising visitors. Also present were Niccolo Tucci, the novelist, and Ugo Stille, New York correspondent for what was then Italy's best newspaper, *Corriere della Sera*. Steinberg had been a student in Milan in his early years, was absolutely fluent in Italian, and had been with the American services in Italy during the War. He knew Italy and Italians well, and had observed them with that oblique sharpness of vision which is peculiarly his own. Stille had also done some liaison work for the American forces in Italy. The conversation I walked into was anecdotal and rollicking. The whole War seemed to collapse into a swarm of amusing stories about Americans and Italians confronting each other in comic and pathetic misunderstanding. Each of us there, in his own personal way, was aware of the desolation and misery that the War had visited upon the Italian peninsula; but in the mood of the moment we could let these things be forgotten. The War was behind us, and we could even dare to look at it in amusement.

Not so long ago I happened to run into Steinberg at an academic gathering, where he was receiving an honorary degree. When I recalled this earlier conversation to him, the memory of it came slowly back. I told him that I remembered the liveliness of the conversation that afternoon rather poignantly now because it seemed typical of that whole period in its exuberant confidence that a great new world lay before us. Then, as his memory focused, he gave me that sharp and reflective look of his, like a jeweler squinting sidewise at a questionable gem. "No," he said, "there was something else there too. Something simpler beneath all our big ideas. It was the simple feeling that we had survived."

The nation, of course, had survived, and was never more powerful than at this moment. But beyond that, each of us—in his own particular and private way—had managed to come through; each of us had saved his own skin. Was our euphoria, the great lure of a promising and splendid future to come, merely a disguise of that other more ele-

32

mental feeling of relief at the sheer fact of self-survival? Had we paused to think of this, perhaps some of our hopes would have been less exalted, and we might have been less disappointed in what the next few years would bring.

Chapter Two

"Analytic Exuberance"

I.

In the fall of 1945, then, I came to sit in on my first editorial meetings. The small office was in the old building, the Bible House, long since torn down, near Astor Place. In many ways it seemed like an offshoot of the nearby tenements of the East Side, as if the editors in choosing this place were returning to the locale of their forebears. The office was so cramped that conversation on any intimate matter could not be kept from the girl (secretary, proofreader, general workhorse) who was in the next room, and usually the meetings, when more sensitive matters needed to be discussed, overflowed into lunch at some nearby restaurant or cafeteria.

For the most part I sat quiet during these first meetings, for I had a great deal to learn; in a way I was still carrying over the attitude of a student, this time studying the three minds before me. Up to now I had been mostly in the academic world—as student and teacher—and I had watched the academic mind at work; but now I was confronted with a different type of intelligence. What is intelligence, anyway? I have long since come to the conclusion there is no such thing separate from the rest of the personality. We see things in our own way, and our mind bears the stamp of our whole person upon it. Each of my co-editors bore a unique intelligence of his own that I have been a long time deciphering.

"William Phillips and Philip Rahv are two of the most intelligent people in the country," Clement Greenberg told me—meaning at the same time to warn me of the limits, the peculiar twists and turns, of that intelligence. He meant it as a kind of warning to me, but it was one which I was not able to heed or really understand at the time. I was too much in the throes of my personal revolt against academia, and so joyful at my temporary deliverance from it, that I was ready to fling myself into the intricacies of literary bohemia.

It was an odd quirk of fate that the names of William Phillips and Philip Rahv should be perpetually linked, and that they should be bound together over the years in a long and close intimacy not unlike the stresses of matrimony. One of the office girls at one period, who had spent considerable time observing them—how could one avoid it in an office so tiny?—remarked to me one day that it was too bad William and Philip were not of opposite sex, for then they could have gotten married and had babies instead of *Partisan Review*. She didn't specify who would be male and who female in this remarkable trans-formation; but her point was well taken, for their child, the magazine, was the issue which held them together through the various dissen-sions of personality. And when they had finally and definitely split years later, each carried something like the grudges of a divorced cou-ple, complaining how he had been put upon by the other over the long term of their union.

The closeness of friendship, however, was still there, or at least the residues of it, when I entered upon the scene, though the explosion was very shortly to take place.

Of the two, William Phillips was indeed the more put upon, in terms of personal and moral deception. It was he who was pushed into the shadow by Rahv's more aggressive and blustering personality. In a sense, there were two William Phillipses: one that presented it-self to the public world of strangers, and the second that revealed it-self only at home in the company of a small group of friends in whose affections he felt secure. The first was a rather tense, nervous, and fidgety person, who could leave you uneasy even when you knew he was trying to be nice to you. The second person emerged and shone fully mostly at his own home, when he felt thoroughly at ease with the "family," a few friends who, he felt, were really bound to him. Then he became expansive, warm, and witty; his conversation flowed like a radiant and sparkling stream. Many nights, when we were walking away from his house, Delmore would observe with affectionate sadness, "If only William could get all that into writing!"

Delmore's wistful lament here named the essential tragedy of Phillips's life. He had, some years back, given up the possibility of an academic career, for which he already seemed to show promise, in order to become a writer. Then something had happened: that fearful thing —a writer's block—had descended upon him and would not relinquish its grip. At the same time there was an escape ready at hand in the excitement of radical politics in the early 1930s, and he could throw himself into that. He was a dissident Marxist, an anti-Stalinist Communist, and he could become absorbed in the missionary role of converting some of the misguided faithful away from Stalin. Brilliant in argument, he could at least become a dialectician if he were not after all to be a writer. The long nights during the 1930s, and indeed much of the days, had been consumed in argument; and while there had been zest and excitement in it at the time, there came the later moments when it all would seem suddenly hollow. "I pissed my life away in talk," he observed ruefully to Delmore and me one night.

In good part the tragedy may have been the self-defeating fruition of his own powers of intelligence. He had, as I've said, a mind brilliant and quick at argument. He could enter into a discussion, even when he had not read the materials at issue, pick up the main themes from the other disputants, and soon be directing the flow of argument, skipping nimbly from one side or the other as it pleased him. But this brilliance to argue either side of a question exacted its toll; it brought with it a certain quality of detachment and sterile skepticism that had more hold over him than he was aware. Apart from the circle of personal friends to whose loyalty and affection he was deeply attached, I doubt that he had any strong beliefs generally, though he himself probably did not know it. And this is something very surprising to say about a man who was so essentially kind. One exception was his hatred of Stalin, which had for him the firmness of a conviction of principle. So much so that when Stalin died, William told me that he felt strangely empty—almost as if something central to his life had gone.

My own friendship with him at this time had become, for me at any rate, something warm and close. Once I had been permitted past the barrier of his tenseness, of his Persona Number One, he had adopted a kind of paternal relationship to me: I was the "kid" younger in years and more innocent than he, and I in turn flung myself into the role, taking and soliciting his teasing. Much of our jesting back and forth took a Jewish turn—his own humor, even at its most sophisticated, had almost always an inescapable Jewish tinge. The tags of Yiddish which I'd picked up at City College revived in our conversations, and much of his joshing of me turned about my own personal ambiguity as to whether I was or wasn't Jewish. In the heat of an argument, he would smile at me and remark, "Sometimes I forget you're a Jew." One time, in a more serious mood, when we were alone he suddenly said very shyly and *apropos* of nothing, "You know, you're the first gentile I as a Jew ever felt completely at home with." I do not know how he would have felt about this later, or how his corrosive mind might have dissected it analytically, but at the moment it came, and with the sudden and unexpected shyness in which he said it, the remark touched me deeply.

Any such confession in momentary diffidence, at least as far as I can imagine, would never have crossed the lips of Philip Rahv. In this, as in so many other respects, he was the antithesis of his partner. Rahv seemed always to exude forcefulness and self-confidence, as if the mask of a man in thorough command of the situation could never fall from him. "Philip is a manic-impressive," William had once quipped about him, the joke having a particularly poignant edge at this time because we had been talking about the manic-depressive moods—the alternating phases of elation and gloom—through which Delmore Schwartz was passing. Delmore was then immersed in the Freudian literature, trying to figure out his own case; and we were all more or less saturated with psychoanalytic jargon. Psychoanalysis was at that time very much in the air, and everybody seemed to be in it or contemplating it. Once Delmore—with that point-blank impishness of his —had asked Rahv why he didn't try analysis, and the latter had merely shrugged in reply. Privately, William Phillips commented that there would be no point in Rahv's consulting an analyst: "Most of us, under analysis, break down and admit our shortcomings. Philip would break down and confess he was a great man." He would be manic-impressive even in a situation of confession.

Yet smile at him as we might (and our jesting at this point was not altogether unkindly) we had to recognize that Rahv was in his way a very impressive figure. And it was for this side of his character—the suggestion it carried of authority and power, and therefore masculinity—that women were attracted to him. And that attraction was real enough. Even William Phillips, years later when he had very little good to say about his ex-partner, had to concede it; but William had to add his own qualification, "Yes, he fascinated women, like Jack the Ripper." From the woman who did become devoted to him Rahv was likely to exact the last full measure of devotion. She would have to enter into the duplicities of his mind and become, as William Phillips put it, "Rahv's alter-Iago." Indeed there was often something menacing about Rahv's impressive manner, as if he were capable of being quite ruthless if he had to. This quality of possible ruthlessness in him was something I felt quite early. It made me uncomfortable in my first weeks around the office when I wasn't at all sure of my status there. On the occasions when he and I happened to be alone there—in a "little" magazine there are no regular nine-to-five office hours—he would, if the mood were on him, merely grunt at me or sometimes talk to me as if he were looking through me like a menial. Though he could, on occasions that called for it, go through the gestures of a grand gentleman to the manner born, he was also one of the rudest men I've ever known.

But his bearing toward me was to change quite a bit after the scene of "the great confrontation"—as Delmore Schwartz came to call it afterward.

II.

There was no definite indication that anything like a confrontation was coming. I knew of course that some kind of "sides" were being drawn, and that in some general way William Phillips recognized me to be on his "side," which meant at this stage no more perhaps than that he was beginning to be more relaxed and at ease with me. And for my part, to be on his side—whatever that might come to mean—accorded with the fact that I was more comfortable with him than with Rahv. And Phillips was extremely scrupulous about not talking to me against his partner; whatever jokes he may have made about Rahv were offered in good humor and without spite. The nearest thing to an advance disclosure of what was brewing came indeed through William Phillips's effort to keep me out of it. On a few occasions when I had come in on him and Delmore in conversation, he would stop their talk with the remark that he didn't think I should get mixed up in those matters. And it was remarkable—it seems even more remarkable to me now—that Delmore held his tongue, since he usually spilled everything to me. Perhaps he thought I wouldn't be present at the scene when they finally did confront Rahv, and he would have the gorgeous opportunity later of telling me all about it, with all the dramatic ornamentation that only he could add.

In any case, when it did come, the confrontation arrived quite unexpectedly. We were leaving the office for lunch when William Phillips suggested that we wait a few minutes: "Clem Greenberg said he'd like to come down and have lunch with us."

Rahv grumbled and was restive. It was unusual to have an "outsider" sitting in on our informal editorial luncheons. Not that Clement Greenberg was exactly an outsider; he had been an editor of *Partisan Review* not many years before, and he was now writing on art for the magazine, and was its more or less unofficial art critic. Moreover, he was now an editor of *Commentary,* and the relations between the two magazines at that time were cordial. What bothered Rahv was not so much that Greenberg was an outsider, but that, on the contrary, he might be on his way to becoming too much of an insider; that he might be pushing his past ties with the magazine, and his present friendship with William Phillips, into some kind of quasi-editorial status. Had Greenberg come in time, he would have seemed merely to be casually dropping by, and nothing would be thought of it. But now every moment of waiting heightened the feeling of strangeness. William Phillips mumbled something by way of explanation: "Clem gets tired of midtown, and he thought he'd like to come down here for a change." But everybody was fidgeting till he arrived.

Presently, then, all five of us were marching down Second Avenue toward a Jewish restaurant, this one a little more elegant than we usually chose, and this choice itself seemed to mark this as a special occasion. I had no inkling of what was to come, but I cannot recall that day now without a sense of what was later to happen; I now sense that walk to the restaurant, and indeed the whole episode that fol-

lowed, under the somber and melodramatic image of the mafia chieftain, the *capo*, being led to execution by his rebellious lieutenants. To
be sure, there would be no spraying of machine-gun bullets around
that quiet restaurant, but when the affair was over the place would be
littered with the corpses of several dead friendships and things would
never again be as they had been. There was even a certain appropriateness that a Jewish restaurant on the Lower East Side should
have been chosen; the mafia gangster meets his end always in an Italian restaurant. There was even the appropriateness of the proper ritual in William Phillips's withholding any intimation of the meeting's
purpose till the luncheon was ending. The mafia chieftain is always allowed to complete his meal and is gunned down only when he has
come to coffee.

William Phillips pushed back his cup, cleared his throat a few
times, always a sign of nervousness with him, and began. The magazine, he said, seemed to be entering on a promising period, there were
some likely possibilities of financial support, and we therefore ought
to get some personal matters straight in order to pull together. All of
this came out very haltingly, but Rahv was fully on the alert. To follow in the mafia image, he was like the *capo* who sees danger immi-
nent and makes the first move, either darting for cover or overturning
the table and pulling his own gun first.

"What is this, a plot!" he roared, even before Phillips had got to the
point. But Rahv's hand, despite the bluster of his voice, was shaking
so that he could hardly light his cigarette.

What prompted his fear was the presence of Greenberg. For Rahv,
as I was to learn later, despite his bluster, was a physical coward who
shrank from even the idea of blows or violent physical contact of any
kind; and Greenberg had lately gotten a reputation of someone "who
goes around socking people" (which was Delmore Schwartz's way of
putting it). In fact, the reputation was highly inflated. There were two
cases in which he had in fact come to blows, but there had been provocation. The incidents had been much talked about, and a good many
people condemned Greenberg's resort to violence as crude and barba-
rous. One of his staunchest defenders, however, was Hannah Arendt,
who for the moment sounded like a protective mother hen. Greenberg's actions, she felt, showed a certain sense of honor; the trouble
with intellectuals was that with them everything became a matter of
talk, talk, talk, in the course of which the moral issue gets blunted or

41

disappears. When she spoke of Greenberg, she referred to him as "this young man," and she sounded almost protectively maternal. "This young man," she said, "has some sense of manliness and honor." And she invoked the name of Camus (whom she personally admired) and the latter's sense of a "virile ideal." Greenberg himself followed this line: he did not apologize for those incidents, there had been principle involved, and he had struck with due deliberation. One can imagine, then, why Rahv should now be trembling.

But no blows were struck that day. Instead, the confrontation became—in the usual pattern of intellectuals—talk, talk, talk. In its final effect, though, it was nonetheless deadly for being that. The burden of complaint, as it tumbled out in various minute particulars, was that Rahv had talked too freely against the other three behind their backs, and particularly to the wrong people—publishers and editors who might thus be dissuaded from allotting certain favors, or heads of foundations who were in a position to dispose of certain grants. Against all this Rahv moved agilely in his own defense, his point being that everybody in the circle talked and that it was a characteristic of literary intellectuals to dissect the personalities they knew. "Everybody does it," he concluded.

"But not like you," Clement Greenberg insisted; and he pressed him further, almost pleading, "Why do you do it?"

Pushed into this corner at last, Rahv was far from defenseless; his answer was so simple and matter-of-fact that it stopped his accusers in their tracks: "I suppose, it's just analytic exuberance." In short, he had simply been carried away by his own overflowing analytic powers, as if neither malice nor destructiveness were involved.

("Analytic exuberance" was to become a choice item in Delmore's treasury of phrases, one that he would trot out from time with great glee. "Analytic exuberance—Philip Rahv's euphemism for putting a knife in your back.")

Throughout the confrontation, it became clear that William Phillips had been the one most put upon. The points that Delmore himself brought forward were largely to show how Rahv had perpetually shoved his partner aside in getting the benefit of whatever prestigious contacts might come through the magazine. Since Rahv usually got to the office before anyone else, he had first go at the mail, and sometimes pocketed certain things for his own advantage. Yet it was William now who struggled to keep this confrontation on the level of a reprimand to a friend. He still had hopes of reclaiming Rahv.

Talk always exhausts a subject—for the time being at least—and this was no exception. The tension wore down, or wore the participants down, and a gentler and invisible impasse had been arrived at. Clement Greenberg announced that he had to get back to the *Commentary* office, and left. Then, in a very abrupt shift, Rahv remembered suddenly that when we got back to the office, there was the business of firing a new girl who had been hired only a few weeks ago. She had not worked out well, we were all agreed, and there really was no need for an extra girl after all. But who would do the firing? Rahv cowered before this task as much as from the confrontation he had just passed through. It was another one of the ironies of this impressive figure— this "intellectual he-man," as Sidney Hook called him—that he quailed before any unpleasant encounter of this humdrum kind. It was as if he were born to be an aristocrat who assigned such tasks to the stewards of his estate. "Philip pushes the dirty work off on somebody else," Delmore once remarked; and in this long and close association, William Phillips—indolent as he was in so many other ways—had been the one who was there to take these unpleasant burdens on his shoulders. Now, when we had got back to the office, we would hear him in the next little room, where he had called the girl, clearing his throat and stammering as he began to tell her, as soothingly as he could, that the mistake was ours and she wasn't really needed after all. William was infinitely more softhearted than Philip, and yet it was he who had to do the nasty jobs like firing.

On the way back Delmore lagged a little, and I with him, as we watched William and Philip walking ahead, with William apparently doing most of the talking. "Look at William," Delmore said, "he's trying to win his friend back again." Kindhearted William Phillips was probably doing his best to make Rahv feel better, to assure him that the whole scene had really been enacted in the interests of friendship —"if we were out to get you, we would have acted behind your back, we wouldn't have brought matters out into the open." Delmore shook his head ruefully, as if the whole confrontation had been doomed from the start.

And he was right. The break was not healed. For a while—and not a very long while at that—the differences were hushed up, and things would go along quietly, but the tensions between the two would grow and become more vocal, and the relationship became more and more like a strained and bickering marriage. What was started that afternoon at lunch ended more than a decade later in a lawsuit over the ownership of the magazine.

Delmore said no more on the way back, but that night he had me over to his flat for a rehash of the whole confrontation. "It could happen this way only among Jews," he began; and suddenly he was off on a theoretical exploration of a theme—the difference between Jew and gentile—that preoccupied him a great deal at this time. "The gentile lives by wearing a mask," he went on. "The Jew by taking it off. He has to get everything out in the open." He was in a phase of discovering his Jewishness in a new and more somber sense. He had always been acutely conscious of being Jewish, and had made much use of it in his writings, but mostly in an ironic and self-mocking way. Hitler and the Nazis had made him think more somberly about the whole issue. If Jews were so persistently and terribly persecuted, there must be a reason, and perhaps they were as bad as the Nazis said. But maybe the key turned the other way: the Jew was persecuted because he was superior and therefore feared—and Delmore sought to find this superiority wherever he could. In these musings, consequently, he would become more antigentile as he waxed more pro-Jewish. With me he could be outrageously frank in these explorations because, though I was gentile, I somehow belonged to the Jewish camp; and this duality added another piquant touch to our relationship. Delmore could not have gotten quite as much zest out of attacking the gentile with another Jew.

For my part, I was not so sure about his high-flown interpretation of the scene at lunch. Certainly, it would not be the way Philip Rahv would look at that confrontation. From his point of view it was a display of weakness on the part of the adversary. If they wanted to crush him, they should have proceeded by other means; as it was, they had merely indulged in some "psychological aggrandizement" in order to humiliate him, but that in itself was a sign of his superiority. They had been three to one, and he had faced them and come through. Rahv did not believe very much in friendship, but he did believe in power. Of course, he seemed somewhat chastened for a short while, but he was really going about his business more warily and cautiously. Presently he was his old self again, and I have no doubt his tongue began to wag just as freely in whatever places he chose to drop his wisdom.

It would have been impossible for Rahv—more than for nearly any-body I've known—not to be himself. The only time I knew him to be really crushed was when he read Mary McCarthy's cruel caricature in her novelette *The Oasis*. But that was in print and had the authority of the written word behind it, for which he had always a special respect; moreover, it represented him as ridiculous rather than evil; and, finally, the blow was struck by a woman of whom he had once been the lover, and for whom—according to Delmore—he had never ceased to nurse a special attachment.

When William Phillips had nervously cleared his throat, I had shifted to the edge of my chair to leave, sensing something unpleasant was on the way but not knowing what. But then the whole thing had burst into the open so quickly that I was overcome with curiosity to see how it would end and remained as if pinioned to my chair. Nevertheless, the nagging doubt came now that the right thing for me to have done would have been to get up and leave, since as a newcomer I should be party to this particular personal wrangle. William Phillips sensed my doubts on this score, and later apologized for not sparing me the whole scene. It was typical of his fundamental sensitivity toward other people that he should have felt this. On one thing, however, there was no doubt in my mind at all: henceforth the circle of the magazine was divided into the party of Rahv and the party of Phillips, and I would now belong to the latter. I would have been drawn this way simply by my friendship with Delmore, who was now on the side of William Phillips. Even on my own I would have been led to take William's side, for his kindness and good humor toward me had already won my affection. Rahv, I felt, was a powerful and fascinating figure, but at this stage of our relations he struck me as forbidding and bleak.

Yet, however my sympathies lay, I had to wonder about Rahv's side of the argument. Had he been right, after all, when he said that the destructive talk he was being charged with was part of the literary life of a whole circle—that "everybody" did it, and perhaps he was only a little more exuberant and impressive in scoring his points? Certainly, people gossip; the main topic of human conversation, as Jane Austen remarked, is the failings of other people. But there was a certain glee, an intellectual savagery, with which this circle went at the dissection of character. Was it the spirit of the Jewish ghetto, as Delmore maintained, where everything has to hang out in the open, perpetuating itself now in a new country? Or the rawness of the American spirit, unused to the refinements of a salon, going about producing one with its own point-blank and destructive energy? Or both at once?

These questions were with me during an editorial meeting not long after the confrontation. Unlike the latter, however, this was one of exceptional good humor. Whatever tensions there were had disappeared, for the time being at least, far below the surface. Delmore and Philip Rahv were enjoying each other's sallies uproariously. When animosities were pushed aside, these two could appreciate each other's qualities of mind enormously. The subject—or target?—in this case was Alfred Kazin, who was not a personal favorite of the editors. The sources of their hostility against him were never fully clear to me. Perhaps his association with *The New Republic*, with which they had been doing political battle at the time, made him suspect in their eyes. But I think the animus against him came from his personal tone: Kazin was too earnest and serious in conversation to leave the *PR* editors comfortable. "Alfred insists so much on sincerity when he's talking to me," William Phillips laughed, "that he makes me feel insincere."

Nevertheless, Kazin's abilities as a writer were recognized, and a contribution from him was usually welcome; and it was one at hand now that provoked the present dissection of his character. He had been in Italy, and sent in some pages of an "Italian Journal," which the magazine was already sending to the printer. Why an Italian Journal? "Well," Delmore ventured, "Goethe wrote an Italian Journal, and Alfred decided he would have to do one too."

The characteristic handling of wit in the circle was not merely that a *mot* would be remembered, but that it would also be recalled with the name of the person who originally said it (which is not a bad way to start feuds). Thus Rahv, presently trotting out an old remark that had been made about Kazin years ago when the latter first appeared on the scene, was careful to identify its original source: "Alfred is always ambitious—the starry-eyed opportunist, as Diana Trilling called him."

Coming a little more up to date, Delmore reported that he had just run into Mary McCarthy, who had wondered out loud why "When Alfred had been in Italy, they didn't press all the olive oil out of him."

The session was now launched and pleasant. Rahv announced that he had just heard Kazin was turning to the subject of Melville. "I wonder what Alfred will make of *Moby Dick* when he turns all that Jewish schmaltz loose on Captain Ahab and the White Whale."

Delmore leaped to his feet and took the stance of the harpooner ready to strike at the cry of "Whale ahoy!" Then he lunged, hurling the invisible harpoon, yelled "Gefilte fish!" and collapsed back, giggling, into his chair. Rahv was giving off bass chuckles. When he was really amused, his laugh was Russian, Slavic, from the belly.

All of this was so exuberant that it was almost free from any malice, and even carried a certain affection for the victim. They were expressing a certain Jewish self-irony at one of their own and a representative figure at that—the earnest young man on the make. Moreover, it had been done *en famille,* and where else has one the right to discourse on the foibles of others if not in the bosom of the family? The trouble was that remarks made in the family did not always remain there but had a way of getting noised abroad and passing into circles where their effect would be malicious and damaging. The question was whether Rahv ever observed this distinction— whether he would not deliver his personal observations wherever he pleased. On the other hand, it was a question whether his accusers, from the simple fact that they too participated in the circle, would not acquire dirty hands themselves. Rahv stood so much at the center of the circle, he embodied it so much in his single person, that his own negative attitude could hardly keep from spreading to the whole.

Certainly, the sheer intensity of the group itself could be enough to drain one's energies—especially away from writing. The writer is always secretly seeking some seduction from the painful loneliness of his desk. The excitement of ideas and intellectual talk are potent temptations. You may even come to believe that you have accomplished something for the day when you have rounded off a phrase or succeeded at last in making your point in an argument. But between such phrases made or points scored in argument and the written paragraph there is an abysmal gulf; and sooner or later the writer comes to know he has wasted his time.

Besides, there was a danger for creative writers particularly in becoming too deeply involved in a circle where every item of experience was intellectualized. James Agee felt this chill and withdrew. He had been a contributor to *Partisan Review* in its early days, and he was an old school friend of Dwight Macdonald, and by all odds should now have been within the fold. But in these post-War years he resolutely kept his distance while inveighing against "intellectuals" and "highbrows" generally. Agee and Delmore Schwartz had their first real meeting in the summer of 1939, and I remember it as one of the most exhilarating afternoons I have spent. Both were just about to burst forth into literary acclaim: Delmore's first book was just published, and Agee was completing *Let Us Now Praise Famous Men*. I thought at the time that here were the two best literary talents of their generation, and the talent in both was essentially poetic. That afternoon they talked as poets together, without inhibition and without artificiality. They really seemed to hit it off together; I expected they would form a close friendship, and for a while during his first years at Harvard, whenever he came to New York, Delmore would visit Agee in his house on King Street in the Village. But when Delmore became intricately involved with *Partisan Review*, the friendship faded out. Agee felt the close-knit atmosphere of the New York intellectuals as an alien one and did not wish to get too near it, even when the contagion might be carried by a fellow poet.

One writer whom the circle could not intimidate in any way was Mary McCarthy. The human and personal tensions within the group, which might upset some writers and get in the way of their work, were the kind of things that set her creativity flowing. She had left *Partisan Review* years before, and she was not now officially connected with the magazine. But she moved in and out of the circle as she chose; and these entrances and exits were rather regal, and more often than not attended by some small storm. I see her indeed in the image of a Valkyrie maiden, riding her steed into the circle, amid thunder and lightning, and out again, bearing the body of some dead hero across her saddle—herself unscathed and headed promptly for her typewriter. But in this respect Mary McCarthy was almost superhuman, and not everyone could command her powers of resilience.

Elizabeth Hardwick, for example, who had recently entered the circle, was rather troubled by the personal cross-currents she found there. She was then in the position of the young writer who has come to New York to make it, having trouble with and doubts about the novel she was writing, as well as being in the difficult position of a very attractive young woman alone in the city. Plunged now into this intense intellectual milieu, she had a good deal to cope with, and for a while it seemed touch and go whether she might not head back to Kentucky. But, as it turned out, she had enough talent, brains, and human resourcefulness to cope with all these difficulties, and she has survived—magnificently so. Nevertheless, I believe—and this is a purely personal impression—that the possibility of a simpler and more direct kind of fiction that she was then exploring became permanently closed to her by her immersion in this intellectual circle.

But it was Saul Bellow who was the past master at protecting himself in his relations with the group. Whenever he was in New York, he made contact with the *Partisan Review* circle, but he did not let himself get entangled in it. He needed to observe the New York intellectuals, to be stimulated by them, and learn from them what he wanted—that was his job as a writer, and Bellow was a full-time writer. But he moved always at the edge of the circle. He was wary and guarded—above all, guarding the talent and concentration of his vocation. At this time he was gestating *Augie March,* and when the book came out I immediately recognized the hero as one part of himself that Bellow carried openly before the world. He was the kid from Chicago, carrying a chip on his shoulder, and ready to show these Eastern slickers that he was just as street-smart (intellectually) as they were. He made me think at times of the great Chicago welterweight Barney Ross, who had come to New York a few years earlier and beaten all the Eastern contenders. Not that there was anything raucous or overtly aggressive in his behavior; on the contrary, his manner was civilized and gentle; but the chip of self-confidence was there on the shoulder just the same. And Bellow never faltered in this single-minded dedication to his muse; the solid body of work he went on to create is to be admired as, among other things, a triumph of character.

I wish now I had reflected a little more on his strategy of self-protection. But at the time I was too taken up by the intellectual intensity and excitement generated by the circle to heed the warning note of the scene I had just been through. With the "confrontation" I had at last arrived; whether I would be able to cope was another question.

Part II

Sojourn

Chapter Three

The New York Intellectual

I.

The rift between the two editors was, in an odd way, to make my relations with Rahv closer than they otherwise might have been. He needed an audience for his tirades, whenever the oratorical mood came upon him, and I happened to be at hand. After the confrontation, William Phillips and Delmore Schwartz would not be as sympathetic listeners as once they had been. Besides, even apart from the presumed hostility that the confrontation would have left behind it, they were used to his harangues and were in that respect a somewhat jaded audience who had heard it all before. At least I was a fresh ear, however unsatisfactory I might prove in other ways.

"A mouth in search of an ear," was Mary McCarthy's phrase for Meyer Schapiro, professor of art history at Columbia. Schapiro was one of the great lecturers of our time, and the flow of his eloquence was not confined to the classroom. Encountered almost anywhere, on a street corner or a subway train, his discourse would pour effortlessly forth as if all the while he had simply been waiting for your receptive ear. Rahv's eloquence was of a different order, and his need of an audience more inconstant and sporadic. He would go long stretches silent or laconic to the point of rudeness; and indeed this taciturn and dark side was part of the somewhat menacing *persona* he could present to the world. But when the need hit him, almost like a physical urge to deliver himself of something festering inside, Rahv would become, in Miss McCarthy's phrase, very much a mouth in search of an ear. And for several years I was to become a receptive ear, simply because I was closest at hand, though he may also have been encouraged by the eagerness with which I listened.

But my first encounter with him of this sort was to prove rather unsettling. It happened only a few days after Delmore Schwartz had burst in on me with the startling announcement that I was "now one of the editors of *Partisan Review.*" (It was delivered like that, a *fiat*; I was never asked whether I would like to join the staff.) I received the announcement with a mixture of emotions, of which diffidence and uncertainty about the role I might play on the magazine were a good part. Some reassurance, however, came a day later from William Phillips. He called on me in the afternoon, embarrassed, I think, at the dinginess of my flat but perhaps more at finding words for what he wanted to say. The substance of it was that he wanted to reassure me there was a place for me on the magazine, that I would indeed be able to contribute something, and that *PR* could use some fresh blood. The point that struck me then, and even more strongly as I later recalled it, was that William had the human tact to sense what my uncertainty might be, even though he had not talked with me since Delmore's announcement.

But Philip Rahv, I imagined, would be a more formidable obstacle to face. Though I had met him a few times in the past, we had never had any real conversation together and I stood in awe of him. For someone younger in years and many years younger in experience, Rahv was quite overwhelming in the impression he made. But as it happened, our first encounter took place in an abrupt and unexpected way for which no preparation of mine would have helped. It was only a day or so after William Phillips's reassuring visit, and before I had yet attended my first editorial meeting, that I ran into Rahv in Washington Square. I was to run into him there a lot in the next years. He was, when the mood struck him, as lazy as a cat, and the long afternoons when he should have been working he would let idle by in some ramble through the Village. The area he patrolled was only a few square blocks, and he usually ended on his way home by going through the Square.

He mentioned nothing about my coming on the magazine but instead launched into a long harangue. It seemed to me strangely impersonal, as if he were talking through me or else spelling out instructions to some newly hired hand. His principal subjects then were either Stalinism and Soviet expansionism or the *Kenyon Review* and the evils of the New Criticism. They were the chief *bêtes noires* (in a private world peopled very much by *bêtes noires*) that could launch him on his oratory, and he could become as passionately inflamed against the one as against the other. Stalin and Stalinism enraged him because they had distorted the whole nature and meaning of Marxism; and the New Criticism, since it sought to examine the work of literature as a self-contained object, tried to escape from the broad claim of Marxism that the literary work cannot be torn from its social and historical context. On both of his pet subjects, then, his point of view claimed to be consistently Marxist.

I have compared him to Meyer Schapiro in this need to pour himself out to a listener, but there could scarcely be any greater difference than between the talk of these two men. Schapiro's was a smooth and foaming flood, almost ecstatic in self-surrender to its own eloquence, with each sentence chasing swiftly on the heels of the preceding one. Rahv's, by comparison, was a very choppy current indeed, punctuated by grunts and sighs; he seemed to prod his individual sentences along, sometimes chuckling at them for having spoken out well, or slapping one of them on the back to make it speak up louder. And yet in their own way his tirades had eloquence too; the whole menacing and angry person who was Rahv came at you in these gusts of language.

His topic this day was the political one, and he spelled it out for me in its simplest terms as if I should get this basic instruction correct at the outset. The War had just ended (this was September 1945), and a revolutionary situation existed in Western Europe. A revolution would be good; but the left-wing elements were all decadent and corrupt minions of Stalin, and could be expected only to lead any revolution straight back to Moscow. In the generally disordered state of Europe

Stalin's power could potentially extend from the Baltic to the English Channel. Except for one thing, and one thing only—and here Rahv paused to drive home his point. Except for the power of the United States. That was the only thing that stood between the present confused situation and the Stalinization of the whole West. The intellectuals here were stupid in not recognizing this fact. They talk in the air, they're *Luftmenschen* (a favorite word of his), they don't have their feet on the ground. They don't realize their own existence depends on the continued presence of the United States. But—and here he snorted—when the chips are down they'll come running back to Mama.

I have to emphasize again the impersonality of all this; Rahv and I were scarcely acquainted, and I was about to join the magazine that was his heart's blood; but he had made no venture into any preliminary small talk, any gesture toward clearing the middle ground of a preliminary acquaintanceship, before he had plunged into his speech. And I, for my part, made no effort to break in, out of timidity and diffidence, and because I had not heard the international situation summed up so bluntly and forcefully before. But as he went on, I began to feel physically uncomfortable. It was a late afternoon in September, unseasonably cold, colder than I had thought when I left home, and I had put on no coat. I was beginning to shiver a little as the shadows in the Square lengthened, but Rahv paid no attention, having captured a passive ear and riding in the full flood of his oration. He was always, or nearly always, worth listening to, and I was fascinated—but freezing. I can't remember by what excuse I managed to make my escape.

Rahv was promptly ready with his verdict on me, and I got it back from Delmore Schwartz, almost immediately, a day or so later. "Will has no ideas," he told Delmore. I wondered how he could conclude this when I had hardly said more than two words. It also struck me, faintly then, but strongly through later experience (this first encounter was several weeks before "the confrontation" of our last chapter) that Rahv could be singularly incautious, for surely he must have known, if he'd stopped for a moment to think, that Delmore would report his words back to me. When the mood was on him, which was often, he could and did speak witheringly about people he knew, and more than once the words got back to the original person. For a man whose mind was so filled with plots and counterplots, he could be very incautious.

Still, I was puzzled about this business of not having ideas. It was—as Mary McCarthy notes in her affectionate memoir of him—a constant judgment Rahv made of other writers and intellectuals. Edmund Wilson, for example, was a target. "Wilson is a good writer," he would say, "but he has no ideas." Wilson was something of an obsession with him—"like a boil on the brain," to use one of his own expressions—for reasons of a quite personal nature. But Wilson had a body of work behind him, on which, rightly or wrongly, Rahv's judgment might be made. But why pick on me, and for so few words spoken? And what, after all, did Rahv really mean by "ideas," what kind of "ideas" specifically did he have in mind?

I persisted in this latter question with Delmore, because it had begun to interest me. "Well, you know," Delmore finally said, "something like 'Redskin and Paleface.'" This is the title of one of Rahv's best-known essays, in which he explores the American mind as exhibited in our literature. That mind, he found, was pulled toward polar opposites—the cult of raw experience, on the one hand, and, on the other, the cramping inheritance of the Puritan spirit and of the Genteel Tradition in its pursuit of high culture without roots in the native soil. The American writer thus tends to be either a Redskin, a primitive thirsting for simple-minded and direct experience, or an overcultivated Brahmin surveying the world through his borrowed culture. These points, or suggestions of them, had been made many times before and by numerous critics; but no one had brought the matter so compactly together and placed it in judicious focus as he had done. These, then, would be the "ideas" Rahv meant when he judged other intellectuals by their presence or absence. Delmore was very perceptive here. The "ideas" that concerned Philip Rahv were always concrete and intuitive, usually dramatic and colorful simplifications of already known but diffuse literary and political perceptions. He had little liking and in fact very little capacity for abstract ideas as such. This was a weakness, however, which he turned into a strength, for it kept his feet on the ground and his mind attuned to the concrete. Still, it was ironical that he who so readily condemned others for not having ideas was always uncomfortable with an intellectual like Harold Rosenberg simply because of Rosenberg's dazzling facility with ideas.

I bring Rosenberg's name in here because he has a bearing on the central point of this chapter. Were I to fall into Rahvian language, I would say that he and Harold Rosenberg represented "polar opposites" within the mythical archtype of the New York Intellectual. I had begun to wonder about this figure of the New York Intellectual about whom one seemed to hear so much. Did it—or he—really exist? What were his qualities, and who really represented him? Was he short or tall? Harold Rosenberg was big and husky, built like a fullback. When he and Clement Greenberg had had a disagreement on the subject of art, Greenberg (who had been prone in other cases to use his fists) came away saying, "I'm not going to tangle with that guy, he's too big." Was this mythical intellectual Jew or gentile? The consensus seemed to be that he was Jewish; and even the phrase "New York intellectual" in some mouths had a certain suspicion of anti-Semitism. Yet four of the six people who had launched *Partisan Review* were gentile. This intellectual would have "ideas," of course; but what kind of "ideas"? Like those of Philip Rahv or of Harold Rosenberg? Did this intellectual really think or merely cerebrate? I had begun reading the Existentialists and this distinction had begun to force itself on me. A few years later I would read Heidegger's *What Is Thinking?* and that made the question more acute. It was difficult at times to make out just what Heidegger meant by thinking, but I could take guidance from one thing: whatever it was Heidegger meant, thinking as he understood it was not done by the New York intellectuals I knew. Genuine thinking, according to Heidegger, ends in silence. That would not quite apply to Meyer Schapiro or Philip Rahv or Harold Rosenberg.

These questions were not so explicit to me at the time, but the whole question had begun to occupy me; and from time to time I explored it in desultory fashion with Delmore Schwartz. There was one side of the question on which Delmore was very definite: Why was the usual phrase "the New York intellectual," why not "the American intellectual" or, more simply, "the intellectual"? The reason, Delmore said, was that New York itself was not really an American city—it was "the last outpost of Europe" on these shores—and the intellectual life does not fit in with our native American habits. I think there is something to be said for this point of view.

In any case, there seemed to be other grounds for Rahv's irritation with Rosenberg than the simple difference in the configuration of their minds. At one point in a meeting I had brought up Rosenberg's name in a certain connection, and my mention of it was greeted with an abrupt and heavy silence. This puzzled me, and I asked Delmore privately why Rosenberg wasn't writing for the magazine at this time.

"Didn't you know?" Delmore replied, and gave me the story. Rahv, who had been one of the leaders in the Henry James revival, had put out a collection of James's stories. Rosenberg, glancing at the book, had remarked to someone, "The Henry James delicatessen," and the remark had gotten back to Rahv. From that time on, Rahv swore, Rosenberg would never appear in the magazine again. Though at times he could walk quite callously over other people's sensitivities, Rahv was morbidly sensitive to any slight to himself. "You better not bring up Rosenberg's name in his hearing," Delmore warned me, "or he'll have a mild hemorrhage."

But Rahv himself, in our talks, would bring in Rosenberg's name from time to time without any particular convulsion. Rosenberg was brilliant, if you cared for that kind of thing, but he was a *Luftmensch* (again that word), who blew intellectual soap bubbles but never got down to solid earth. Rosenberg had been along the way a poet and had committed himself to a volume of verse, *Trance Above the Streets*, and in Rahv's view he had remained where this title indicated ever since. In short, Rosenberg was after all just a bohemian intellectual; he lacked a base, whereas Rahv had that base in a magazine for whose policies he had to take responsible and sober judgment. I wonder what Rahv would have said later on when in fact Rosenberg did secure such an institutional attachment and became the art critic of *The New Yorker*, a position from which he could and did exercise considerable influence.

II.

What if one went further afield in one's search for this representative intellectual? Might not Edmund Wilson be a stand-in for the type? That might seem strange according to the view of Wilson in our circle. But for an earlier decade, the 1920s, Wilson had been a decidedly intellectual figure for his contemporaries. To Scott Fitzgerald, for example, he had certainly been the intellectual par excellence. For years, Fitzgerald tells us, Wilson had been his intellectual conscience. And one gets the sense from Wilson's own writings, and from other records, that he moved amid the Village life of the 1920s as the arrogant young intellectual passing judgment. This would even seem to be the point of the anecdote told by Allen Tate. Wilson had come to visit the Tates in the South, and no sooner had he arrived and deposited his grips on the porch than he turned and flung out the question, "Now where are the sharecroppers?" Among other things the story would seem to illustrate the tendency of the Leftist urban intellectual to impose his own abstract framework upon the more organic and concrete situation of the Southerner.

These thoughts crossed my mind—I did not voice them—one day in conversation with Rahv. Our talks together had now reached the stage where they could be called conversations in the broad sense of that word—at least I got in words of my own. There were even subjects on which Rahv seemed to want to hear what I had to say—and this was particularly the case on the subject of Edmund Wilson.

I had gotten to know Wilson in Rome toward the very end of the War, and it had come about with the abruptness that was to prove typical of him. The phone in my office rang, and the voice at the other end said, "This is Edmund Wilson." I had difficulty placing the caller altogether, for Edmund Wilson was hardly a person expected to turn up in this situation and be asking for me. But after identifications had been established, I made a date with him for lunch. Thereafter, I was to see him off and on throughout the weeks that he stayed in Italy.

He was there as war correspondent for *The New Yorker*. This in itself seemed to me a very strange assignment for a man of Wilson's age and temperament. It was odd to see his short and pudgy figure, above which the face of Herbert Hoover looked intently at you, dressed in the khakis of a military correspondent. Wilson himself must have insisted on the assignment; it was part of the figure he cut as the complete man of letters; he had written criticism, history, fiction, poetry, and worked as an editor, but he needed now to add the final role of the war correspondent in the tradition of Stephen Crane and Ernest Hemingway. Not that he would be expected to file stories of actual combat, of blood and guns and the red badge of courage. The War must be really over, it struck me, if *The New Yorker* is sending Wilson out as a correspondent. For readers back home the War had so definitely moved into its conclusion that they wanted *The New Yorker*, in its usual style, to provide them with stories of atmosphere and local color. My informal job was to help Wilson find some of that local color.

I had done my Baedeker very diligently in my spare moments, and I

knew the city fairly well. Wilson said that he had only visited Rome
once, when he was a boy, and that his memories of the place were
very faint. I took him to the more traditional parts of the city first. But
I soon found out that Wilson would see only what he wanted to look
at: his mind moved amid the words of some piece he was projecting
and any perception could register only as it fell in line with what he
might come to write. He had, he said, an especial desire to see the
Forum. He had been taken there as a boy, and he remembered being
very moved by it, but his memories of it were now very vague. When
I took him through it, however, I noticed that for the most part he
walked along watching his feet. His walk itself was something memorable; I think I learned the meaning of waddle from it, or rather the
possible varieties and nuances of a waddle; Wilson moved with swift
short steps, and his waddle was something of a trot. There must have
been something comic in the pair of us: myself in the role of *cicerone*
with this little man toddling rapidly beside me, picking his way over
the stones of the Forum, watching his feet all the while.

At one point, since these ancient stones did not rouse his interest, I
thought to arrest his attention by a literary reference. There is, near
the Capitoline end of the Forum a medieval house said to have been
occupied by Cola di Rienzi during the time he was trying to restore a
Roman republic. It is remarkable for the layers of time the structure
incorporates: ancient tufa stone at the base from the ancient Roman
republic, limestone and tags of marble from Imperial Rome, and on
top of that the old red brickwork of the Middle Ages. "It makes me
think of Joyce's *Finnegans Wake*," I said, deliberately aiming at something that might get a rise from Wilson. "Here the layers of time are
superimposed in brick and stone, Joyce excavates them in language."
As soon as the object before us had been transferred into some literary
context, Wilson's interest quickened and he looked up. "Gosh, yes," he
said. He had recently been reworking his essay on Joyce and *Finnegans Wake*, and I had touched upon something that was a literary
project of his own, and therefore he could get interested.

Wilson saw what he wanted to see. One morning a troop of Russians—men and women—appeared in my office. They were refugees
who had fled before the advancing Russian armies and somehow had
made their way down into Italy into one of the nearby Allied camps.
They were now in something of a panic because Soviet officials had
begun to go through these camps looking for Russian nationals, whom

they then shipped back to the Soviet Union. I tried to allay their fears: this could not really be happening in a camp run by the Allies, the Allied officials would not permit it. The Russians shook their heads No; they had already seen it happen to some friends of theirs in a nearby camp. We were all jabbering away in an assortment of pidgin languages. I tried to get a girl from the American Embassy who was fluent in Russian to come over and process their complaints; but she would not be available till the next morning. I told the Russians to come back on the following morning, and we would do what we could for them. Meanwhile, I tried to be as reassuring as I could.

That day at lunch I told Wilson about the Russian refugees; it seemed to me a kind of lead that a journalist might want to look into. But he never followed it up; there were other things he wanted to see, and he soon forgot it. I myself forgot it after a few days. The Russians themselves never came back—whether they took to their heels, distrusting Allied protection, or had been pounced upon by the Soviet agents and transported to Siberia, I do not know. I bring up the incident not to tax Wilson's memory with it; he was a literary man reporting on atmosphere, not an investigative reporter ready to dig up a scandal; besides, none of us at the time suspected the story was as big and awful as it turned out to be. I recall the incident here because it bears upon the question of who started the Cold War, and whether the Russians did not merely respond to our gestures at playing tough. In fact, the Allies—Britain and America—leaned over backward in allowing Soviet agents to repatriate their own nationals. Nothing must be done to shake the wartime amity with the Soviets. The result was one of the worst blots on the Allied record in that war: millions of Russians were denied the right of sanctuary, and were returned "home"—a euphemism for being deported to Siberia. Stalin was Stalin and operated as Stalin at every moment during the war. He did not have to wait to be provoked.

Wilson saw what he wanted to see—even when it wasn't there to be seen. He was an avid student of languages, but not always, as Vladimir Nabokov pointed out in another context, as accurate in the language as he thought. I had arranged for him to take a few lessons in Italian with a university student I knew, and within a few days he felt he had the language in hand. The North of Italy had been liberated by this time, and there seemed to be a great ferment going on in Milan. Wilson became persuaded somehow that there was a great countermovement against the Left taking place, and he went up to check. One piece of evidence he brought back was about a sign in the window of a bookstore in the center of the city that read: "Socialist books are not sold here." Wilson took this as an indication of how strongly the Right was now reacting in that central city. A few days later I had to go up to Milan, and I checked on the bookstore. The phrase in Italian was *libri scolastici*, which means scholastic books, or textbooks, as we should say, not "socialist" books at all; and the sign had simply served notice it did not sell school texts, to keep out swarms of students from its shelves. Months later when I was back in the United States, I looked up an old *New Yorker*, and, sure enough, Wilson was telling its readers that Rightist sentiment was running so high in Milan that bookstores would not sell socialist books.

Rahv pumped me for whatever trivial incidents I had to tell, for they somehow fattened his own ego against Wilson. But there was one remark I did not tell, though it got back to Rahv anyway. When I saw Wilson after I was back in America, I told him I had joined the staff of *Partisan Review;* he merely laughed and remarked of Rahv and Phillips "Potash and Perlmutter." He was citing an earlier comedy of his own playgoing years. Potash and Perlmutter are the eternal pair of bumbling Jewish businessmen, yoked together and perpetually querulous about each other, but somehow managing a business that survives by the skin of its teeth. Wilson's remark was intended to be humorous, not malicious; there was much anger but no great malice in the man that I ever noticed; but when the remark got back home it had changed coloration. I had told it secretly to Delmore, but he leaked it. And Rahv's retort on this occasion was pithy and vigorous: "The shmuck!" he said of Edmund Wilson.

"How could you talk with him?" Philip Rahv asked me now. It was on the tip of my tongue to answer, "The same way I talk with you. I listen, and then if the silence gets too awkward, I try to fill it." But I could imagine very well what Rahv meant. Wilson had evidently been a very trying person in New York circles, truculently silent or abrupt and very difficult to make any kind of ordinary conversation with. Rahv, of course, had dealt with him socially under the most formidable and chilling circumstances. Wilson had stolen his girl, Mary McCarthy, and was a nationally prominent man of letters. Here were two barriers of inferiority which even a Philip Rahv might find it difficult to surmount. Rahv had married—on the rebound, it was said—

a Vassar friend of Mary McCarthy's, Nathalie Swan. In the interests of restoring good feeling the two couples occasionally socialized, whenever the Wilsons came to town. With the various undercurrents in such a foursome, these occasions must have been gruesome. And the situation was made worse when the older man out of some impulse of generosity sought to give the younger man advice about the latter's writing. That was almost like rubbing Rahv's nose in the dirt.

But I had met Wilson under very different and more relaxed circumstances than New York circles can ever be. I was not an aspiring young writer thrusting myself upon him; I was a nobody who had simply turned up in his path—a nobody who had a certain amount of interesting and useful information for him, and had read enough books so that I understood his thoughts whenever he chose not to be silent. There was thus no ego contest going on beneath the surface. Moreover, I liked Wilson personally; and the other person, whether he knows it or not, usually responds to his being liked, so that social intercourse is made that much easier. Beneath his eccentric and gruff exterior, Wilson had great integrity, and also—something that usually has not been noted—kindness and good will. As he grew older, he was claimed more and more by the older American virtues in which he grew up. No—I reflected to myself during one of these conversations with Rahv—Wilson would not do for the type of the New York Intellectual. However he may have passed as the intellectual for a previous generation in Greenwich Village, he would not fit in at all with New York intellectual circles in which I was then moving. Wilson was too much in the American grain to serve now as an exemplar of the type. The New York Intellectual connoted something faintly alien to our native American roots and native habits. Perhaps Delmore Schwartz was right in a way: the intellectual, in popular journalistic references, was so often labeled the New York Intellectual because New York itself was a kind of foreign city—"the last outpost of Europe"—and the intellectual life was really alien to our native habits and traditions. I did not know. The more I pursued this myth, this ideal archtype of the intellectual, the more puzzled I seemed to become.

But why not take a further step in pursuit of the phantom? Why must this imaginary figure always be pictured as a man? Why could not this mythical intellectual be realized as completely in the person of a woman? For the popular imagination, of course, this figure of the

New York Intellectual, however vague it might be in other respects, was always definitely of the male sex. But in this, as in other matters, the popular consciousness might well be wrong. And if one let one's mind take this step, and dared to imagine the typical intellectual as a woman, then it seemed to me there could only be one person on whom one's choice could light—Mary McCarthy.

Certainly, the intellectual impulse plays as dominant a part in her writing as in any male's; and in her fiction particularly, this impulse takes such a grip of her that it finally stifles the life out of her characters. This is the only reason to explain why her novels and stories are not greater than they are; they have every other gift—wit, sharp observation, extraordinary intelligence, an unflagging brilliance and elegance of language; they lack only the simple virtue of feeling. It is feeling, in literature as in life, that allows the other person to be what he or she is; the intellect must compress the personality into a concept or formula. Her characters are all so uniformly and brilliantly lighted that we can see them only as flat. Her sentences move forward elegantly and gracefully without ever missing a beat; they never shade off into any indefinite or mysterious depth. When a writer has sacrificed so much on the altar of sheer intelligence, perhaps she deserves to be regarded as the intellectual par excellence, the exemplar of that mythical figure I had been trying to explore.

Miss McCarthy plays a small part in this memoir. She was not at this time actively connected with the magazine; her political sympathies seemed to lie in the direction of Dwight Macdonald's *politics*, and her chief literary energies, for very good economic reasons, were directed to writing fiction and autobiographical sketches for *The New Yorker*. Had she been an active figure in the magazine, her presence might very well have overshadowed everyone else's, and this memoir would accordingly have had to take a different shape. I am rather glad that she was not, for it would require three volumes at least to begin to do justice to this extraordinary woman—one of the most extraordinary, I believe, of our time.

Miss McCarthy was not altogether disconnected from the magazine; from time to time she contributed pieces on current drama. These short reviews and essays were perhaps the most lively and sparkling writing we were then printing; and they strike me as among the best things she has done. They were relatively short, for one thing, and their brilliance therefore did not exhaust or bewilder the reader. For another thing, she was in her element, and she had a message. Dealing with the contemporary theater as it was then represented by Broadway, she was involved above all in matters of style, diction, language, bearing, and performance; and these were the things that were her real subject matter as a writer. What a pity this woman was not born into some time when style was the essence of life itself, the Court of Versailles or a salon of the eighteenth century! She would have produced an imperishable comment on human beings and human nature without having recourse to the subterfuge of fiction, the machinery of which often creaked in her hands. And, writing on the theater, she had a very plain and central message to deliver: the language of our current American drama had forsworn literature; as written, it could hardly be read; and as spoken from the stage, could hardly be heard. The famed Method acting, which had become a kind of sacred fetish among the professionals, was really a training to teach actors how to mumble. The great moment of revelation came in a movie of Shakespeare's *Julius Caesar* in which Marlon Brando appeared alongside of John Gielgud; Brando, in the best non-style of Method acting, mumbled his lines as if he had marbles in his mouth; from Gielgud's lips Shakespeare's language flowed with its clear and pristine freshness. At times Mary McCarthy may have wielded her hatchet with more even than her usual exuberance; but this might be justified as the traditional rhetorical device of hyperbole, and besides, there must have been moments of desperation when she felt she was the only critic around who cared whether plays were decently written and spoken. It might seem slightly exaggerated, for example, to say that Tennessee Williams's *A Streetcar Named Desire* is about a man's difficulties in getting into the bathroom because his sister-in-law is always occupying it; but the remark is near enough the truth to puncture the claims of profundity which so many critics were making for that play.

Just as, in the role of intellectual commentator, she herself was always the leading character in her fictions, so her best book still remains her first, *The Company She Keeps*, in which she is at once protagonist, crusader, and expositor. Indeed, the young heroine of this fascinating series of adventures is almost a dramatized thesis in herself. She has taken as her motto the saying of Chaucer's woman, "I am mine own woman well at ease." Carrying this Chaucerian blazon into the melee of the New York publishing and intellectual world requires the great courage to risk making a fool of herself; she has entered a man's world and, faithful to her motto, she intends to hold her own with men—both intellectually and sexually. We did not know it then, but she was in fact firing the first salvo in the feminist war that now rages within our society, though I doubt that the movement has since produced any weapon of equal class and caliber. It was also something of a shocking book, or seemed so at the time. Delmore Schwartz privately referred to it as "Tidings from the Whore." However, he was at bottom a rather thoroughgoing Puritan, though not always aware of it, and he tended to regard Mary McCarthy as something of a fallen woman. But even *Time* magazine, as I remember, lamented that the book seemed to exhibit "the morals of a kennel." Rereading it now, we are struck rather by a certain quality of naïveté and innocence about the book. That may be because we have since advanced so much further, or sunk lower, in our moral laxity. But I think that is not altogether the reason; there is in fact a certain shyness, an innocent honesty, about Miss McCarthy's heroine; if she is one of the girls who kisses and tells, she does so because she feels it her moral duty to instruct the world about what it doesn't know. Beneath the surface I felt this odd shyness in the author herself when I met her socially; her laugh, which might have seemed hearty to some, was really, more often than not, nervously self-conscious.

To enter a man's world and to hold one's own there—intellectually and sexually! Mary McCarthy certainly did that intellectually, and from what one would gather from her writings, as well as from other reports, sexually too. So much so indeed, that she rather struck terror into some male bosoms. I remember being at some party or other, sitting beside two older men who suddenly froze as she entered the room. This struck me as a very curious response: here was this attractive and engaging woman, all smiles, and their recoil was as if an ogress, booted and spurred, had entered the room brandishing her whips. And in fact, from the point of view of her possible victims, she did carry a stinging whip—that impeccable syntax with which she might lash out in print at any time. And presently she was to strike home. In 1948 she brought out a satirical novelette, *The Oasis*, which caricatured the whole *Partisan Review* circle. Worse still, it appeared first in *Horizon*, the English magazine which was rather the opposite number to *Partisan Review*, and this was as if she had gone across the street to tell her bad news in a rival home. The circle gathered around like a group of mourners. "The woman is a thug," Diana

Trilling said. Neither she nor her husband, Lionel Trilling, had been
lampooned in McCarthy's story, but Mrs. Trilling felt it necessary to
deliver her disinterested moral judgment. The most upset of all was
Philip Rahv, the central figure in the whole caricature, and clearly
identifiable through the slightly changed fictitious name. It would not
have been so bad if he had merely been represented as evil, but he
was made ridiculous, and that wounded him to the quick. For a while
he went into virtual seclusion. For a whole week he did not come to
the office, and that was a rupture in his habits so violent that it could
be produced only by something on the order of a catastrophe. He
needed that daily walk to the office, the satisfaction of curiosity in fer-
reting out the mail (not always his own), and above all the escape it
provided from staring at the typewriter in the pangs of authorship. He
saw only his wife and . . . yes, William Phillips. For it was only the
latter from whom he could draw consolation at a moment like this.
William assured him that he was not discredited, that nobody around
town took the caricature as accurate, and, finally, that Rahv wasn't really like that at all.

For a moment Rahv could sink back on the breast of their former
and unsullied friendship. And for that moment Mary McCarthy had
come within a hairsbreadth of accomplishing what neither Delmore
nor I thought even remotely possible: she had *almost* healed the rift
and brought the two editors together again. Almost . . . But William
Phillips's consolation worked well (he was a practiced hand at it), and
very shortly Rahv was himself again and things took their inevitable
and appointed course. What was amazing was that there was no real
break in his friendship with Miss McCarthy. For his part he could
come to regard her act of writing as the play of a very brilliant child
who does not quite know what she is doing. And for her part she
probably had not thought her victim would be wounded, for it was all
in such fun.

Perhaps this childlike side accounts in part for the incredible energy
of her career. This amazing woman could ride through earthquake
and thunder, pass through the most dire upheavals in her personal
life, from which another woman might have collapsed in hysteria—
and her typewriter would go on indefatigably tapping. There are, of
course, hacks who go on pounding it out no matter what, but Miss
McCarthy is of another class; the energy of her writing always came

out unwearied, buoyant, and polished. Perhaps a certain adult ballast never weighed her down.

III.

No; despite her formidable claims to the title, Mary McCarthy cannot be considered as our ideal embodiment of *the* New York Intellectual. She is too much a law unto herself—too much her "own woman well at ease," or even when ill at ease for that matter—to serve as the paltry embodiment for any type.

Must we then give up our search for this phantom intellectual? We have found that his spiritual physiognomy varies too much from person to person: from mind to mind (Philip Rahv and Harold Rosenberg), from decade to decade (Edmund Wilson and Philip Rahv), from sex to sex (Mary McCarthy and Philip Rahv). There seems to be no sharp outline, no definite and clear-cut center, to this collective image of the intellectual. Shall we not then, in the spirit of a hard-headed empiricism, renounce this figure as a myth altogether, a concoction of the popular imagination and the phrase-making of journalists? To puncture a fantasy may often be an admirable and a necessary duty, but sometimes the removal of the myth leaves the world a little more flat and uninteresting. You wait discreetly and patiently a certain number of years until you can tell the child No, there is no Santa Claus; but then you find you have left its world that much emptier. Better perhaps, in some higher and more symbolic sense, to brace yourself and say, Yes, Virginia, there is a Santa Claus. Yes, there is such a figure as the New York Intellectual, and he is, or was, Philip Rahv.

In saying this, of course, I am proceeding somewhat like the mathematician who declares: Let P be the point we select in that domain. Which point? A multitude of others might serve. In a sense, the choice is arbitrary; but the choice once made, the characteristics of the point are neither arbitrary nor haphazard; they are essential; they help define the domain in which it stands. So Rahv illuminates essentially the period and the milieu in which he came to be. Even the narrow orbit in which he moved serves to throw a sharper light on things. He was, with William Phillips, co-founder of *Partisan Review* in 1934 (though the magazine began its real life in 1937, when it broke free of the Communist Party); and thereafter continued as an editor during the following two decades. He might thus seem to be a figure of purely local and circumscribed interest. But we should remember that during the time of his editorship and particularly the first two decades, he was at the center of most of the intellectual currents that flowed through and around New York, which is to say the currents that were to prove most significant for the nation as a whole.

He was also a product of the Depression, and the intellectual of the thirties had a distinct kind of identity that by now has virtually been lost: he floated free and institutionally unattached within the society at large. To be at loose ends was an unpleasant fate which that period inflicted on many, but for some it became an art of life to be followed along whatever paths one chose. Rahv used it to educate himself, again without the benefit of any institutional attachment, unless you call the public library at Jackson Square his college. Fred Dupee—who knew Rahv in the old days and retained a warm but judicious affection for him—pointed out the library to me as "Philip Rahv's alma mater." "They should have issued him a diploma," Dupee continued, "and there should be a bronze plaque on the building." The remark was intended as a tribute. There, day after day, sheltered from the Depression, Rahv read away, acquiring a literacy that was quite formidable. That he had done it on his own gave him a certain secret arrogance toward intellectuals who had had to acquire their education by taking degrees.

He was thus a reincarnation of the nineteenth-century intellectual, who floats freely within society, not imprisoned in any slot, cultivating his famous alienation, usually in the form of some kind of rebellion or other. This kind of intellectual is on the way out; the rational organization of modern life, which Weber pointed out, proceeds inexorably, and we all get assigned to some place or other. I was recently at a social gathering of New York intellectuals (rare for me now, since these days I am out of the world) and what struck me was that all the men present had their distinct, socially acknowledged, and fairly highly salaried positions within society—a few even within government.

At times Rahv seemed indeed to be a character who had stepped out of a nineteenth-century Russian novel; he made one think of Bazarov, the dissident freethinker in Turgenev's *Fathers and Children*. Atheism and irreligion in his lips still had the freshness of discovery that they carried in the previous century. But there was also something of a paradox in this nihilistic attitude of his, for his two favorite Russian authors—the ones to whom he felt closest and on whom he wrote best—were Dostoevski and Tolstoi, both intensely religious men. From time to time Delmore Schwartz and I pointed out this discrepancy to him, and Delmore even used to tease him about it, wondering whether Rahv were really as antireligious as he professed. Philip usually shrugged off the question; but once he declared, and with dead seriousness, that he had settled the religious question for himself when he was nine years old. To which Delmore immediately shot back: "And what other brilliant ideas did you have at the age of nine, Philip?"

I think now underneath his bluff exterior Rahv had his own *pietas,* his own religion—and it centered in his Marxist faith. On occasion he could question Lenin and Trotsky, and there was that blasphemous moment when he declared to me, "Lenin and Trotsky lied like hell." But he could not push further back, and question Marx himself. That was a step he could not take. Marxism was too much woven into the fabric of his being, it was the framework within which he took in experience, and he could no more have placed this framework in doubt than any other true believer can step outside his faith and question it. In retrospect, there was something touching about his Marxism; it provided the emotional center for his life, unifying in feeling his early years of poverty, the breadlines of his youth, his skirmishes with the Stalinists within the Communist Party, and his general dissatisfaction with the society around him (which, Rahv being Rahv, he would have felt for any social system in which he happened to find himself). For the present (the 1940s and 1950s) he let this framework recede into the background while he did his best work as a literary critic. But it was always there, and it is well to remember this when we try to understand his radical reversion in the tumult of the 1960s.

A man who has built himself up so painstakingly, who has tenaciously constructed bit by bit a center of culture within himself, is likely to be marked by some deeply conservative streak, whatever his beliefs. And Rahv was no exception. Even his gifts as an editor were really those of a certain conservatism. By this I don't mean any conservative ideology, but a conservatism of literary temperament. He had staked out, slowly and laboriously, a world for himself, and he wanted the magazine he edited to live within it with him. Mary McCarthy observes in her memoir of him that for Rahv literature began with Dostoevski and ended with Joyce and Eliot. At the time I first knew him he had not read *Ulysses* through; but he was reading at it, bit by bit,

71

and enough to gauge its power. He had the shrewd gift of triangulation, marking out his course like a good navigator in terms of his acknowledged landmarks, and gradually he could make room for Joyce. But Miss McCarthy is right; he wouldn't budge much further. Sometimes this conservatism of temperament shut him off from new currents. He did not want to hear much about what might be going on in the other arts, and he would gladly have turned his back, as we shall see, on Abstract Expressionism, which was the great breakthrough in painting at the time. He had a similar lack of interest in pop culture. Anatole Broyard, now literary critic with the *Times*, was in that period a young explorer of Village life and had written a piece on "The Hipster," which was then a very new phenomenon. I called it to Rahv's attention, it was printed, and Rahv liked it when he read it again in print. But he did not make much use of Broyard thereafter. The latter represented to him another generation and new things with which he did not want to cope. His mind was turned backward, rehearsing the sacred canon of the Great Moderns.

We have been in search here, innocently, I hope, for the New York Intellectual and have chosen Rahv as the case that might explain the type. But if the type is somewhat unclear to start with, do we make very much advance when the individual who is to explain it brings us in the end to paradox and mystery? There always remained something secretive and hidden about Rahv. In all those long conversations that went on between us he remained in a curious way impersonal about himself and his background. And this was not simply in his talk with me, for he left with other people whom he knew this same impression of something kept hidden. He had a brother living in Providence, who resembled him a good deal; when I was teaching at Brown I had seen his brother in the street, and thinking it was Philip, had gone up to speak with him but quickly found out my mistake. I told this to Philip, and he merely grunted; he did not want to talk about his family or background, and one had the impression at times that he might have come into existence full-blown as he was without antecedents. What he divulged of himself to the women with whom he was intimate, I cannot guess.

And what was not secretive in Rahv seemed to fling itself at you in a kind of flamboyant paradox. After he had done something outrageous one might grind one's teeth in anger, but one found it hard to hate him unwaveringly as a villain, for even there he had a certain charm of paradox about him. I think it was this side of his character that most fascinated Delmore Schwartz. I am speaking of Delmore now at a time before his rapid decline, when he was still one of the most perceptive minds around. Rahv fascinated him because Rahv made such a good subject for his own aphoristic wit. The *bon mot* inevitably simplifies and dramatizes a bit, but Delmore on Rahv was never completely off target. For example, one that particularly pleased him and that he delivered with perfect timing: "Philip Rahv does have scruples," said very reflectively and gravely; a judicious and reflective pause; then, with a sudden wide grin, "but he never lets them stand in his way." Extreme, yes, but not altogether without its point; and in its own way as good a brief summary of the moral side of Rahv's character (if it can be called that) as you can get. Delmore originally handed the remark out to me as a warning not to get too charmed by Rahv in the conversations I was having with him; but even in the warning itself he could not help being amused and charmed by the person he was warning me against.

But if one has doubts about the individual who is supposed to explicate the type, one is also turned back in doubt of oneself. When I rake over the ashes of a dead friend, are my own motives as pure as I might like them to be? The shade of Philip Rahv, gloatingly intoning *Schadenfreude*, joy at another's discomfiture, at me, rises before my vision. *De mortuis nil nisi bonum*, we should speak only good of the dead, runs the old maxim. It is a maxim to which I would subscribe with a few reservations. Our charity is needed more by the living, who are still struggling to cope with things, and who are easily upset by any disobliging remark. And when can one try to be candid about other people except when they are not listening? On the other hand, one should not write about the dead out of malice and hatred; or if one does, one should make clear that these are the premises from which one writes. After Delmore Schwartz's death Rahv did a rather devastating piece on him in *The New York Review* that fairly took my breath away. It astounded me that he should have written it at all. After their long period of mutual fascination the two had come to loathe each other, and that loathing was one of the things that made meetings at *Partisan Review* distasteful in my last days there. The piece in itself was not at all a bad critical performance, but it presented Delmore personally as a rather sniveling and whimpering neurotic in the period of his very rapid decline. And Rahv knew this was not the whole story; he had known Delmore earlier (and indeed courted him then) when Delmore had the being of a poet, vibrant and alive. So I must emphasize that I have not been writing here out of hatred or any desire to tear Rahv down. His death would not have released so many memories if I had not been deeply moved by it. But he was a complex, often self-contradictory and secretive character, and any tribute that failed to notice this complexity would be insipid. I admired his gifts; at times I liked him as an engaging ruffian even when morally I felt I shouldn't; at other times he frightened, irritated, and depressed me. The trouble was if you had to have constant practical dealings with Philip Rahv. No man is a hero to his valet, Goethe said; and Rahv, who tended to push his collaborators into the category of servant, must bear some of the consequences of the servant's-eye deflation. In the end, it was only after I had left the magazine and I then met him on an altogether different basis that I could put together the pieces of impressions into an affectionate whole. And it is in that spirit, and as a tribute, that I now offer them.

So, dear Philip, I lay this poor wreath on your grave; and if it does have some thorns, never mind; you would be even more suspicious of my motives if it did not.

Chapter Four

"The Liberal Fifth Column"

It is time that the United States
awoke to the truth that nothing is
gained for us vis-a-vis Russia by
"getting tough".
              —*The New Republic*,
                 April 22, 1946

I.

Despite their personal differences, the editors were still bound together by the common causes they served. I would not like to leave
the impression from what has been said so far that they merely

75

suffered from a sense of bondage in being yoked together in the chore of getting out a magazine. They were still enthusiastic about the ideals it served: on the one hand, to maintain critical standards against the deplorable leveling of taste promoted by commercial culture; on the other hand, to advance a generally Leftist position in politics, which would not, however, be subservient to the needs of the Soviet Union or the distortions of the Communist Party. I think it was this latter that bound Rahv and Phillips together most passionately. If any feeling of theirs could claim to be pure and spontaneous, it was their holy hatred of Stalin and Stalinism. They were in this particular matter like two believers who may not know what the good life is but have caught some terrifying vision of the Devil, and are at least unified around that center. Nothing holds people together like having a common enemy, and at the moment Rahv and Phillips had foes in plenty to fight. For in the post-War atmosphere of the late 1940s there had been a remarkable and pervasive resurgence of Stalinism and fellow-traveling that had, subtly or openly, captured the minds of Liberals.

But to grasp this, one has to take a step backward and see how it had come about.

The love affair between American Liberals and the Soviet Union had gone through varying fortunes from the 1930s to the end of World War II. The Depression decade of the 1930s, as a generally Leftist period, was dominated by Fellow Travelers of one shade of intensity or another—but all fundamentally well disposed toward Stalin and the Soviet Union. To be critical of the Soviet Union, in that general climate, was to be immediately consigned to the Right, where in fact most of the doubts of the Soviet Utopia were then being expressed. On the Left only a handful of intellectuals, of whom the editors of *Partisan Review* (I was not then a member) were the most notable examples, had continued to be vigorous and consistent critics of Stalin and his regime. And perhaps those early years of the magazine were in fact its most shining hour—certainly, its period of greatest courage.

The honeymoon between Liberals and the Soviet Union was sadly terminated when Stalin signed a pact with Hitler in 1939, setting the latter free to invade Poland and launch the Second World War. The rhetoric of Fellow Traveling had always drawn heavily upon anti-fascist slogans—fascism was the arch-enemy of our period, against which we should forget our smaller partisan differences; but now suddenly the "Worker's State" was in alliance with the arch-fascist of all. Even the die-hard Fellow Travelers were daunted, though only a little, for they were quick to find a defense for Stalin: he needed the protection of this pact with Hitler to safeguard the precious Socialist Fatherland, and besides he had tried but could not get sufficient guarantees of security from the capitalist regimes of France and Britain. For the less ardent and less disciplined Fellow Travelers the pact was too much of a blow, and there were not a few defections. Where pro-Russian feeling continued among Liberals, it was at least more muted. Significantly, the movies out of Hollywood at this time began to show an isolationist tinge: the war in Europe was a capitalist affair with which we should not become involved, or else it was represented as a conflict of time-worn nationalistic rivalries that did not rightfully concern us. All told, it was a restive and sullen interval for the Liberal Left that lasted for two years.

In 1941, however, when Hitler turned on his erstwhile friend and invaded Russia, everything was suddenly changed. The honeymoon was on again; and the movies now became anti-isolationist and pro-war. And when at the end of 1941, after the bombing of Pearl Harbor, the United States entered the War, the Russians had now become comrades in arms, and our sympathies with the heroic struggles of the Russian soldiers could easily be transmuted into favorable feelings toward the Soviet Union as such. The overflow of amicable feeling could even extend to the personality of Stalin himself, who suddenly emerged as "Uncle Joe," a genial, pipe-smoking elder. In the first months of the invasion there were immense surrenders and defections among the Russian ranks, but then the Red Army braced itself and fought stubbornly. For some people, the bravery of the Russian soldiers seemed to be taken as a sign of the validity of the Soviet regime itself. Of course, this inference from military bravery to the value of the regime for which the soldier is fighting was a dubious one: the German soldiers fought bravely, but one could not take that as evidence of the soundness of the Hitler regime. But it would have been bad taste to insist upon a logical point like this at that time. In any case, our feelings toward the Russians and the Soviet Union were at their warmest and most fraternal during those war years, and the warmth also extended to our official policy, particularly under Roosevelt.

But the defeat of Hitler and the ending of the European part of the

War signaled another turn in the road. With the removal of Germany as a threat, Russia now seemed to have the security of its borders that, according to its apologists, had always been its goal. The great socialist experiment was now safe against invaders. To be sure, Russia was still in the War and it had something to gain thereby: it was to gobble up Manchuria in a quick thrust in the last days, as Japan sank into defeat. The War thus still served a purpose, and anti-War feelings were out of order. The real turn in the road came with the explosion of atomic bombs on Nagasaki and Hiroshima. The War was now ended, and America had revealed in its last days the possession of a frightful new weapon—a weapon, moreover, that the Russians did not yet have. The bomb had blown away the fragile structure of wartime amity; and in the imagination of the American partisans of the Soviet Union what emerged from its ruins was the dread picture of Russia insecure under a possible atomic threat. Liberals suddenly began to express pacifist feelings and to stage peace rallies.

At the same time, however, Russia was hardly behaving as a meek and frightened power. It was pushing its influence aggressively into Europe and was in the process of setting up puppet regimes in Eastern Europe. American Liberals promptly arose to defend these Russian moves as necessary to safeguard the Soviet borders against a possible attack from the West. Thus a pattern of apology was set up that persists to the present day: any apparently aggressive move on the part of the Soviet Union was to be understood as a purely defensive countermove to some possible threat on the part of the United States.

Such was the atmosphere, the general background of the time, when I joined the staff of *Partisan Review*. For myself I would not have been unduly aroused; left to my own, like most casual readers of the newspapers, I probably would not have spotted what was going on in Europe. The great mood of the country was one of relief at getting over with the War, eagerness to return to one's own private life, and an unwillingness to be disturbed by any thoughts about international tensions and hostilities; and in this general mood I shared. My mind and my interests for the moment were turned in another direction from politics: I was trying to catch up on the reading from which I had been away during the War.

But Philip Rahv would not let me rest in that ivory tower. He read the Liberal weeklies and the New York *Times* indefatigably, and the more he read the more apoplectic he became. "Those goddam Liberals," he fumed, "they'll end by giving away the whole of Western Europe to Stalin. He won't even have to push for it, they'll make a present of it to him." These conversations were part of my education; and if I recall them now, it is against the background of later revisionist views that America launched the Cold War and Russia only responded in kind. The sharp eye of Rahv, a practiced Marxist, could spot Soviet moves that newspaper reporters or indeed American officials failed to notice.

"Why are the Russians doing it?" I asked in my innocence. "Don't they realize the mood of the West is one of such great good will that they can have all the security they need?" I still labored under the liberal opinion that the Russian moves were always of a defensive nature.

Rahv shrugged: "There's a power vacuum in Europe and the Soviets move in to fill it." The explanation even then seemed to me too mechanical, but it is only now that I can understand why he could not push further. That Stalin might be trying to export the Revolution did not square with Rahv's view of Stalin as the dictator who betrayed the Revolution and was interested only in his own bureaucratic power. For Rahv it would have been impossible to think that the bureaucratic apparatus might have its own momentum, and further, that its ideology was still Marxist and revolutionary, without raising fundamental questions about Marxism itself; and this far he could never go.

He was not alone in his concerns. William Phillips, though quieter, also fussed and fretted about the duplicities, as he regarded them, of the Liberals in their drift toward appeasement. For these two veterans of the anti-Stalinist battles of the 1930s, the Second World War had now come to an end with them back in harness together fighting their own small war—but this time against a Stalinism that wore much more subtle and various disguises. In meeting after meeting in the cramped little office the haranguing would go on, the international and local situation would be dissected and redissected again, always ending with the stale sense of frustration at the stupid drift of things. I had by this time been an editor for several months, and felt confident enough to put in a word or two of my own now and then. "The magazine should have an editorial on the subject," I suggested one day, after Rahv had been venting his fury with more than usual eloquence. The suggestion was immediately taken up, and the two editors were suddenly plunged into an intricate discussion of who should write that much-needed editorial. Whatever their personal tensions otherwise, Rahv and Phillips on these occasions fell into tandem like a smooth and practiced pair, alternately like two talmudic scholars exploring the fine points of a text or a team of borscht-circuit comedians milking the quirks of personality involved, until the practical point of the whole discussion almost got lost in the sheer fun of caricature.

Who, then, was to write this editorial? In England George Orwell and Arthur Koestler had been fighting much the same battle against the pro-Russian factions of the British Labour Party. But for our present purposes their polemic would have too much to do with their own specifically British situation. The editorial we needed would be something that addressed itself more directly to the American situation, and particularly to the milieu of New York, where liberal opinion was being fabricated. But the American possibilities—names like Sidney Hook or James Burnham, who were then close to the magazine—seemed out of the question for other reasons: they might want to bring in points of view of their own with which the magazine, friendly as it might feel toward them generally, did not want to be saddled. And so, after long and gossiping haggling, the discussion trailed off. A dead end, as before. Silence.

For my imagination that momentary silence was filled with the presence, or rather absence, of Dwight Macdonald. He had been an editor in the early days of the magazine, but had left after a public difference with Rahv and Phillips on the policy toward the War against Hitler. Macdonald opposed American involvement because the powers arrayed against Hitler, namely France and Britain, were capitalist societies. Rahv and Phillips, though Marxists, were willing to bend principle and support the Allies because Hitler and the Nazis represented a break with Western civilization that had to be opposed. But Macdonald, then a Trotskyist, insisted on being a purist: the War was essentially a struggle of capitalist powers and we should stay aloof and watch the disease take its course. Neither side in the controversy would budge, and eventually Macdonald quit the magazine.

But his effectiveness was sorely missed. He was a journalist of superb and facile talents, ready at a moment like this—if his heart were in it—to bat out a sparkling polemic. Now that he was gone there was no one to take his place. Rahv himself was on occasion no mean polemicist, but his energies were now directed toward polishing up a collection of his essays for his first book. Composition came slowly and laboriously to him, and he could not now spare the time for an editorial task. As for William Phillips, he was still in the grip of his perpetual writer's block. And Delmore Schwartz? I think we were all—myself most of all—under the impression that Delmore was doing some important writing on his own, that he was continuously, if for the present secretly, productive—even amid the personal disruption and the turmoil of his life at the moment. He had now returned to teach at Harvard, but was constantly shuttling between Cambridge and New York—and, it may be added, between two or three personal lives he shared. There were two girls he was involved with in New York, beside what other attachments crossed his path in Cambridge. "The trouble with Delmore," William Phillips observed, "is that he gets married to the girls he is carrying on an affair with." No doubt he was scribbling away all this time, but whether it would come to anything remained to be seen. For my part, out of love and admiration, I had no doubts. It never entered my mind at the time to doubt that all the extraordinary, even meteoric, brilliance that he had exhibited at the beginning of his career seven years earlier was only the prelude to something greater and more substantial. I never noticed, I never even for a moment dreamed that his life had already secretly taken a turn, an inexorable step, from which he could not retrace his path, so that he would never be the same again. In any case, on the present occasion it was clear that he would not be available for so prosaic a chore as writing a political editorial.

So, speaking into the absence of Dwight Macdonald, I was surprised to hear my own voice saying, "Maybe I might take a crack at it"; and I even ventured a title for the editorial, "The Liberal Fifth Column." Rahv was pleased, and more than delighted with the title, which was aggressive enough to satisfy him; and he promptly set about coaching me on what to say.

The editorial appeared in June 1946, unsigned—which was proper, since I was not writing for myself personally but for all of us and as part of the voice of the magazine itself. I have just reread the piece with some embarrassment, aghast at how strident it is, like a man shouting at the top of his lungs. I had had no experience in political polemic, and naturally drifted into the heavy-handed abuse that I had picked up from my earlier Marxist training. There is also a period ring to the title itself that probably would not have the same echo for readers today. We were close enough to the Spanish Civil War to remember Franco's remark, as he was mounting his final offensive against Madrid by sending four separate attacking columns against the besieged city, that he had another even more powerful force, a Fifth Column, operating within the citadel itself. The American Liberals, as the pro-Russian party, would then be the Fifth Column within our nation.

But if, on rereading, I am embarrassed by the crudity of the piece, I am also brought up even more sharply by the facts themselves which the editorial brought forward and many of which, in their detail, I had forgotten. Here, indeed, one has the sense that nothing has changed, that one is seeing the same play and characters with somewhat—and only somewhat—different settings and costumes, and that more than thirty years later we are facing the same alignments. Throughout this memoir I have been haunted by the thought that the reader may wonder whether it is worthwhile dwelling on the infighting within a small circle of intellectuals, whose influence on the life of the nation seems to have been slight (in point of fact it was not), and whose feuding in consequence might look petty and incestuous. Yet, precisely here, in this encounter with Liberals and Liberalism, there is a story to tell that has a central bearing on the life of the nation over the last half century. The quarrels of that time have a greater significance in the light of what followed. Consider, for example, the quotation from *The New Republic* that stands at the head of this chapter in the light of what has happened since then. Suppose Kennedy had been persuaded that there was no point in getting tough with the Russians when he faced the Cuban missile crisis of 1962, and had backed down. There would now be an atomic artillery pointed at the heart of America from ninety miles off our shore. Or—to move back more closely to the spring of 1946 when the Liberals of *The New Republic* made their bold statement, and when in fact it was directed toward the formation of actual policy—suppose that Truman had followed their advice. There would have been no Truman Doctrine and no Marshall Plan; Europe would have persisted in a condition of economic chaos and political confusion—a "power vacuum," to use Philip Rahv's expression, into which the Soviet Union would have moved easily. Thus Western Europe as a whole might very well have passed into the Soviet camp if the policies advocated by some Liberals at the close of World War II had been followed, and the chances of the survival of liberty in our time would be that much diminished. Nor has this peculiar Liberal temptation—this drift into compliance with pro-Russian tendencies—been confined to those particular years of the 1940s; on the contrary, it persists as a continuous history into the present. And it is the continuity of that history that I find so perplexing and disturbing—especially since I consider myself a liberal.

II.

Though they were struggling against what was then the main current, at least in intellectual circles, and the struggle seemed at times a very lonely one, nevertheless Rahv and Phillips were not absolutely isolated. There were kindred spirits fighting the same battle, and a glance at some of these may help round out the political picture of our circle at the time.

In England, as I've already mentioned, George Orwell and Arthur Koestler had been fighting Stalinists and Fellow Travelers right through the War; and these two were in fact valued contributors to the magazine. Orwell, in particular, commanded a singular power for downright plain English that was remarkably effective because it seemed to be spoken at the reader directly. Koestler was brilliant logically, but his personal aggressiveness and exuberance were such, as he revealed on a visit to New York, that he could sometimes make enemies of those whom his logic had almost persuaded. But both these men were British, and in Britain, and to that degree remote from our more local quarrels. Nearer home, and in fact very much of the *Partisan Review* circle at the time, were Sidney Hook and James Burnham, two remarkable and representative figures who do not deserve to be forgotten, as they seem to be by the present generation.

Sidney Hook is not exactly a forgotten figure, though in comparison with the position he once held and the force he once exerted in public discussion, he would seem to be consigned by some to the limbo of the irrelevant. Within the *Partisan Review* circle itself at this time his position was already subtly on the wane. He was still a friend and a trusted ally, but he was no longer the indispensable intellectual support he had been for Rahv, Phillips, and Macdonald in the 1930s. Hook had been the leading Marxist scholar of that earlier period, and the editors had all leaned upon his knowledge. In a flash of memory now I hear Dwight Macdonald in his kitchen arguing with some more orthodox Marxist: "Look, there are a hundred and twenty million peo-

ple in the United States"—(how far back *that* number now sounds!)—
"and Sidney Hook is America's Number One Marxist. That's good
enough for me."

Hook not only knew the Marxist writings, but was a close and dili-
gent student of the Russian Revolution and all the steps of Stalinist intrigue in its wake. As a youth in Brooklyn, he was already an ardent
socialist when the October Revolution occurred, and like Lenin himself he marked each day that it survived, even—though he was only to
learn this later—echoing Lenin's statement "Now we have survived
another day beyond the Commune" (referring to the short-lived
Paris Commune of the revolution of 1870), "and now another day,"
and so on day by day. It is necessary to invoke this earlier radical
image of Hook against the almost quasi-official role he was to fill as
the premier anti-Communist of the 1950s; and perhaps to insist that
there is not so much discontinuity between the two images as might
seem. Hook had to be courageous in the early 1930s. The term "premature anti-Communist" had not yet been coined, but he would have
been one of the earliest to fulfill that insidious description. However,
it is important to note that he broke with Stalinism very early because
he was a dedicated socialist, and believed that the cause of socialism
had been betrayed in the Soviet Union. He had reached this conclusion on his own, as a meticulous student of Russian affairs since the
Revolution, and though his criticisms in part ran parallel to Trotsky's,
he was never to be an orthodox Trotskyist. And once he had made up
his mind, he was aggressive and vocal about it, no matter how un-
popular a figure he might cut. The denigrators of Hook as a semi-
official anti-Communist during the 1950s (when anti-Communism became more common) might do well to summon up the early image of
Hook as a young instructor at New York University being hissed by
Stalinist students as he walked through Washington Square. Not that
anything like public hissing would have deterred him for a moment
from his self-appointed course, for he had the absolute integrity and
courage of the single-minded.

It was this single-mindedness, indeed, that was now making him
more questionable in the eyes of Rahv and Phillips. Hook, they felt,
had become a kind of Johnny One-note, clear and forceful but also
monotonous in the one issue he was always pursuing. When the question came up one day of Hook's possibly doing an article that was
then needed, Rahv rejected the suggestion in his usual corrosive and

reductive way: "No. Sidney will only tell you once again that Stalin stinks." Yes indeed, Hook had become something of a Johnny One-note, but it has to be said now with the clarity of hindsight that the one note at which he was perpetually hammering away was a momentous one and seemed almost forgotten by Liberals: that socialism, so-called, was meaningless without political and individual liberty, and that indeed it was not socialist at all. This was the meaning and the tradition of socialism for which Hook spoke, and for which he was always to speak. Whatever advantages the socialist arrangement of the economy might bring (and none of us then doubted that there would be such advantages), they had no value at all if liberty were absent. And it was the Liberals' tendency to forget this point that accounted for their benign attitude toward the Soviet Union: in their apologies they would fall back time after time on the phrase that it was "after all socialist"—an actual quotation from *The Nation* at this time.

Most of us followed Hook in this point; we had been brought up to believe that socialism and liberty were inseparable, that a socialism without liberty was meaningless, and even further that liberty itself—liberty in the fullest and most complete sense—was only realizable under a socialist regime. It was only years later that some of us took the step, which Hook himself did not at this time, of doubting whether the two could be so blandly and confidently linked, and even further to wonder whether they might not be after all incompatible ideas. Did the control of the whole economy under socialism involve a concentration of power to which limits could then be set in other areas of life? Must not the abolition of economic liberty curtail political and civil liberties all along the line? These are very urgent matters that the whole experience of the twentieth century now thrusts upon its intellectuals, since the dictatorial course of socialist revolutions can no longer be dismissed as an aberration due to the personality of Stalin. But at the time of which I write—the late 1940s—our socialism was an article of faith that seemed to reassure us on all these points, largely because we had never put the troubling questions to ourselves.

James Burnham, as I look back, was one of the casualties of American intellectual life. This is not to say that he collapsed in impotence and simply ceased to produce, or that he personally destroyed himself in the impetuous fashion of some other literary figures; indeed, for a certain conservative sector of American opinion, he was to win a solid and respected place. Still, it was not the place that his own impressive gifts might have brought him if the intellectual climate in America, and particularly in its politics, had been different. He himself in this post-War period seemed to me to envisage some possibly larger role. He had just come back from Paris, where he had had a long session with André Malraux, and I think he may have dreamed of some such independent intellectual position of power as the latter commanded. Malraux was then in his early Gaullist stage: that is, his position had not yet congealed into any official form, but he was urging a general direction for France that De Gaulle was to bring into power shortly. Meanwhile, Malraux carried enough personal aura from his adventurous career on the Left so that he could not be regarded as just another run-of-the-mill conservative on the Right. Indeed, Malraux criticized these routine notions of Left and Right as obsolescent and no longer applicable to the political realities of the twentieth century: "The Communists are not of the Left," Malraux declared, "and when they attack me, they do not establish me on the Right." Burnham quoted these words with obvious relish, as if they marked out for him the possibility of forging an independent line of political thinking that would cut through these worn-out clichés. And it would have been a good thing; it would have been good if he could have helped dispel those old spectral clouds of Left and Right, which still hang like a pall over our thinking today.

But it was not to be. Part of the reason for his failure lay in the vast and diffuse power of Liberalism in the intellectual climate of that time, which virtually confronted people like Burnham with the choice, if you are not for us you are against us, so that eventually he felt forced to opt for the Right. But a more personal and perhaps deeper reason why he failed to play the independent role he dreamed of lay in the quality of his own mind—he was too sweeping and schematic in his tendency to extend an intellectual formula into a prophecy of things to come. *The Managerial Revolution,* for example, was an original and brilliant book when it appeared, and it anticipated by a good number of years the discovery of the "New Class," which now absorbs the attention of sociologists and political analysts. In a technical society, Burnham indicated, the technicians play a special and indispensable role, and consequently come to occupy a place not recognized in the classic Marxist opposition of capitalists and proletariat. But where more recent writers are tentative and hesitant, for what impresses them above all else about the New Class is its indecisive and heterogeneous character politically, Burnham on the other hand rushed into the breach with the prophecy that there would be a radical transformation of politics in our time as a result of which the technicians, the managers, would come to power. Alas, politics seems to plod on in its old and immemorial ways; the technician is still subject to the political boss, the corporations bow before Washington.

This sweeping character of his thinking, this need for black-and-white simplifications, may have been the legacy Marxism left with Burnham. In any case, his encounter with Marxism is revealing in one or two other very crucial points. When he became converted to Marxism in the early 1930s, he threw himself into the movement and became an active Trotskyist. He kept his mind free, however, to scrutinize the philosophical bases of Marxist theory, and at a certain ripe moment the influence of Sidney Hook fell upon him. Hook had written a devastating critique of the Marxist dialectic, one of his most brilliant philosophic performances, a job of demolition, by the way, that he accomplished more than a decade before Sartre was to direct a similar polemic against French Marxism. According to the dialectic, History (always with a capital H) moved inexorably in a certain logical pattern, in the course of which capitalism must eventually give way to socialism. In rebelling against capitalism, then, socialists were simply cooperating with the inevitable march of History; they were on the side of the future. Hook showed that the dialectic was an arbitrary metaphysical construction, with no basis in fact or logic, and his argument convinced Burnham. The latter, however, was still a socialist and wished to remain one. There must be better grounds, then, for subscribing to socialism than that you were simply siding with the inevitable march of History; one's socialist sympathies were prompted by the moral aspirations toward a more just and humane society, and thus socialism represented a moral ideal that one freely chose to pursue. And having reached these conclusions, Burnham promptly gave them voice in the Trotskyist organ, together with the added recommendation that the whole Historical Dialectic be dropped as part of the Hegelian inheritance of Marx that was now thoroughly superannuated.

From his retreat in Mexico, Trotsky thundered furiously. Moral ideals indeed! Where had he heard such talk before? It was a typical petty-bourgeois reaction to worry about moral ideals, and Burnham's was only one more case in the recurrent distemper of petty-bourgeois revisionism. Whereupon Burnham was promptly read out of the Party.

With this incident, the scales fell from Burnham's eyes. First of all, the revelation of Trotsky himself had been shocking: someone who had to be accounted among the great men of the century, one of the heroes of our imagination, had shown himself in controversy to be crude and coarse, as rigidly committed to dogma and as impatient with individual disagreement as any dictatorial Stalin could be. But there was a further point in logic beyond Trotsky's own failings, and Burnham's mind was nothing if not logical. Even if one accepted the Historical Dialectic, if one accepted the inevitability of the passage from capitalism into socialism, one's attitude could take one of several different directions: one could go along listlessly with the march of History, one could cooperate actively and energetically with it, or one could choose to resist the general drift of things. But this factor of free will and the moral reality of the individual who makes his free choice were precisely anathema to the Marxist mind. And here the fault was not just Trotsky's personally but deeply ingrained in the whole Marxist way of thought. When one pared away all the fancy trimmings, it was a fairly crude materialism after all.

Burnham's response—an indirect but nonetheless potent one for that—was an essay, "Lenin's Heirs," that appeared in *Partisan Review* in 1939. Trotsky and Stalin were here represented as suitors in a court of chancery for the right of succession to Lenin. Within the anti-Stalinist Left, Trotsky was usually portrayed as the dispossessed prince, the rightful heir of Lenin, and Stalin as the upstart who had seized power, introduced a reign of terror, and generally betrayed the Revolution. But Burnham pointed out that, on whatever grounds you chose, Stalin was a legitimate follower of Lenin. The Terror had begun with Lenin, not Stalin, and as for the cunning manipulations of power within the Communist Party, Lenin himself had been a past master of the art. Burnham's essay was the boldest bit of thinking that had yet appeared within this circle. Hitherto, the name of Lenin had been protected almost as a holy relic; the blame for any miscarriage of the Russian Revolution had been shunted over entirely on the head of Stalin, who thus provided a ready-made excuse for not locating the fault within the nature of Marxist doctrine itself. That may be why Burnham's article, though brilliantly written and incisively argued, did not produce any radical converts. We would have required a fundamental change in the premises of our political thinking, and for that we were not yet ready.

Personally, I came to like Burnham very much when I got to know him in the 1940s, and I admired his mind more as it exhibited itself in conversation than in his writings. He was from Princeton and Oxford, and bore the stamp of the gentleman in his bearing—so much so that in comparison with some of the more raucous types of the New York Intellectual he appeared almost shy and diffident. He thus created in person a very different impression from the image of the power-hungry and power-obsessed mind that some readers, including Edmund Wilson, claimed to find in his writings. His conversation was enriched by the great range of his culture. One of his special courses at New York University, where he taught philosophy, was in aesthetics, and it was long rumored that he would do a definitive work on the subject. The book never materialized; it was pre-empted by politics, which for some writers who stray into it is often a path of no return. Delmore Schwartz had been a student in that course; and though Delmore was inclined to be skeptical of his elders, and was particularly hypercritical of any discourse on the nature of art and beauty, which were his own special terrain, nevertheless he continued always to admire Burnham for what he had learned from him on those subjects. As it turned out, Burnham was soon to take his own giant step to the Right; but while his presence graced our midst, in those few short post-War years, he added a different and original note to the circle.

Dwight Macdonald had quit the fold some years before, but he had hardly disappeared from sight—or from hearing. He would occasionally barge into one of our informal sessions at William Phillips's house, and plunge into argument with everyone. Outnumbered and outgunned in such arguments, Macdonald nevertheless seemed to be in his element and thoroughly enjoying himself, unmindful of the barbs and sometimes heavy-handed jibes that were thrown his way. I admired his courage and openness, and his willingness to put himself on the line, but he was not very good at argument, for he stammered. In his case the pen—or, rather, the typewriter—was mightier than the tongue; and where in written polemic he could spear his victim with a single deadly phrase or sentence, in oral argument on the other hand he would become excited and reduced to an incoherent stammer. In these verbal free-for-alls Delmore Schwartz was usually the most abusive, but there seemed some unwritten agreement between the two by which Macdonald accorded him *carte blanche*. Indeed Delmore's regular conversation with Macdonald was a running stream of teasing insults, which the latter usually took with amused giggles. It was the channel through which a real affection passed back and forth between them. And this pattern in his relationship to Macdonald seems to have been one part of his personality that Delmore was able to maintain coherently through the awful disorder of his last years. So much so, in fact, that Macdonald never perceived that he was quite as mad as he was, as long as the old teasing patter still flowed as it always had.

Macdonald still loathed Fellow Travelers and Stalinists, and in this respect certainly he was still with us and on our side. I don't know whether he coined it, but it was from his use that I learned the word "Liblab," which he liked to throw around at that time. The word was a compound of Liberal and Labor, and, accordingly, "Liblab" was meant to designate the knee-jerk Liberal who was a patsy for pro-Soviet propaganda. But though Macdonald despised the pro-Soviet Liberals, he was not about to join party with us in any systematic attack upon them. That would be too mundane and common, for the nation generally was beginning to become aware of the Cold War and, now that the wartime feeling of comradeship with the Russians had cooled, a certain mood of anti-Communism was beginning to spread. And Macdonald desired above all that his politics be pure and avant-garde, detached from any vulgar alignments of power.

He was at this time publishing a little magazine of his own, *politics,* which was interesting mainly as an exhibition of his own extraordinary energies and skills. Macdonald, like Burnham, had been a Trotskyist, and he too had been roughly handled by Trotsky in a matter of intraparty dispute, as a consequence of which he had abandoned Marxism altogether. He was now searching for another and purer political ideology in Anarchism, and his guru in this search was Nicola Chiaromonte, one of the more quiet and striking figures around at this time. Chiaromonte had lived through, or actually fought in, all the major conflicts of the time about which most of the intellectuals of New York had only argued. As a young man, he had fled Mussolini and fascism in Italy, fought in the Civil War in Spain, after Franco's victory escaped to France, where he moved among intellectual circles in Paris; then had fled France in 1940 when Hitler's armies broke through the French lines and overran the country; and finally—and only after a series of hair's-breadth escapes—had somehow managed to make his way to America. Unknown and not knowing anyone, Chiaromonte would have been lost amid the flood of refugees that reached New York in those days except that Dwight Macdonald adopted him and took him into his own intellectual fold. But he in turn seemed to have adopted Macdonald intellectually, and was instructing him in the principles of some of the classic Italian anarchists. It was more apropos of his case than anyone else's that William Phillips at this time delivered himself of a *mot* about Macdonald: "Dwight is looking for a disciple who will tell him what to think."

But whatever the source of his ideas, Macdonald pursued politics with a passion and purity that were all his own. Anarchism now provided him with a purer atmosphere, a loftier ether, in which he might give his wings full flight. Philip Rahv, as the entrenched Marxist, sneered at Macdonald's magazine *politics;* besides, it could be a rival to *Partisan Review,* and like a very doting parent he instinctively hated all possible competitors to his own offspring. Today I think I would be inclined to a more favorable view of Macdonald's magazine, for he was touching on issues that have since become more and more troubling: the question, particularly of Statism, and of the constantly expanding role—true everywhere in modern civilization—of government in regulating the lives of its citizens. But his way of going about these questions was troubling; he could never accept that political discourse must be plodding and prosaic, that politics itself deals with a middling region of reality where ultimate and sweeping generalizations are almost never possible. For him every venture into politics was a leap toward the Absolute. He and James Burnham had had a quarrel in print a few years earlier, in the course of which Burnham had accused him of being a "dilettante" in politics. Macdonald heatedly denied the charge of dilettantism, pointing out all the time and energy he poured into political activity; to which Burnham had sagely replied that dilettantes were well known for the time and passion that they spend on their consuming hobby, whether it be "esquimaux dolls or whatnot"—implying by this odd example that Macdonald's time and labor might just as well have been spent on some such trivial item. Burnham was right about dilettantes, but there was something more to Macdonald's pursuit of politics. He was a kind of Don Quixote or Galahad, alternately tilting at windmills or in quest of the Holy Grail. Politics for him, I think, was really a groping for salvation of some kind.

Thus he was entirely consistent with his own past in not joining our particular anti-Stalinist line. In a similar way he had opposed American participation in World War II. Unlike a good many isolationists who were not unduly troubled by the thought of the Nazis, or even may have covertly admired Hitler, Macdonald hated Hitler and the Nazis as passionately as anyone could; but the opponents of Hitler were capitalist powers and they were therefore not pure enough to be accepted as allies in a war. Now, in the post-War period, he continued to loathe Stalinism and Fellow Travelers as he had always done; but he withdrew from any policy that would acknowledge the power of the American nation as one of the foremost safeguards in the struggle to contain Stalin.

III.

All that we have reported so far might seem only the intramural bickering within the intellectual circles of New York, but in fact the issues were soon to erupt before the nation and become questions of national policy.

In 1947 Truman enunciated the doctrine that became known by his name, to support free peoples who were resisting the spread of Communism, and a few months later the Marshall Plan for the economic reorganization of Western Europe followed. The United States was now adopting a policy which Philip Rahv had been urging privately since the end of the war in 1945. It is necessary to step back for a moment to underline the irony in this situation, for it may be somewhat blurred to later readers. We were Marxists and socialists, yet at this particular turn of time we were for measures that would stabilize the shaky capitalist economies of Western Europe; for if those economies were to collapse, the whole of Europe would slide into the grip of Stalin and the Soviet empire. We thought it preferable that the European peoples should have liberty under capitalism rather than slavery under Stalin. And, oddly enough, the government of the United States, a capitalist power, had been very tardy in moving toward the point of view of us socialists!

This shift in official policy should have given Rahv great joy, and it did, insofar as it brought discomfiture to the Liberals of *The Nation* and *The New Republic;* but it also left him faintly ill at ease. A political policy which had been avant-garde was now about to be contaminated by being taken up by the *hoi-polloi.* The term "avant-garde" was originally borrowed from the military, but there is a profound difference between its application in the military and in the intellectual world. In a military campaign, when the small advanced contingent wins a position that then comes to be occupied by the main body of troops, it is cause for congratulation all around. Not so in the intellectual world. For the intellectual the avant-garde position may lose its special enchantment when it becomes commonly accepted: after all, it may be held now in a vulgar way and not for his lofty reasons. There is then the temptation to develop some more *outré* position just to be different. It is another form in which he is tempted to play the truant—to cultivate politics as if it were a purely aesthetic discipline. But Rahv's incipient uneasiness, as the general mood of anti-Communism became more widespread, did not burst forth into print until much later on in the 1950s.

Meanwhile, two other events—the Hiss case and the advent of Senator Joseph McCarthy—brought the issue of Communism even more sensationally into the public domain. Alger Hiss had occupied a sensitive position in the State Department, during which time—according to the accusation of Whittaker Chambers—he had been an agent in the service of the Soviet Union. Chambers was then a senior editor of *Time* magazine, and a complex and interesting character in his own right, so that the confrontation of the two personalities, Hiss and Chambers, invested the whole case with a kind of high drama. And even something more garish than that, as Delmore Schwartz pointed out, if you considered the name of one of the protagonists: "Hiss, a villain in some old Victorian melodrama."

Yes, a villain for some, but strangely enough a sudden hero for many. For what was surprising about the Hiss case was not only the amount of passion it generated, but also the direction this passion took, such that the innocence of Alger Hiss virtually became a Liberal crusade in some quarters. Why should the Liberal Mind feel itself so involved in the Hiss case and why should its involvement take this turn? Philip Rahv watched, waited, and then on the publication of

Whittaker Chambers's book *Witness*, delivered himself of judgment on the Liberal Mind:

> The importance of the Hiss case was precisely that it dramatized that mind's struggle for survival and its vindictiveness under attack. That mind is above all terrified of the disorder and evil of history, and it flees the harsh choices which history so often imposes. It fought to save Hiss in order to safeguard its own illusions and to escape the knowledge of its own gullibility and chronic refusal of reality.

This is Rahv in one of his more oratorical bursts, but the oratory is compact of much experience and infighting with Liberals, and well earned. The Liberals find it hard to believe in the reality of evil. As children of the Enlightenment, they regard evil as only relative ignorance or misunderstanding. Thus they found it hard to think of Stalin as an active and conscious agent of evil, as they find it hard to think now that the Politburo is intent on our destruction. And so too they found it hard to think of Alger Hiss as a traitor. Hiss had been to the right schools, had always made the right social impression, and accordingly had risen in the State Department. It was hard for nice, genteel, middle-class Liberals to believe that such a man would be guilty of betraying his country. It would place their whole world in question. But then, even if he had, would that have been so bad? In the Soviet Union democratization might not have proceeded as far as we would like, but after all they did have social programs there. The Liberal Mind seems unable to entertain the possibility that the regime itself may be intrinsically and energetically evil. Which may be why Liberals have turned their back on Solzhenitsyn. The facts he tells us, after all, are by this time well-known; but what he gives us as a writer is the human face of that evil as he himself had to live with it. And this the Liberal does not want to see.

McCarthy was a disaster for the Liberals. Not that he wreaked such great personal or material damage to the Liberal body. There were some personal harassments and blacklistings, which were bad enough but not nearly on a scale to justify inflated rumors that concentration camps were about to be set up, and that the United States in that period was in its way as totalitarian as Soviet Russia. And McCarthy himself was defeated by the democratic process. A seedy and unpleasant character, he was censured by his own legislative body, the Senate, and his influence was eclipsed; and presently he disappeared from the scene. The real disaster to the Liberals was that their public opponent in this case should be so unwholesome and irresponsible a demagogue that the issues which were raised, or should have been raised, became more thickly veiled in the general confusion. An enemy so unpalatable and disreputable only confirmed them in their own sense of self-righteousness, which is one of the Liberal temptations anyway. Where there might have been an opportunity to do some soul-searching, and to rethink their position particularly with regard to its pro-Soviet leanings, Liberals could now easily throw out the accusation of "McCarthyism" at any critic of those tendencies. And the result is that Liberals have continued in these attitudes, with some more or less minor variations, to the present day.

That continuity seems to me one of the more disheartening aspects of our whole post-War period. This memoir has been centered mainly about the decade immediately following the Second World War, though the present always keeps coming in. Those early years, and particularly at their beginning, as I've said, were a time when the world seemed opening up to us and we looked forward to a promising future. Looking back now, I seem to meet my own gaze looking forward, and I find that the period between falls into a unity. Yes; the post-War period from 1945 to the present is a distinct historical entity, a unified era; and nowhere is this unity exhibited more markedly than in the continuity and stability of the Liberals' attitude toward the Soviet Union—the disposition, to put it at its mildest, always to give the Soviet Union the benefit of the doubt.

Why this should be so, remains one of the puzzling questions of our age that we cannot even begin to answer here. We only note, by way of conclusion, three periods in which this aspect of Liberal history may be divided:

The first belongs to the 1930s and early 1940s, when the struggle was to establish the facts about the Soviet Union: in particular, that it was not the "workers' democracy" which the Liberal imagination dreamed of but in reality a bureaucratic dictatorship, and a very brutal one at that. Questions of American foreign policy, or of a defense posture, did not enter the picture at this stage. The debate was over the internal character of the Soviet regime, in relation to its own people; and the quarrels were mainly confined to intellectual circles in and about New York. The aim was to clear the air, and make it possible for an independent Left to function here. Progress was slow, but the facts did get through and there were some changes of mind. However, when the accumulated evidence became so overwhelming that the Soviet myth could no longer be maintained, the acknowledgment might take a very muted form. Lillian Hellman's wistful remark, "We were mistaken about the degree of democracy in the Soviet Union," is really precious when one considers the distortion, cover-up, and conniving that went on in order to perpetuate that myth.

The second phase begins from the end of the war in 1945. The debate is now no longer a family matter among intellectuals; questions of official government policy enter the picture as the United States must seek some way of containing Stalin's expansive drives toward Western Europe and the Middle East. By the late 1940s the facts about the Soviet labor camps—that vast network of internal prisons Solzhenitsyn was later to call *Gulag*—had been clearly established, and there was no doubt that the Communist regime had exercised a grim and systematic terror over its own citizens. Yet a curious inversion of logic now took place with some Liberals. Though the internal regime of the Soviet Union was indefensible, its motives and actions on the international scene were to be looked at benignly as those of a legitimate power. Somehow the evil of a regime stopped at its own borders, and its actions beyond that were all sweetness and light. Thus a certain mentality of appeasement set in.

The third phase in this Liberal history is where we are now, and it is continuous with the second. The new note that has been added is the ever-mounting anxiety about the possibility of atomic confrontation. It is understandable that people would shrink from this possibility and seek whatever ways of accommodation may be tolerable. I have little sympathy with those who lightheartedly throw about the possibilities of atomic war. Even a limited nuclear war—and "limited" has a strangely ironic ring here—would cause 125 million casualties and unimaginable destruction to the environment, and there is good reason to draw back from such a possibility. Indeed, it is conceivable that in the ultimate confrontation between the two superpowers, the more humane power (presumably ourselves) would give in rather than bring about such awful destruction to the race and the planet. The morality of this course of action may be debatable but it is not necessarily despicable. However, if this should in fact become our final choice, there are two considerations to keep in mind. First, let us not lie to ourselves about the nature of the power to which we would be capitulating and begin to find reasons why the Soviet Union may not be so bad as people say. Second, and from a practical point of view more important: that ultimate confrontation may be a long way off, and may never come about if we push prudently but aggressively for the containment of the enemy now. In fact, not to pursue this latter course would hurl us all the more quickly and dangerously toward that ultimate confrontation. We need not capitulate before we have to. The course that Liberals are now pursuing seems nothing less than a policy of premature surrender.

We are entering a period in which liberal values may be on trial, and will have to be struggled for more stubbornly than at any time in the recent past. It would be well if Liberals could enter this struggle with all the strength they can muster. It should, after all, be their chosen role and traditional cause. But so long as they remain tied to their past, with its pro-Soviet leanings, their efforts are bound to be compromised and therefore less effective than they would otherwise be.

Chapter Five

Foreign Visitors and Existentialism

I.

Hannah Arendt was not a visitor, strictly speaking, since she had been settled in this country since 1941. Just one skip ahead of history, in 1933 she had escaped from Germany and Hitler to France, from which she then had to flee Hitler's invading armies after the French defeat in 1940. But she could have been among us twenty years and she would still be something of a foreign presence. One part of her never quite became assimilated to America. Not that she did not know the ropes; she was adept at that, she had to be in order to survive as a refugee in Europe and in those first years in the United States. But she was always conscious of coming from elsewhere—of speaking for something older and deeper that she understood as European culture, something she guarded at her center. So that for us she could become a kind of incarnation of the European presence that began to be felt more and more in New York during the 1940s.

Indeed, my first meeting with her had to do with her in her chosen role as interpreter of European culture to Americans.

During the War, the continent of Europe had been cut off from us in all the usual modes of communication. We knew about the gross and large-scale facts of history: invasions, troop movements, areas occupied, frontiers shifted. But we knew nothing of the lives of the people under occupation. What were they thinking? Were they secretly writing things that would be worth reading? Or painting pictures that broke through into some new style? Would some new consciousness or movement come out of this dreadful War? Then, after 1941, we ourselves were in the War, and too actively involved to have time for such questions, except perhaps at rare moments of reflection.

With the end of the War, however, the channels of communication were opened, and—perhaps more important still—ordinary travel between the two continents could be resumed. We who were so possessed by the feeling of a new period opening with the end of the War, and were looking everywhere for some new message, failed to notice some of the obvious things that would transform the life of the future. Air travel, for example. At first a trickle, then a gathering flood, air travel shortly became the accepted and normal link between Europe and America. The old ocean voyage by ship rapidly became a thing of the past. And that in itself was to mark a subtle and deep change in human consciousness. Whoever has crossed the Atlantic by ship will have gathered a sense of the ocean that is not granted to younger travelers who have taken it at one brief jump in an airplane. Traveling close to the sea for a week, even the most jaded passenger in one of the old steamers would experience some sense of the ocean as that great watery tract between two worlds as it was known to the old explorers. The ocean—as a felt and imagined reality—has disappeared from the consciousness of the present generation. The young traveler boards an airplane in New York, passes several hours in reading or looking at a movie, perhaps occasionally catching a tiny peep of blue surface between clouds, seen from five miles up, and that is what the word "ocean" means to him. So technology transforms our consciousness of the planet on which we dwell.

The idea of "future shock" became popular a few years ago. Nothing could be further from the truth about the way technology subtly and imperceptibly transforms our human consciousness. People are not shocked by technical novelty; they gobble it up like so much cotton candy. And they are scarcely conscious of the way in which they are transformed in the process. The shock, when it comes, proceeds from something else. In 1949, I made a short visit to Paris and dropped in on Saul Bellow, who had been living in Europe for a while, testing how it was to work away from home. He asked me what was new back in America, and I remember telling him, among other things, that television seemed to be gaining ground. There was no "future shock" in the reaction of the American people; on the contrary, they ate it up, and in the process it ate them up. Television became a permanent component of the American consciousness. The shock, after all the technical transformation, comes from encountering the residue of the old and immemorial that is still with us—the core of life that has not changed and that technology cannot master, the old emotions and the old quandaries. It is not the future that shocks us but the past we harbor in ourselves.

In sifting through these memories of the last thirty-five years I am perpetually brought up before the question what has changed and what has abided in the world as we knew it. And the "shock" for me is not in the scientific transformations of the period but that the old political attitudes and philosophic uncertainties persist unchanged.

Which, appropriately, brings us back now to our little band of intellectuals waiting for the cultural news from Europe in 1945, and Hannah Arendt as our interpreter of it.

Naturally, our expectant eyes turned toward France and Paris. Our generation had been brought up on the remembrance of the 1920s as the great golden age of the avant-garde, whose focal point had been Paris. We expected history to repeat itself: as it had been after the First, so would it be after the Second World War. And it seemed for the moment almost as if history were not going to disappoint us: there was indeed "hot news" from Paris of a new movement—Existentialism —whose spokesman was a young Frenchman, Jean-Paul Sartre. Nobody here knew what the word really meant; Philip Rahv, as an alert editor, felt that this was something that had to be explained to the American intellectual public, and he had got in touch—how he found her among the crowd of refugees then in New York I never did know —with Hannah Arendt, who might do an explanatory article on the subject. Accordingly, all four of the editors met with her for lunch.

She was a redoubtable woman, and that first meeting still lingers in my mind. She knew Rahv only slightly, and she was thus cast into the

101

situation of confronting four strangers—and possibly four antagonistic males—but she never faltered. She was wary but hardly shy (it would be hard to imagine her ever shy), and in very short order had locked horns with Rahv. His usually authoritative manner could not pass muster with her, and he was thrown off stride by encountering an aggressively intellectual woman who talked back to him. It was a novelty for me to hear him becoming somewhat faltering and tentative in tone. He, who usually laid down the law to other people, now rather put himself in the role of the inquiring learner. The upshot of the meeting was that she agreed to write an article on Existentialism; the only difficulty was that she still felt very uneasy in writing English, and on a subject so subtle and intricate as this, she felt she could only express herself adequately in German. That was all right, Rahv suggested, like an army sergeant immediately "volunteering" me and my services: "You write it in German, and Will here will translate it."

The translation, however, proved a boon to me, since it was the means by which we became friends. The article, subsequently printed in the magazine as "What Is Existenz Philosophy?" (the German word, she insisted, had to be kept in the title), dealt only tangentially with Sartre and the French Existentialists; for the most part it was a straightforward presentation of the thought of Karl Jaspers, who had been her mentor and friend in Germany and remained one of her intense personal loyalties even when her thought later turned more in the direction of Heidegger. I brought my translation to her, for she had insisted she would want to look it over before printing; she liked it, and the occasion was a very long and pleasant afternoon with her.

What impressed me was her great gusto and the vibrancy of her character. She came at things with energy and eagerness. She was dressed rather informally that afternoon, with her hair set back loosely. And finding herself at ease with me, she was much more womanly than I had expected. She was also much younger then and more attractive than her later photographs, when she became a more public figure, could show. I couldn't help thinking throughout that she was a very handsome woman indeed. Later I reported this judgment to William Phillips, who pondered it judiciously for a moment and then declared, "I think of Hannah rather as a very handsome man." He could only think of her as the stern figure in intellectual argument.

Delmore Schwartz came in on the same subject from a different angle; in a moment of good-natured pique, remembering her resistance to one of his anecdotes, he spluttered, "That . . . that Weimar Republic flapper!" I could never see her thereafter without remembering Delmore's remark. Behind the façade of the stern and intellectual woman there lurked the ghost of a beautiful young girl who had done all the *risqué* things of the 1920s—dared to smoke cigarettes in public, have affairs, charm and tantalize men—and managed to be a very brilliant student at the university. In a way, perhaps, some of that adventurous vitality never left her.

That afternoon we quickly put the business of the translation behind us (there were only a few changes she wanted), and the rest of the long day she gave to me. I was almost unknown to her, and yet she poured herself out on any topic that came to mind. In view of the fact that she was later to become a controversial figure, particularly after her book on the trial of Adolf Eichmann, some of her remarks that day were prophetic. She was a tough woman. She had had to live by her wits from the time she had fled Germany and Hitler; and much as her mind dwelt on theoretical matters, on large and sweeping ideas, she was nevertheless a very down-to-earth person. She also had her fair share of prejudices, which entwined themselves about some of her fundamental attitudes. Above all, she was a German Jew, with the peculiar double loyalty which membership in that gifted minority conferred. The German Jews had been the most assimilated of the European Jews; and the cultivated ones among them had been among the staunchest guardians and partisans of high German culture. Hannah Arendt remained such a partisan. In some quarters of American Jewry, consequently, her Jewishness became somewhat suspect.

This pride in her origins as a German Jew—and indeed a very Germanic German Jew—led, understandably enough, to a certain arrogance. After fleeing Germany, as refugee in France she was without money and had to find domicile in the Paris ghetto. The French Jews, she told me, had shocked her, they were so inferior to the German Jews. "They were nothing in comparison." These Jews seemed outside the pale of French life. In the Weimar Republic, on the other hand, in which she had grown up, the assimilation of Jews and gentiles seemed, at least in intellectual circles, almost complete. She harbored a nostalgia for that condition and that period. In restrospect, she could not quite get used to the idea that the worst persecutions of Jews in modern history had broken out in Germany of all countries. On this catastrophe she could not take the rigid view of historical determinism

and inevitability. "Of most things in history," she remarked, "you feel
that they were bound to happen. But this, I still feel, was something
that should *not* have happened." This remark came, remember, from a
scholar who had reflected long and deeply on the origins of totalitarianism.

Some of her arrogance—partly conscious, partly unconscious—was
directed against America and Americans. America was still a raw and
uncultured country in her eyes. She was certainly better educated
than the New York intellectuals, and she had grounds for feeling their
insufficiencies of understanding. One reason, I suspected, why she was
so flattering about my translation of her essay was her surprise that an
American could understand anything at all of the matters she was
talking about. She was dismayed by the prevailing atmosphere of
American academic philosophy; and when she learned that I had been
through the academic mill, she let out a blast: "I can't understand
why you Americans have taken to these second-rate European positivists that have come here. In Europe people like Carnap and Hempel were jokes. They were at the level of gymnasium, not the university. Here you take them seriously." She had grown up in the exciting
philosophical atmosphere of Germany in the 1920s, the period of Hus-
serl, Scheler, Heidegger, and Jaspers; and judged from that level,
these positivists whom American philosophers were honoring were
stale repetitions of nineteenth-century errors tricked out in a new
technical lingo. It was what one could expect of America as a new
country; we were intellectual novices, eager to absorb any cultural
influence, and consequently sometimes undiscriminating about what
we absorbed.

This arrogance toward American intellectuals became mitigated in
the years that followed, but I think it never entirely left her. She became fond of her adopted country, but this sense of superiority toward things American still remained. And despite all her shrewdness,
in some ways this sense of intellectual superiority got in the way of
her insight into American life. She never quite grasped, I believe, the
realities of American politics—a failing which she shared, of course,
with a great many American intellectuals. She was a European Social
Democrat, rather to the left in that political category, and a German
Social Democrat to boot; and her politics were, consequently, of a
high and sweeping kind, always ideologically slanted, though the slant
in her particular case might be quite original. She had little taste or
feeling for the humdrum and gritty actualities of American politics.

And this was a shortcoming on which Rahv, ever eager to spot any-one's shortcomings, promptly seized. "She doesn't really have political insight," he observed. And from time to time he would take her on in argument, in his usual ranting fashion; but she could usually cow him, leading him into the deeper waters of ideas, where, autodidact that he was, he was suddenly unprepared and beyond his depth.

But this sense of herself as having emerged from a particular class, the German Jews, and her pride in so belonging, were not matters of any narrow and sectarian attachment. On the contrary, her feeling about the German Jews was connected with the highest and most uni-versal motives: these Jews had been, above all else, "Good Euro-peans," the dedicated bearers of the intellectual culture of the West. In this she followed Nietzsche, who had extolled the destiny of the modern Jew to be a "Good European," lifted above the narrow con-straints of nation and class. Later on, she was to say, when pressed by the more Zionistically inclined among American Jews, that her iden-tity lay in "German philosophy." Her intent here was not to affirm any nationalistic bias; she meant that aspect of German philosophy in which it had once expressed the loftiest and deepest aspirations of the European mind. It was not an attitude, however, that won her much favor among some Jewish circles later on when the quarrels broke out on the subject of her book on Eichmann and the Holocaust. It was an attitude that seemed neither partisan nor passionate enough to satisfy some.

In any case, she served as the "Good European" for us in those years. In the time she had stayed in France before coming to America she had absorbed a great deal about the French. She had a fine appre-ciation of French culture, though it was somewhat after the fashion of the highly cultivated German: the French were exquisite and elegant, but for profundity one had in the end to go to the Germans. Never-theless, she helped us understand the ferment that was seething around Sartre and his existentialist circle in Paris, and she stood at our side as the foreign visitors arrived, quite ready with a salty or sympa-thetic observation as the case might warrant.

II.

But if our minds were turned toward Paris and France in expectation of some message for our new post-War world, some manifestation that

105

would confirm Delmore's hopeful cry of "1919! 1919!" it was the British who arrived first.

Sometimes they slipped in and were gone before we were almost aware of it. T. S. Eliot and Bertrand Russell came and went without any great fanfare. In fact, no one would have known about Eliot's visit at all if, on the night before his return to England, he had not called Dwight Macdonald and asked to drop in. Eliot had become interested in Macdonald's theories of pop culture and wanted to meet their author. But there were no intellectual sparks struck that night, for when Eliot arrived he complained of a strained back and asked to lie down on the sofa. The only message Macdonald could bring back to us was a report of how wonderfully modest and simple Eliot's manner was: there was no "side" or affectation to the man at all.

We did not see Russell, but Sidney Hook had him in tow for a good part of the time and kept us informed. In private circles Russell was then pushing the theory of a preventive war with the Soviet Union, and his arguments for it, as usual with him, were very simple and rational. Russian behavior after the War was so aggressive that it was a threat to the West; why not, then, deal with the threat now when the United States enjoyed a monopoly of atomic weapons rather than later when we could expect that the Soviets would be similarly armed. It is interesting to remember this particular stage in the great philosopher's shifting opinions in contrast with his later denunciations of the United States during the Vietnam War. Lord Russell's opinions, philosophical as well as political, never moved in one static groove. But if it is interesting to remember this position as part of his intellectual biography, it is more important to recall for the record—in view of later misrepresentations of the United States as an incurably aggressive country—that Russell made very few converts among Americans. Among the intellectuals of our circle no one ever soberly advanced the idea of a preventive atomic war with Russia, however vigorously anti-Stalinist these intellectuals might be. Philip Rahv might rant at moments as if he personally would have liked to drop an atomic bomb on Stalin's head, but he was too shrewd not to recognize that Russell's purely rational argument was unsound concretely and politically. For one thing, the American people at the moment were in a mood in which they did not want to hear about the idea of war.

Not all British visitors, however, slipped in and out so unobtrusively. Some of them indeed arrived in a rather unbuttoned mood.

In coming to America, after all, they were visiting "the Colonies," and perhaps they could not restrain the old traditional attitudes of the relaxed lord on tour. They were also escaping from the gray austerity of England in those post-War years when rationing was still severe and quite ordinary luxury goods were scarce. At the time, New York in comparison with London was a very lush city, and the British—to the limit of their economic means—threw themselves into it.

Cyril Connolly, the editor of *Horizon*, a magazine which had a considerable vogue on both sides of the Atlantic in those days, was perhaps the most intense socializer of all the visitors. Partly this was his own gregarious mood, but in part he was still functioning here as the energetic editor trying to meet new people and possibly gain new contributors. Since Connolly's own memoirs rather call attention to the more sensitive and languid aspects of his personality, it is well to remind ourselves of the service he performed as a very active and able editor. From the start the British had been more totally involved in the war than we, and their war effort had had to be far more total than ours, in effect claiming the energies of the whole nation. Those are not conditions favorable to such marginal luxuries as the concern with literature. The achievement of Connolly's magazine was to help keep a certain civilized literacy alive during those years of British strain. I have referred earlier to *Horizon* as a kind of British counterpart of *Partisan Review*, but the differences were perhaps more marked than the similarities. The English magazine was more urbane, less political and contentious, more relaxed about drawing an intransigent line between highbrow and middlebrow. At this distance of time I am not sure that this latter quality is not an advantage; for if we sought to be purer about our standards, we were also more strident about them. In all of these qualities the British magazine was an expression of Connolly's own personality.

But if he was an intense socializer while in our midst, he was also something of a puzzle when taken on short notice. Hannah Arendt, for example, could not quite make him out. I suggested the reason might be he was English and she was more familiar with Continentals. "No," she answered, "the trouble with this Englishman is that underneath it he's really an Irishman, and I can't make out which is which." With his broad, ruddy face Connolly did indeed look like an Irishman who would be perfectly at home in a Third Avenue bar; instead he took immediately to the Oak Room of the Plaza, as elegance demanded, but when he once quarreled loudly with a waiter there, he seemed perfectly in character as the Irishman starting a quarrel in his pub. It was hard to grasp that the other aspect of this man was a complex and neurasthenic aesthete. He had quoted, applying it to himself, Stendhal's remark that inside every fat middle-aged man there is a slender youth wildly signaling to get out. In Connolly's case the slender young man seemed to date from the period of Aubrey Beardsley.

However, it was in neither of these two aspects but in the character of the traditional British lord on tour that Connolly managed on one occasion to provide the crudest act of visiting arrogance. The Trillings had him to lunch, for which Mrs. Trilling had prepared a chocolate mousse, which was one of her specialties and in which she took great pride. Connolly ate one or two spoonfuls and then lit a cigar. The conversation dawdled on for some minutes and as they were repairing from the table to the living room, Connolly very carefully stubbed out his cigar in the uneaten dessert. Diana Trilling said later: "He knew what he was doing, it wasn't a fit of absentmindedness." According to the old British definition, a gentleman is someone who never does anything rude unintentionally. In the light of this definition, then, Connolly would have been behaving as the perfect gentleman; but Mrs. Trilling could never forgive him.

A far more gentle but in his way an even more unbuttoned and casual visitor was E. M. Forster. He had slipped into the country quietly, for he did not want any publicity: he was here for strictly private pleasure and relaxation, traveling with his boyfriend, a London policeman. It was inevitable, however, that a meeting between him and Lionel Trilling would be managed. Trilling had written beautifully and eloquently about Forster, arguing his claims to be considered a major novelist of the century; and he had actually succeeded in getting people, intellectuals particularly, to read Forster carefully. It was only natural thus that the two should come together. But the manner of their meeting was very shocking—to Trilling. I heard the story from Philip Rahv, who came to my flat with the news hot and fresh. Rahv told it with great glee, fairly dripping with *Schadenfreude;* but there was something so frank and open, and for the moment good-humored, in his relish of the situation that one felt one could hardly condemn him for it. Trilling had met Forster at an apartment-loft somewhere downtown in the East Village in the midst of a party of homosexuals. And in this gay atmosphere Forster let himself go entirely. Trilling's beloved idol came on simply as an elderly queen camping all over the place. Here he could be more abandoned even than the traditional Englishman going to seed in the colonies. Forster would never have behaved like this in India, where the official eyes of the British *raj* would have been upon him. In America, however, there were no British civil service or colonial police to bother one, and the queen could come out of her closet. "Lionel was simply aghast," Philip Rahv crowed. "Imagine his naïveté—that he shouldn't have been prepared for something like this."

Should he have been prepared? I confess the story was something of a shock to me on hearing it. The works of Forster we knew, those which remain his really important works, did not then include the later more explicitly homosexual writings. In those principal works there were evidences, if one had the mind to suspect, that the author would be homosexual. He had written with engaging freshness about male friendship and camaraderie; but perhaps even more to the point, he had written so delicately and exquisitely from the woman's point of view that one could easily suspect that there must be some pronounced feminine component in the author himself. Still, there was a great gulf between those traces in the then published writings and the spectacle of the aging queen turning on in public. There was indeed something shocking in the discrepancy between the image of the author one carried away from his works—the image of the truly civilized mind, perhaps the most civilized of twentieth-century authors, wise and balanced in his perceptions of human feelings and character—and the image of the sexual grotesque that Rahv's story evoked. Perhaps we all become grotesques when our sexuality becomes a public spectacle. Trilling, of course, was a man of depth and resilience, and he could very shortly absorb the bizarre episode and place it in context. He was to see Forster again, and under different circumstances, and they were in time to become friends, as Trilling himself was later to inform his readers. One is happy for that, and particularly happy that Rahv's *Schadenfreude* did not have the last word.

Yet one cannot leave this episode without bringing up some reflections on the vexed question of sex and literature, and the possible desirability of keeping sex in the closet. The body of Forster's writing that makes up his literary reputation was produced while keeping his own homosexuality in the closet—at least so far as the writing itself was concerned; what Forster did in his own private life has interest for the biographer but no bearing at all upon the value and significance of what he wrote. Indeed, we could hardly get the exquisite qualities of the writing, particularly in its delicate handling of the relations of man and woman, if the author's sexual idiosyncrasy had been thrust at us. The later explicitly homosexual writings of Forster are, by comparison, slighter in substance and inferior in quality; the homosexual theme becomes obsessive and narrowing. And this point—that literature, under certain conditions, may benefit from the author's keeping some aspects of sexuality in the closet—seems to me to apply equally well to heterosexuality too. Of course, to be able to write frankly about sex has been one of the great breakthroughs in modern literature. But for writers like Lawrence and Joyce the candid treatment of sex had a definite meaning; for Lawrence it was part of an intellectual thesis about the nature of modern civilization, and for Joyce part of the artist's project to render ordinary life in its full concreteness, with its bathos and sordor as well as its more ideal moments. But now that they have been given freedom of expression, writers have turned it into a dubious gift. Where invention fails, try to hold the reader by the titillations of sex. If sex were to become a more private and personal affair, writers would have to interest their readers by other means and they might even end by being less boring. Of course, in our life as well as our literature, our society has become possessed by a sexual mania; and a future civilization, if it were to be more balanced, might very well judge that we are deranged on the subject. Once, a few years back, when homosexuals in demonstration marched up Fifth Avenue, I expressed distaste to a friend and was rebuked for being intolerant; I replied that it was not a question of tolerance but that I would feel the same distaste if a crowd of heterosexuals were to march up Fifth Avenue with their flies open. It might not be a bad thing all around if sex for the most part were to pass back into the private sector where it belongs. What was so bad about the closet anyway? It was warm and cozy there.

From these few episodes I would not want to create the impression that all our British visitors were badly behaved. Even Connolly himself must have generally socialized well, for he was able to launch a large and glittering party of his own as a farewell gesture just before he left. It was held at the hotel One Fifth Avenue, which then still retained something of its original elegance as a residential hotel. (In-

deed, Greenwich Village as a whole had a kind of elegance which it
has since mostly lost.) There were a great number of guests, and they
were drawn from all parts of the New York cultural world—from some
areas, in fact, which we rarely penetrated. Many of these guests might
never encounter each other in their own habitual circles; it had taken
a stranger to the city to bring them all together. Doors that were usually shut to us had been flung open to Connolly, who carried the
rather snob value of England with him. *Horizon* might be something
of a counterpart of *Partisan Review,* but after all it was published in
London and it had the cachet of being British that opened doors for
Connolly. And he in turn had made the most of his opportunities.
Even in the time of a short visit he seemed to have made all the
rounds and touched all the bases, and this glittering party as a farewell thank-you was the result. I do not remember, however, seeing
Diana Trilling among the guests.

By comparison, I had to reflect, the social life of the *Partisan Review* circle was a rather narrow affair. However intense in its personalities, and however cosmopolitan in its ideas, it was the social life of
a sealed-off circle and it seemed to transpire largely below Fourteenth
Street. "Midtown" was for us the name of an alien territory, the haunt
of the middlebrows and philistines of the cultural world. And carrying
this ghettolike mentality with us, we were not likely to widen our circle of acquaintance within that uptown world. Besides, we were severely limited by the physical means at our disposal. The small cheap
flats of Delmore and myself were not suited for any kind of social entertainment, and we had to depend upon the apartments of our fellow
editors Rahv and Phillips. Accordingly, we socialized, as Delmore put
it, either *du côte de chez Rahv* or *du côte de chez Phillips;* and this division in our social life inevitably became affected by the growing es-
trangement between the two editors. Rahv usually entertained a few
guests, and one often felt they were carefully selected, almost
screened, for the particular occasion. After his proletarian past, he was
now very conscious of personal status and position, and in this connection he was aware of the growing national stature of the magazine he
edited. He tried to catch visitors to New York who had some voice in
the American literary establishment, and who might at some time or
other put in a good word for him with one of the Foundations. Moreover, he kept these possibly influential guests to himself, treating his
fellow editors more or less as questionable members of the family who

had to be kept out of sight lest they make a bad impression upon the visitors. Thus he had systematically cut out William Phillips from meeting these people over the years of their joint editorship—a fact which Delmore rather sharply brought forward in the middle of the "confrontation"—and this was a sore point that secretly rankled with William Phillips. An evening at the Rahvs', consequently, tended to be a more sedate, careful and calculated affair; and, depending on the particular guests, one sometimes had to tread warily. The late Isaac Rosenfeld—a young and promising novelist and critic who, sadly, died before his promise was realized—was an occasional guest until Rahv decided he was on the skids and was no longer a "winner." Isaac once described a typical evening there pretty accurately: "It was like throwing darts."

William Phillips, on the other hand, entertained much more informally. The guests were not selected, or not markedly so, as a maneuver to advance the host's career. They were there for the purposes of conviviality, and when the early guests departed, those of us who were left felt that the real party had begun and we flung ourselves into the general verbal melee. Rahv was not excluded from these parties, and when he was present he was one of the more boisterous participants in the arguments. He seemed, in fact, to be more uninhibited and at ease as a guest at the Phillipses' than as host in his own home. I do not remember, however, that I ever saw William Phillips at one of the Rahvs' *soirées*. Rahv worked constantly at dividing himself from his fellow editor. Given this difference of atmosphere, it was only natural that for Delmore and myself the Phillipses' apartment should become the center of our social life during those years. And many of those evenings still remain a pleasant memory. There in the late hours, when only a handful of guests remained and William felt himself surrounded by trusted friends, he came to life in a way that most people who did not know him in these moments could hardly imagine. These were his moments of redemption, and his wit and lucid argument could at times lift and transfigure the whole evening.

So far as the visiting English were concerned, we felt we had nothing new to learn in the way of ideas. However interesting as individuals, they seemed to bring with them recognizable attitudes with which we were familiar. Besides, Britain was in the doldrums, in the midst of the gray austerity of rationing, exhausted after the War and under the Labour Government muddling its way toward some kind of

normality. As radical intellectuals looking for something new and revolutionary to emerge in our post-War world, we felt that the English
situation had no possibilities of any development that would enlighten
us about the deeper matters of modern history or of social theory. We
were wrong of course—as intellectuals usually are in their confron-
tations with actual history. In its quiet and stodgy way, Britain was
then in a process of socialization, of radically extending the Welfare
State, as a result of which some twenty or thirty years later it would
emerge as a second-rate industrial nation in comparison with West
Germany. The British were victors in the War, yet proceeded to lose
it economically. Germany was the defeated nation, and its industrial
plant so decimated that we Marxists were convinced that the aid
offered by the United States through the Marshall Plan would prove
only a futile effort—"a drop in the bucket," as Rahv put it—to restore
capitalism there. But capitalism, when left relatively unhampered, was
to prove viable and productive beyond the dreams of earlier economists. In the space of a decade Germany was thriving and Britain was
in decline.

Nor did the redistribution of wealth, toward which the tide of socialism moved in Britain, seem to bring any greater happiness to the
majority of the people. The benefits which the State confers on the
disadvantaged seem never sufficient to take away their resentments,
and these benefits usually come with strings attached. On my last visit
(in 1975) I sensed more class resentments in the air than ever before.
More and more as the British became wards of the State, there
seemed to be an erosion of traditional British characteristics that once
were so attractive to visitors. London seemed almost as rude and un-
civil as New York.

For intellectuals committed to socialism, as we were then, here is a
whole chapter of history from which some simple and profound lessons might now be drawn. Of course, at the time this was a chapter
that still lay in the future. But even today, intellectuals—not to speak
of economists and politicians—seem unable to draw these lessons.

III.

Would Existentialism have made such a splash in the news at this
time if it had not come before the public under this puzzling and im-
posing label? I doubt it. The big name provoked curiosity, and

seemed to imply some special and portentous message it had to convey. Existentialism was the rage in Paris, and might become a fashion here; and therefore one would want to be in on it. On the other hand, it might bring some new way of looking at things, some new twist or gimmick, like a new style of psychotherapy. The modern public is characterized by its perpetual curiosity about news, its hunger for novelties, and at the same time its preoccupation with techniques and gadgets, any means whatever to escape the human condition. Modern technical civilization is in good part the blending of these two impulses. It is the fate of any serious idea, when it enters the market place, to be taken up in one or the other, or both these aspects. I remember being asked very aggressively at the time, What is Existentialism?, the question being backed by the insistence that I answer in one or two sentences, and on the spur of the moment I replied, "You are alone and you die alone." I could see my questioner's face fall. Only that! Then it had nothing to teach him.

I could have given him any number of different formulas of course; his face would have fallen in any case. But no formula would have encompassed the vivid variety of personality in the four French emissaries of the movement—Sartre, Merleau-Ponty, Simone de Beauvoir, and Camus—who visited us soon after the War.

Jean-Paul Sartre had already been installed as the high priest of Existentialism, whatever it might be, and he was already so much in the public eye that he swept by us in his quick tour of America in semi-official tow. We did not have a chance to get to know what the private Sartre would be like at firsthand. We saw him mostly on public display, on the platform and before an audience. He was a formidable orator, a torrent of words; and in his whole career he was a veritable volcano of words. It was altogether appropriate and in character that he should later entitle his sketch of an autobiography *The Words*, as if the whole reality of his life had been to drink them in and pour them out. And all the more deeply and ironically in character coming from the philosopher who did not believe in fixed character.

Merleau-Ponty, on the other hand, was very accessible personally, but managed nevertheless to keep himself personally hidden in his intercourse with us. He was well-mannered, pleasant and witty, almost suave enough to suggest something of the diplomat, confining himself for the most part to small talk and generalities. He was relaxing socially, of course, and may very well have wanted only to enjoy casual conversation; but I suspected there was a deeper reason for his reserve. At this time the news of Stalin's labor camps was beginning to break upon the world. The existence of these camps had been known of before, but now their full and horrifying extent was being disclosed and documented. The news was upsetting to intellectuals everywhere, and produced some extraordinary dialectical writhing. Merleau-Ponty was then associated with Sartre in editing the magazine *Temps Modernes*, in which he published a justification of these camps. It was a position, however, that left him uncomfortable, and he was uneasily moving away from it. He did not want to discuss it with us; he was a guest and wished to avoid bringing a noisy quarrel—which would certainly have come up if the subject had arisen among us—into the company of his hosts. So he deftly steered the conversation around that minefield. Years later I was to read his fine essay on Machiavelli, and I recognized the mind that had been at work that evening—subtle and devious enough in its own right to comprehend the great Florentine.

But if Sartre was unavailable, and Merleau-Ponty skirted our questions, Simone de Beauvoir was ready and willing to give us all the answers—and indeed more answers than we asked for. She had good features, but of that peculiarly French kind that inevitably suggests a touch of the maiden aunt or the governess. And toward us she often came on as the schoolmarm or governess who has to explain matters to the benighted children. Her devotion to Sartre and his doctrine was touching. She would interrupt the person speaking, not obtrusively but patiently and sadly, to remark "If you would only read page 329 of Sartre's *Being and Nothingness*, you would get that clear"—and one almost waited for her to produce the text from her purse. Someone had relayed to us the joke going around France that Simone de Beauvoir was "la Sartreuse de Paris"; and observing her in action, I could see that the joke had its point.

Unfortunately, she did not know English so well as she put on, and she often got large chunks of the conversation all wrong. I found this out later when I read her book about her tour of the United States. I had been present at several of the gatherings which she reported, and she simply got the whole drift and intent of the talk wrong. But what could one do? The woman insisted that we speak in English to her. She wanted to learn the language, and she pretended she was following perfectly what was said. This kind of faking is a good device when you are trying to become fluent in a foreign language, for you learn to swim forward with the current of the conversation and pick it up later when the drift becomes a little clearer. But it is not particularly advisable when you are later to report authoritatively on certain conversations, especially when the conversation may happen to touch on rather complex matters.

Indeed, "authoritative" was the word for her on most subjects. We were glad to have her explain Sartre's doctrine to us, but it became somewhat irritating when she proceeded to lecture us on the true nature of America and Americans. The French were then going through a love affair with "the American novel," as they called it, though they were in fact dealing with a rather curious slice of American writing. They had had the benefit of an early and good translation of Faulkner, whom they read seriously and closely at a time when attention to Faulkner in this country had waned and his books were allowed to go out of print—and in this the French critical intelligence was operating with its traditional acuteness. But the French then went on to swallow in one indiscriminate bolus all our "tough-guy" literature—Hammett and Chandler and the thrillers of James M. Cain—tricking these writers out with all kinds of elaborate philosophical and literary motifs; and out of this amalgam they constructed an America of the imagination which they took for the real America—a country more eerie and violent even than we really are. And American intellectuals? Well, they were a handful of very lonely palefaces adrift on a continent of savage redskins, to use Philip Rahv's old terminology. At bottom, every American intellectual is as ghostly and lost as Bartleby the Scrivener. Such was the general picture that De Beauvoir carried with her across the Atlantic. I wondered at times why she had come here at all, since she already had her case complete on us and our country. Perhaps it was only to add some confirming details to the picture she already had. She seemed to me like a traveler carrying an invisible visa form in which all the main items had already been entered and she had only to fill in a few blanks.

Or perhaps she came for some possible adventure on the road in the style of the lonely American hero of our fiction. In any case, the adventure came—a love affair with the novelist Nelson Algren in Chicago, which she later reported in detail in her book. After all, it was good literary material. When Algren later read her account, he shrugged in embarrassment: "She made too much of the episode. She got it all wrong." I could well believe him.

Camus was a welcome change, wonderfully appealing in his sheer modesty. He listened, he did not come carrying the prefabricated dope on us; he gave us the impression he was intent on learning from us as much as he could. "Writers aren't people really," Scott Fitzgerald remarks somewhere; and in my own experience of them I have found this observation true for the most part. Writers can be quite real as people in one aspect, but then there is that other side of them that is always looking at the real side and questioning it, so that they remain suspended in a kind of aesthetic unreality. But Camus, at least so far as I knew him, seemed one notable exception to Fitzgerald's dictum. (Another was Samuel Beckett, whom I met years later, and who had probably paid a crucifying price to retain his human reality.) Camus read English, and loved English literature, but he made no pretense of speaking English; and we carried on with him in our own varied and halting French. But somehow the gates of understanding were open, and I learned more from my talks with him than from any other of our visitors.

Camus and Sartre were still friends at that time (1946). *Partisan Review* had just published a number which was devoted to the French situation and in which some of the fiction of Sartre and Jean Genet first appeared, as well as the opening chapter of Camus's new novel, *The Plague*, which had not yet been published in France. Camus had read through the whole issue carefully (that kind of attentiveness in itself was something quite rare among our foreign visitors), and he found the occasion to chide me, though gently, about a little review of Sartre I had contributed to the number. "You are too severe (*trop dur*)," he said; but then added—rather mysteriously at the moment he said it—"But in time you will be proved right." In my talks with him later his meaning became clearer, and gave me a portent of what was to happen in the relations of the two men, and the deep difference in personal character that really divided them.

Camus and Sartre, among the figures of our period, were almost archtypal opposites as personalities; and from that opposition much can be learned about the mind of our century (which is, after all, the fugitive theme that haunts these memoirs). The break between them is usually attributed to their differences over the Soviet Union and the nature of its Communism. Sartre at this time had begun to be an ardent Fellow Traveler, enamored of the idea that Soviet Communism, whatever its imperfections, still represented a progressive and revolutionary force in the world. Camus had been a member of the Communist Party in North Africa in his earlier years; he knew the treacherous shifts and duplicity of the Party from the inside, and he was now an intransigent foe of the Soviet Union. It was typical of Sartre, by the way, that though he was the most celebrated Fellow Traveler in France, he never became a member of the Party. To join would be to diminish his Freedom—that absolute and somewhat vacuous freedom which his philosophy celebrates—and in this he was consistent with his own system. But the friendship survived even these political differences for a while. The break, when it came, was over more deeply personal and at the same time universal values.

The difference between the two men seems to me wonderfully revealed in a little incident related by the Dominican priest Father Bruckberger, who was active in the French Resistance and was close to both at the time. Bruckberger used to run into Sartre and Simone de Beauvoir at the cafe, the two of them huddled over books and notes and discussing points in philosophy. They struck him, he remarks, like two permanent graduate students (and perhaps, we may add, Sartre remained something of that to the end). They were joined one day by Camus, who was coming away from his labors on *Combat,* the clandestine paper of the Resistance that he edited. Sartre was then in the process of completing his big book *Being and Nothingness,* and he was in the midst of expounding to his hearers the view of absolute liberty which he develops in that tome. This liberty is a possibility we carry around within us like a terrorist's bomb, which at any moment we could detonate in any direction. "Nothing prevents us . . ."—this is Sartre's recurring phrase to indicate that at any moment we can step off into a new direction out of the rut that we have hitherto traveled in life. At that moment a German officer in full regalia walked past on the sidewalk, and Camus, who had been listening in silence, remarked: "Even granted that liberty, there are some things we wouldn't do. For example, you wouldn't denounce me to the Germans even though you had the pure possibility of doing so." The remark, Bruckberger tells us, seemed to disturb Sartre, as if he had never thought of the question so concretely and personally before, and he was at a loss for a reply.

This little episode seems to me to sum up the two men: Sartre the rampant ideologue, and Camus the advocate of what he came to call "ordinary values"—those elementary feelings of decency without which the human race could not survive. There was a quality about Camus which made him something different as an intellectual—a quality indeed that most intellectuals lack: he was a man of the people who remained in touch with our common humanity, and this quality came through even in that first meeting with him. Later on, when his position developed in directions contrary to what they would have liked, French intellectuals began to snipe at him and I had the feeling from what I read that he must have been rather uncomfortable in their presence. Years later I had the occasion to mention this impression of mine to Germaine Bree, who knew both Camus's work and the man himself better than any other critic, and she replied: "Uncomfortable! That's hardly the word for it, Camus came to feel almost physically distressed when in their presence." So much so, she went on, that toward the end of his life he even thought of moving from Paris and settling somewhere else in the country—a move that would have been very drastic indeed, since the French writer is so strongly attached to Paris as the cultural heart of the nation.

And it was Germaine Bree who enlightened me on the deeper personal differences that surrounded his final rupture with Sartre. She had called one day, only to find Camus fuming and brandishing a copy of Sartre's book on Jean Genet, which had just appeared and which he had just finished reading. "That does it!" Camus exclaimed. He could no longer pretend to have any real human understanding or indeed human communication with Sartre after this, for they stood for things that were too different. Sartre's book had been an "existential psychoanalysis" that sought both to explain and justify Genet the man and the writer. Genet had been a pimp, a pederast, a homosexual prostitute, a thief, and a paid informer of the Nazis. He happened also to be a writer of a very special genius—though I believe that genius is cramped and distorted by his vice: after the initial shock passes off, as one goes on reading, one finds a heavy and narrow monotony and, surprisingly, a kind of skewed sentimentality. Some of the more lush passages about the charms of young homosexuals would strike us as mawkish and sentimental if addressed to young women. The effect of vice deliberately pursued, and perhaps sexual vice especially, is never "liberating," but usually quite the opposite: it produces a rigid and narrow obsession, the mania of an *idée fixe*, in the individual who gives himself to it. Nevertheless Sartre had presented Genet's life in a way to justify it. In the Sartrean view, our life is a free project which

119

we launch into the world: we choose the self that we become, and the authenticity of the life is to be measured by the fullness of our commitment to our freely chosen project. Genet had been energetically and thoroughly wicked; he had been committed passionately to the project of his life; and in this respect his life was more "authentic" than that of the tame bourgeois who is bound by ordinary morality. Camus gagged at this intellectualist juggling, at this blindness to ordinary feelings and indeed ordinary instincts. Moreover, he felt it would be impossible at this point to try to communicate his objections to Sartre: the latter would not understand, he had gone too far in encircling himself in the system of his own ideas to see beyond them. The intellectual spider spins his web and cannot come forth from it.

Significantly, the sense of this episode—which expresses the core of the opposition between the two men—is exactly what was foreshadowed in the earlier anecdote of Father Bruckberger.

Sartre later was to write a sketch of an autobiography, *The Words,* remarkable for its candor and its eloquence—all the more remarkable, I think, in that it contradicts his whole philosophy. In his philosophy he had denied the notion of fixed character; the man who asserts roundly that we are what we are is denying the fundamental fact of our human reality, which leaves us always with the possibility of being what we are not; free to create ourselves as the person we choose to be. But the autobiography—and this is at once its strength and its fascination—reveals a singularly unitary and consistent personality throughout. Sartre is there in its pages; he is what he is from the start and throughout. His father died while he was an infant and thus remained unknown to him. Sartre therefore grew up, he tells us, without a superego; without that moral conscience that usually comes through the authoritarian figure of the father. And Sartre is exuberant in telling this about himself: he grew up more free and unencumbered than other young men he knew, who had to carry the burden of their fathers on their backs, like Aeneas lugging the aged Anchises from the ruins of Troy. In a sense, his whole philosophy, with its doctrine of unencumbered liberty, is the expression of a man without a superego: it pursues the notion of an absolute liberty not hedged in by the ordinary restraints of human nature. They are remarkable beings, these men without superego, without an engrained and troubling conscience; they may sometimes be more "moral" than we are, but if so, it is in a different way from most of us; and if they are intellectuals, they can let the head take over completely and fabricate values in the air. Paul Goodman—to descend to a lesser talent and lesser mind—was another such case, whom I knew very closely at one time. Just as Sartre, according to reports, could be very engaging in personal intercourse, Goodman could be amusing and great fun as a companion, but one could never be sure where his head would carry him in violation of "ordinary values." And it is typical of these individuals that when they come to general social issues, they are sweepingly and uncompromisingly "idealistic" and utopian. Perhaps, one suspects, to prove to themselves they do have a moral conscience after all. Camus's last, and to my mind best, novel, *The Fall*, can be read as a parable of the modern intellectual who is without a superego, without a sense of "ordinary values," and develops by way of compensation an outsized, maniacal, but still cerebral sense of guilt.

After one of our meetings I accompanied Camus back to his hotel. In the cab he suddenly shook my arm and said that he was disturbed by us. This came as a surprise, since the evening had seemed to go so pleasantly. No, he didn't mean that, he had had a very good time, but he was distressed because "You people still call yourselves Marxist, and think of yourselves as Marxists." At the time I couldn't understand what he was getting at. His distress seemed to me unnecessary and extreme, a result—so I thought then—of the French habit of formulating intellectual theses too neatly and dichotomously. To be a Marxist in France meant one was committed to a defense of the Soviet Union; liberals who were critical of the Soviets could not really be Marxists. But why this Either-Or? What was wrong with being a liberal or democratic Marxist? Why couldn't one believe in Marxism and freedom both?

Later on I was to understand what Camus meant. At that time his thought was taking a new turn, which would eventually find expression in *The Rebel*. In his first phase, Camus's thinking had turned around the solitary individual who confronts his own death without any religious consolations and must ask himself the question what meaning his life has. Now, his thinking was moving on from the individual to the group, from solitude to brotherhood, from the "I" to the "We." Whence comes our sense of human community? Camus was to locate it in the brotherhood of men rebelling against some oppressive situation. But the Rebel, as Camus sees him, is something very different from the modern Revolutionary. The Rebel is fighting against a definite and concrete situation which he wishes to change or abolish; and because his aims are limited, his thinking consequently is bounded by a sense of limits. The Revolutionary, on the other hand, is unlimited and total in his aspirations; he wishes to transform the whole fabric of society and therefore of human life from top to bottom. And because his aspirations are total, they inevitably become totalitarian. The French Revolution was the first of the modern total revolutions, and the Russian Revolution simply carried on further. And because the revolution that wishes to change human life totally must arrogate total powers to itself, it ends in Gulag or the equivalent. The excessive idealist becomes our jailer.

Now, in retrospect of all the years between, I think Camus was dead right. Our kind of Marxism was a luxury; it never had to sully itself by coming to power, and did not even have to ponder the problem of power generally and its crucial concentration in the modern state; on the other hand, we could keep the purity of our dissent by being detached from what we regarded as the wickedness of American capitalism. We seemed to ourselves to walk the just middle ground between the dictatorial Communism of the Soviet Union on the one hand and the "unprogressive" capitalism of the United States on the other. But in fact we were treading on air.

In reporting here about a particular group of intellectuals in New York I do not wish to give the impression that their inadequacies on this matter were due to their private and personal deficiencies; on the contrary, they were among the keener minds of the time who thought about these problems, and indeed in coming to the proper estimation of the nature of the Soviet Union they were more than a decade ahead of the European intelligentsia. The fault was one of our whole generation. We had inherited the experience of the 1930s, and thought we were doing enough simply to carry it on: we continued the battles against Stalinism and struggled persistently to point out the dictatorial nature of the Soviet Union; but in the process we still wished to think of ourselves as radical Marxists—the genuine radicals—and that prevented us from thinking through to the problems that would come. Intrepid souls like Orwell, Koestler, and Silone had supposedly gone through the archtypal ordeal of the "god that failed"—the title of their book has long since passed into the currency of the language about Marxism—and for our generation that seemed to close a chapter for Western intellectuals. The Communist god seemed so discredited that he could never come to life again for any intellectuals. We were wrong; the god was to rise again; and the cycle of dying and rising god is bound to be repeated again and again so long as we fail to think through what the nature of this god is. The fact is that the god didn't fail at all, he has been a howling success; he now holds half of the world's population in his grip, and threatens almost daily to take over more. It was our deluded expectations that failed. And in this sense we failed the decades that were to come. As the attitude of a liberal Marxism, vague enough to begin with, became even vaguer and more vaporous, it infected the whole of American Liberalism; and was to erupt again as the infantile Leftism of the 1960s.

IV.

What was the impact upon American intellectuals of these existential ideas that the French brought with them?

Very little, it must be confessed, at least at first exposure. The intellectuals, of course, shared the general public curiosity about this new movement. They wanted to know what was going on, and that meant having some approximate understanding of these new ideas, so that one could throw them around, if necessary, in print or conversation. But beyond that, there was no deeper response to the possibility of a new orientation of thought that these ideas might bring with them. Hannah Arendt was very disappointed in the indifferent response to her own article, which we had printed as a kind of introduction to the subject for our readers. She was also surprised and puzzled, for she thought that these were ideas that would have a certain brio and excitement for American intellectuals. I explained to her that the background of American intellectuals was Marxist, and even where not explicitly so, the Marxist influence had colored their mentality so that they were disposed to think in terms of the large, impersonal forces of history. And this disposition did not leave them particularly receptive to a philosophy that placed the reality of human existence in the individual, and even seemed to betray a certain hankering after religion. "Heidegger is the back door to theology," Sidney Hook warned us at the time.

The fact is that Marxism and Existentialism are antithetical, despite the intellectual juggling in some quarters to make the two march side by side. A philosophy which speaks of the radical individuality of human existence, and which seeks to revive some of the thoughts of Pascal and Kierkegaard in however secularized a form, cannot fit into the Marxist state. The French Communist Party knew this immediately, and promptly declared war on the new movement, even though the Existentialists in Paris were all politically on the Left. Communists are usually good judges of what is consistent with their own interests, and we are wiser to follow them in such matters. When they are for Détente, we may be sure that Détente is to their advantage. We would have done better, for example, earlier on if we had understood them when they condemned modern literature and art, instead of trying in schizoid fashion to reconcile the two M's, Marxism and Modernism—an effort that really obscured the nature of both to us. But Sartre in the present case chose the spectacular role of a Don Quixote tilting at a windmill: he sought to show that an existential philosophy was more in accord with the truly revolutionary purposes of Communism. Thus he polemicized philosophically against the Communists, while he continued to support them and the cause of the Soviet Union as an ardent Fellow Traveler—a peculiarly dual role that perhaps only he could carry off.

But if the immediate response among intellectuals here was lukewarm, there was one paradoxical exception in our midst, and that was Philip Rahv himself. (I except myself, since certain peculiarities of my background had already led me in the existentialist direction; and in any case, as the reader may have gathered by this time, and as I myself am more and more aware as I write these pages, I was not typical of this milieu in which nevertheless I sought so passionately to lose myself.) Rahv's sudden preoccupation with Existentialism was paradoxical because at bottom he was the most doctrinaire Marxist among us. To be sure, this Marxism of his was somewhat in abeyance in this period, as he turned his mind toward more literary and cultural themes; but it had not vanished, it was as unchanging a part of him as his bone structure, and later on, as we shall see, it was to reassert itself most strongly. Nevertheless there was another strain in his complex character, and to my mind the deeper and more likable one, that showed itself in his spontaneous love of the great Russian writers. The Russian novel confronted the primal matters of life and death with a directness and energy that Western writers in the nineteenth century could no longer command. This was what fascinated Rahv as the "existential" aspect of the great Russians, and for a long time he had been trying to get a handle on it.

He found it at last in a single passage from Tolstoi's *Anna Karenina,* which seemed to him to sum up the whole matter at issue in Existentialism. The husband Alexey Alexandrovitch Karenin had just begun to suspect that his charming and beautiful wife, Anna, is being unfaithful to him; and here we had better turn to the words of Tolstoi himself:

> He felt that he was standing face to face with something illogical and irrational, and did not know what was to be done. Alexey Alexandrovitch was standing face to face with life, with the possibility of his wife's loving someone other than himself, and this seemed to him very irrational and incomprehensible because it was life itself. All his life Alexey Alexandrovitch had lived and worked in official spheres, having to do with the reflection of life. And every time he stumbled against life itself he had shrunk away from it.

This contrast—indeed this shocking disruption—between our life as it is, actual and concrete, and the "reflections" that we substitute for it in our conceptual systems and social behavior had been the central theme with which Kierkegaard had launched existential thinking. And here it was, surfacing quite on its own, as a central motif in Tolstoi the novelist. The attempt to "stand face to face with life," Rahv later wrote, was the "Existential center of the Tolstoian art." His instincts here were surely right; if only he had followed them and his love of the Russian novel to the end, the Marxist ideologue in him might have found a more subdued place.

Marxism was not the only intellectual obstacle in the way of our American reception of Existentialism. There was also the resistance provided by Positivism, which had just begun to take its grip on American philosophers and whose attitudes had even begun to spread beyond the academy. Positivism was then in its most aggressive phase, and its general appeal, especially for the young, was the apparent tough-mindedness of its stance. All that can be known, it said, was science; and beyond that we may express our emotions but we cannot take those expressions for knowledge. And forthwith the great bulk of traditional philosophy was discovered to be speaking "nonsense." This was a great boon for all those who would just as well forget the past anyway, and an especial convenience for the young professionals in philosophy who were thus spared the trouble of studying those past philosophers. The German refugees Carnap and Hempel (whom we have seen Hannah Arendt lamenting) had brought the doctrine to our shores, but its best-known popular spokesman by far, its veritable Apostle to the Gentiles, was the British philosopher A. J. Ayer, who was then in our midst teaching at one of the local universities. But Ayer was presently engaged in softening the aggressive edge of his doctrine somewhat, and his present mood was that of the convivial visitor about town, preferring not to enter into controversy unless he was provoked to it. Indeed, it was surprising how civilized his conversation was, when he put his philosophic dogmas out of sight. The really aggressive Positivist who sprang upon us unawares was, paradox of paradoxes, a poet—Randall Jarrell.

Jarrell was on a visit to New York to serve as guest literary editor of *The Nation*, a position then of some power and prestige. He would have been welcome in our midst, except that he chose not to be; he belongs properly in this chapter on foreign visitors because he came among us an outsider and resolutely remained such. He was from the South, but he was not like any Southerner I have known. If there is any such thing as the persona of the poet, I have not been able to gather it from my encounters with poets. The persona of John Berryman, for example, was to be or pretend to be stupid (and it was sometimes doubtful which of the two it was). Jarrell's persona, on the other hand, was to come on as the individual with the most glittering IQ you ever met. "He's a regular Whiz Kid," the painter Bill Baziotes declared after meeting him; and Jarrell seemed to be stuck permanently in the stage of the brilliant prodigy. If not told beforehand, one would be unlikely to take him for a poet at all, so intensely cerebral did he appear to be. But perhaps this impression was intensified by the nervousness he felt in this New York milieu. He was uneasy with the New York intellectuals, as if he felt perpetually challenged, whereas he in his nervousness was really the challenging one. He was like the strange gunman who comes to town and must be ready to draw on the slightest provocation lest he be shot down. Had he relaxed for a moment, he would have been feted, both for his own considerable talents and for his temporary position of literary power.

Inevitably, of course, he was at loggerheads with Rahv about Existentialism and the attention the magazine had been giving to it.

Hannah Arendt's article, he declared, was "nonsense"—in the strict philosophical sense, it was "meaningless." Moreover, the whole of Existentialism was philosophically meaningless. Rahv was aghast; I do not think he had ever encountered full-blown positivists face to face before, and he was unfamiliar with their tactic of declaring "meaningless" any rival philosophy cast in a language different from their own. Accordingly, he fell back on the elemental point to which he felt closest; surely, he urged, it was not meaningless to talk about death. But Jarrell did not waver from his ideological obstinacy: yes, all this philosophical talk about death was meaningless.

The argument was let drop there, but the next day Rahv was still turning it over in his mind, unbelieving and puzzled. "Just imagine," he snorted. "Death is meaningless! If there's anything that's real, it's death." And on this subject, Rahv remained thoroughly existential and concrete, whatever other ideological abstractions might take over his mind. Death was real, he brooded enough about it to know; and he was enough of a Tolstoian to know that the reality of it cannot be evaded. But with the other part of Tolstoi's question—"If there is death, what meaning then has life?"—he never really engaged himself, at least openly. Secretly, I think, he had long since answered the question in the negative: he was a Nihilist; but I'm not sure he was even conscious of this.

No doubt, Jarrell might have been unduly excited at the moment and overstated his case; still, there was something very paradoxical in this confrontation of the two minds. That a poet, of all people, and a gifted poet at that, should be the one to insist that the subject of death is meaningless for philosophical reflection, is surely paradoxical. And perhaps more than paradoxical; surely there is something a little crazy about a culture in which a poet feels that he must accept this judgment as the last word of what currently passes for "scientific" philosophy. This small episode gains a very sharp poignancy in the light of Jarrell's own death later. Though the circumstances were somewhat ambiguous, it seems definitely to have been suicide. There was no doubt about John Berryman's suicide: he flung himself from a bridge. Delmore Schwartz committed suicide piecemeal, day by day. They joined each other as the three *poétes maudits* of their generation. In their actual life, at any rate, their death came to be meaningless to them.

Looking back now, I wonder whether the thought of the Existentialists made any deeper contact with the American mind generally than it did with Jarrell's, though he was more explicit and violent in his recoil from it. To be sure, the tags and phrases got about publicly, more than with most philosophies nowadays. For a while the word "existential" would pop up almost everywhere in Norman Mailer's casual writings, though one could not always be sure what its meaning was, beyond being some kind of intensification of what the writer was saying, as if he were to underline his sentence, or collar his reader and exclaim, "Get this, it's very important." And during the 1960s the words "authentic" and "inauthentic" were always on the lips of our flower children. In time, too, Existentialism crept into the academy, courses were given in it, and it became part of the philosophic curriculum—one of the fifty-seven varieties therein dispensed. But there too it was boxed off into its own small corner and had no significant effect upon the trend of the dominant academic philosophy.

Perhaps, though, it is too soon to tell. The significance of the existentialist thinkers and writers may lie less in any finished achievement than in what they were a symptom of, and symptoms may take a long time to work out before the nature of the ailment becomes unmistakably clear. Yet the malady is all around us and spreading; it lies in the sense of drift and meaninglessness that afflicts more and more people in our culture, and that will not be appeased by the various pop-psychological remedies that are now being peddled everywhere. The significance of the whole existential movement seems to me now to consist in its being a symptom of the central question that haunts, and will continue to haunt our civilization more and more as time goes on. This is the religious question, either God or Nihilism; and as such it was grasped by the existentialist founders, Kierkegaard and Nietzsche, in the nineteenth century. In comparison with the depth, passion, and seriousness with which these forerunners grasped *the* problem, the Existentialists of this century, whatever else their considerable merits, seem halfhearted and scattered. In Sartre, to choose the extreme, there was not even serious involvement in the existential themes he juggled dialectically. In an interview shortly before his death he confessed that he had never been an Existentialist at heart, that he had never experienced real anxiety or despair (perhaps the man without a superego does not), and that he had merely borrowed the intellectual vocabulary then current. I think this lack might have been gathered from his writings thirty years before; and it is ironical that he, the least existential in his own personal being, should be the name popularly associated with this philosophic movement. Temperamentally, he was no more an Existentialist than Bertrand Russell; and it has always struck me that among the intellectuals of this century there is a curious resemblance between the two. Though they were poles apart in their background, and though they operated out of a different philosophic tradition, both had the same extraordinary brilliance and facility, together with an amazing glibness and tendency to superficiality. Santayana, who was a sharp observer of men and affairs and had occasion to know Russell pretty well, observed of the British philosopher that "something essential seemed to have been left out of his make-up"—and the remark might be extended to Sartre.

From a strictly philosophical point of view, Heidegger looms as the most original and the major figure to have emerged from the whole existentialist movement. Yet it is questionable whether his thinking does not end in a whisper. He agrees with Nietzsche that the fundamental question this civilization has to face is that of Nihilism. But to confront this question we have to understand and think through the Nihil—the Nothing—in Nihilism, and for this we have to undergo a very long and protracted meditation upon Being. We are not yet prepared to face the question of God until we have recast our fundamental ideas of and attitudes toward Being—the work perhaps of centuries, the passing into a new world-epoch that will succeed the last twenty-five hundred years of Western philosophy that have brought us to our present period of science and technology. And meanwhile? Heidegger is a thinker in the grand manner and his vision bites off huge chunks of time and will not be hurried. Meanwhile? We are in the empty period of waiting between two worlds—"Born too late for the gods, and too early for Being." Meanwhile the number who suffocate from the sense of meaninglessness increases day by day. What can they hope? What is to be offered them? Only this long and excruciating waiting? These are questions that seem not to have touched the late Heidegger in his final years of serene and unruffled meditation.

Such as it was, in any case, Existentialism was the message Europe brought to us in those years. It may not have been what we expected, or even what we wanted, but no doubt about it, it was what was "new." But then again, it would have been hard to say just what we expected or wanted. We would have liked some fresh explosion like the 1920s in the aftermath of the First World War, another *Waste Land* and *Ulysses* and school of Paris in painting, but the century had already exhausted the spiritual and artistic capital on which those earlier achievements of the avant-garde had drawn. Something else too, of which we were not immediately aware, was beginning to happen in the cultural realignment of Europe and America. We were probably the last American generation to go through this old rite of looking toward Europe for our culture. The airplane and modern travel would make the world one in a way it never was before. Cultural innovations might arise here, there, anywhere; and as they arose we might borrow from them; but that older exclusive filial relation to Europe—the sense of Europe as a unique treasure on which Americans must depend—was on the way out. Henceforth, America would have to fend more for itself, in culture as in international politics, where it could no longer escape the role of a world power and had to assume the responsibilities of that position. In fact, the significant innovations in culture henceforth might just as well come from America as from Europe.

And this, of course, was exactly what began to happen now in painting.

Chapter Six

The Painters' Club

I.

The artists themselves spoke of it simply as "the Club." "Painters' Club" was my own expression when I had to identify it for some of my literary friends as the place where I might have picked up this or that odd bit of information. But the addition of the extra word came to convey to me the sense of an alien terrain, a place of very different attitudes and habits from the literary circle in which I moved. So much so, indeed, that it was for a while something of an adventure to go there.

In fact, it was not a "club" in any usual sense: there were no formal requirements or rites of membership. A group of artists had simply pooled their resources to rent a floor-through loft in an old red-brick building on Eighth Street, which in a few years would be torn down for one of the tasteless apartment buildings that were to spring up throughout the neighborhood right after the War. Thus the Club, both in its setting and character, belonged to the ambience of an older

Greenwich Village that would fade and virtually disappear in the following decades. Nor were the members all painters; there were artists in other media, and some with a mysterious and unspoken relation to art that I was never to know and who remained mere nodding acquaintances for as long as I frequented the place. But the nucleus of the Club that was to become famous were the painters later known as "Abstract Expressionists." At this time they had yet to make their big splash before the world and they were not rich, but rents then were very cheap and they had managed enough money for a place of their own to hold meetings and parties. When the party mood was on, an old hand-crank phonograph would turn up with some borrowed records to dance by. Clement Greenberg, the art critic, who was the earliest champion of these painters, nevertheless disdained to socialize at the Club; but I do have one solitary memory of him there once far into the night doing the jitterbug, which was the dance that had come out of the War. It was part of his program for becoming the well-rounded highbrow, the intellectual who can move easily into more popular ways of life.

Sometimes the entertainment was more elevated in tone. A friend of a friend knew somebody at Juilliard, and shortly the Juilliard String Quartet were down to play at the Club. Nor was their playing perfunctory; in that informal atmosphere, they flung themselves at the music with extraordinary energy, and the meaning of "chamber" music seemed to take on some of its old dimension in that loft. There was a thunder of applause at the end, and Willem de Kooning leaped to his feet and presented the musicians with his latest opus, a lovely black-and-white wash drawing, amid a burst of more applause—this time for the picture itself. The incident in itself almost dates the occasion: just a few years later, more likely than not De Kooning's dealer would be on hand to snatch the picture out of his hand. The price of success is the tyranny of the dealer: the artist cannot bestow his works so freely.

Mostly, however, the cultural efforts of the Club took the form of lectures and discussions. The folding chairs would be lined up, the members took their place as serious and intent listeners, and their discussions afterward were heated and lively, though not always directly to the point. It was in this connection that I made my own entree to the Club, to deliver a lecture on the subject of Existentialism. The invitation came through Elaine de Kooning, who was, socially at least,

132

the liveliest spirit of the group, perpetually concocting possible programs and entertainments. I don't think I've ever spoken to a more attentive audience, yet I wasn't sure they heard what I said. That is, they listened to my words, but I'm not sure they heard their meaning. Ideas, abstract ideas, have a way of bouncing off the minds of artists at curious angles and ricochets that are a marvel to behold and a puzzle to try to follow. I was invited to give a second lecture, but somehow the date got mixed up, and in the confusion I was able to get off. In excuse I remember remarking to one of them that perhaps they had had enough of ideas and should stick to their art, and that anyway it wasn't necessarily a good thing for artists to mess too much with ideas. My tone was kidding, but it turned out that I was in fact prophetical. The subsequent history of the New York School was to be, at least in part, an indecent traffic with ideas, in the course of which it is really remarkable that some good painting managed to get done.

There was something quaint and touching in all this bohemian camaraderie. It was at the farthest remove from the literary cocktail party, where each guest measures the other as a possible target in which to stick darts. A cynic like Philip Rahv would have found the activities at the Club corny and naïve, and he would have immediately set about hunting for hidden motives. I doubt that he would have found many, at least at this early stage of the Club's history. The artists were simply bound together by an enthusiasm for art, and particularly the art that they, or some of them, were going to create and bring before the world. In this kind of innocence they harked back to an older bohemian way of life of Greenwich Village earlier in the century, or perhaps before that to the *Vie de Bohème* of the previous century. One of the members, I've forgotten who, sat around one evening with a doleful face; and after questioning, he revealed that he had not been able to pay his rent and his landlady was threatening. Thereupon a hat was passed around and a collection made that was sufficient to bring back a smile to the poor man's face. This little episode might be a scene out of Puccini's *La Bohème*. But would this innocent camaraderie be able to survive the advent of success for some of these artists? The jostling for galleries, the intrusion of the art dealers, and the competition for the favors of rival art critics?

And here, perhaps, I have to warn the reader that the burden of this chapter is a success story, a tale of rags to riches. Memories are more often dolorous than not; they remind us of aborted hopes, unfulfilled aspirations, and blighted careers; but here we deal with a rise that was absolutely meteoric. The group that was centered around the Club was shortly to pass from being unknown to being nationally and internationally famous; they were to be celebrated as the first American artists to have created a truly international style, and with their arrival, it was claimed, the center of art had now definitely passed from Paris to New York. Yet here too, as in life elsewhere, the fruits of success did not mean unalloyed bliss, and their new-found affluence was to bring some of the artists personal problems they had not experienced before. The breakthrough of the Abstract Expressionists was to bring with it a fundamental change in the situation of the American artist within his society. The international acclaim for an American Style was to enhance the status of the native artist, as a result of which the artist's relation to his public, to the dealers, and to the museums, was to undergo fundamental change. The change that was beginning to happen in those years, which of course we could not see at the time, was a radical alteration in the role and position of the avant-garde within modern culture: from its traditional role of the rebel and outsider, the avant-garde now stormed into the Establishment itself, and gradually came to occupy seats of power within the museums and the universities. For the most part, these changes were beneficial to the artists; certainly they were benefited, or some of them, financially; but whether all these changes prove to be for the ultimate benefit of art itself, still remains to be seen.

And none of these rather awesome developments were to be suspected in the humble beginnings of "the Club."

Its founder, organizer, and general factotum was a sculptor, Philip Pavia, whose own works were kept hidden, though I understand they really do exist. No matter; Pavia had his identity as the tireless and disinterested worker in the service of the Club and its members. His two right-hand men in the venture, the two stalwarts who were really the artistic and moral center of the Club, were the painters Willem de Kooning and Franz Kline. "Bill and Franz" were the champions who gave confidence to other members that their own gropings in art might also be significant. Neither had yet attained public eminence; De Kooning was not to have his first one-man show until 1948, and that was at the small Egan Gallery, a transient showplace that seemed almost conjured up for this single purpose; but in the eyes of the other members they had already arrived artistically and it was only a matter of time before the rest of the world caught on.

Toward Jackson Pollock the attitudes of the group had to be more complex. He was looked up to, of course; he had "broken the ice" artistically, as De Kooning himself had said of him, by opening the way to a new style; and he was also in the process of breaking the ice publicly by being the first to come before the attention of the art world. And in both these senses they had to acknowledge him as a leader. But he was a leader who had to be approached at something of a distance; for Pollock would get drunk, and when he got drunk, he would get violent, and so had to be handled cautiously. On one occasion Franz Kline had to stand at the entrance of the Club to keep Pollock from entering. Kline was tough, sturdy, and very strong, and one of the few who could and did stand up to Pollock when the latter was in his cups.

At this time Pollock had already moved from the city to Springs, Long Island, and he used to come into town only once a week for a session with his psychoanalyst. It was an interesting but rather peculiar arrangement, which may or may not be to the credit of psychoanalysis. Pollock's big personal problem was his drinking. So long as he stayed out all week on the Island, he would be sober and working—and this was usually credited to the efficacy of his analysis. Then he would come into the city for his weekly analytic session, after which, as if some great burden had been lifted or as if he were rewarding himself for a duty fulfilled, he would proceed that night to get roaring drunk on the town and tear things apart. Thus I never had any really satisfying conversations with him. When I met him on a few occasions in more formal company, he was sober and chastened, and usually sat through most of the evening in utter silence. On other occasions, he would be in the process of launching himself on his weekly bender; and though he would be affectionate and rambling in his talk, one always felt he was on the edge of erupting into violence. You did not know whether the next moment he might embrace or assault you.

With De Kooning and Kline it was an altogether different story. I saw a good deal of them and got to know them well; I would run into them around the neighborhood or go to their lofts, and I was able to talk with them at length and at ease. For me these conversations were a fresh adventure after the intensely verbal argument or articulate chitchat of my fellow intellectuals. With the painters one moved into

135

another area of sensibility; our talk had a different human and sensuous "feel" about it. No doubt, my intellectual friends would have found many of the ideas of the painters crude or naïve; but then the suspicion was beginning to dawn on me that the way that the intellectuals looked at things might not be the only or in all cases the best way of looking. And, in fact, these conversations with the painters were one of the things, among others, that were feeding this suspicion.

II.

Meanwhile back at the ranch, at *Partisan Review*, some tremors had arrived that something might possibly be going on in the art world, and the news provoked, as could be expected, some very personal repercussions.

Clement Greenberg was our art critic. He was also the art critic for *The Nation*, but his more theoretical and assertive pronouncements appeared in *Partisan Review*, and at this time he had begun to push very strongly for Jackson Pollock and the tendency in art that Pollock represented. And when Greenberg advocated something, he jumped in with both feet. The generosity of spirit in a critic who seeks to assist a movement that is struggling to say something new is certainly to be applauded; and Greenberg's enthusiasm in the cause of the new painting was certainly to his credit. Besides, the audience for art in this country had to be prepared for the large and bold abstractions of this new style. And some of this audience would even have to be persuaded that abstract art as such was a perfectly legitimate style. But Greenberg went on from this minimal argument from legitimacy to contending that abstract art was the only significant style for this time and place. What American painters like Pollock were doing, he claimed, was not merely another interesting experiment; it was the right and historically inevitable—right because historically inevitable—direction in which painting must now move. Painting had evolved to the point where it had at last discovered that it was really about visual form and nothing else. The term "Abstract Expressionism" had not yet been coined; Greenberg used the term "American Style Painting" or "The New American Style," and he had now become the dedicated prophet in its service. But like many another prophet, his pronouncements tended more and more toward dogma, and his tone became more solemn. And here some questioning murmurs began to arise in the *Partisan Review* office.

There was no love lost—to put it mildly—between Philip Rahv and Clement Greenberg. Rahv would never forget, or forgive, Greenberg's part in "the confrontation"; and at times he even thought of Greenberg as the real *agent provocateur* who had instigated that unhappy meeting. After suborning William Phillips's affections for Rahv himself, he had prodded William into planning the whole scene. Worse still, Greenberg had taken his place in those affections: Clem and William had become very close friends, and the thought of this made Rahv toss even more painfully on his bed of uneasiness. Rahv himself knew nothing about the visual arts and did not care very much for them. It is really remarkable that he, the autodidact who had educated himself so tenaciously and scrupulously in the New York Public Library, had rarely, if ever, taken a trip uptown to visit the Metropolitan Museum of Art. Nevertheless, he began to murmur against Greenberg's articles that they were too dogmatic and one-sided. At which William Phillips challenged him, "What do you know about it?" And Rahv, who could himself be so very dogmatic on any matter that came within his ken, had to retreat into the vague statement that he had heard such adverse comments in "certain quarters." He did not name names, but he did locate the sources as in "midtown," thereby implying they came from the art establishment. His wife, Nathalie, was an architect and designer, and undoubtedly had such contacts. After all, there was some ground for saying that in his enthusiasm Greenberg had gone overboard on the new painters.

Rahv, of course, would not have been Rahv if he had not worked out a whole theory not only of Greenberg's motives in his art criticism but also the reasons why he had become an art critic in the first place. Greenberg was pushing the present trend among painters because he expected to ride in on the wave of their success. As for his becoming an art critic in the first place, the reason for that was quite simple: the fact was there were too many literary critics around, and Clem thought it would be easier to avoid the competition by going into the field of art. It is perhaps a blessing to command so simplifying a vision of other people's motives; but in Rahv's case it was a mixed blessing, for it stepped between him and any friendship he might form, and left behind it the taste of ashes.

Delmore Schwartz, for his part, had his own misgivings about

Greenberg, though he did not voice these at any editorial meeting, for he was too aware of the close friendship that had grown between Clem and William, and he did not want to say anything that would embarrass William in his continuing tension with Rahv. But Delmore kept bugging me on the subject. For some reason, he had a certain animosity toward Greenberg, not a consuming hostility as he was to develop toward Lionel Trilling, but a kind of impish desire to see Clem taken down a peg or two. He had written a story in which Clement Greenberg appears as Claude Vermont; and having created a comic persona for Greenberg, he seemed intent on translating this into life. Delmore was nettled by what he thought was a certain pomposity about Greenberg. I defended Greenberg; I didn't think Clem was pompous; he was slow of speech and, in the company of articulate talkers, would have to insist slowly and deliberately on what he had to say—and the effect could come across to some people as pompous.

But whatever his reasons, Delmore found himself amused by making small sideswipes from time to time, and he wanted me to get into the action. At this time Greenberg was reaching out for any corroborating authority for his ambitious theorizing about art, and he was particularly fond of citing Kant's aesthetics in support of his own formalistic views of art. After all, Kant had insisted that the essential and basic condition of beauty lies in the relations of form: the beautiful object is one which, in its own formal relations, conforms to the formal conditions of our own sensibility. There was a special sense of triumph when Greenberg trotted out the reference to Kant; for one thing, the reference was a little arcane, and there was a special cachet in citing a philosopher who did not fall anywhere within the Marxist canon. But sometimes the reference did sound rather sententious coming from Greenberg's lips, and Delmore would growl, "Clem is always putting on the dog—intellectually speaking." And then he turned to rebuke me at my silence: "Listen, you know Clem doesn't know what he's talking about when he mentions Kant. Why don't you show him up?" And then Delmore, his anger gone, would chuckle at the prospect; he had no particular malice here, it would just add to the fun to see Clem embarrassed. Delmore was always fascinated by the aesthetic possibility of some small social comedy happening around him. If for the moment he was blocked from writing the social comedy he wanted to, he might at least help create some of that comedy in his immediate environment.

I never followed Delmore's prompting. For one thing, my memories of Kant's aesthetics, brushed over rapidly somewhere in my graduate studies, were now very vague, and for all I knew Greenberg might be right in invoking his authority. Besides, I had been learning from him as he explored this new painting, and I was disposed to follow him patiently to the end to see where his ideas would lead him. But there was another and deeper reason why I would not then have done anything deliberately to add to his embarrassment: he had befriended me in a number of small but significant ways, and I felt a genuine friendliness in his attitude toward me to which I had responded naturally by liking him. From time to time, and without being heavy-handed and obtrusive about it, he had taken on the role of an older friend offering counsel; and there was one particular occasion, puzzling at first, that was to assume more and more significance for me as time went on.

On that occasion he had taken the opportunity to warn me that I might perhaps be overadapting to my environment. Those were not his words, as I remember, but I am trying now to give the sense of what he said. I had entered the *Partisan Review* world with enthusiasm, and, naïve about its ways, had nevertheless proceeded to identify —perhaps overidentify—myself with the spirit of the magazine and its editors; and that overidentification could be crippling to me. There was nothing malicious in any of Greenberg's words here; he spoke, in fact, with admiration of Rahv and Phillips as editors: they were "two of the most intelligent men in the country." Yet in all that intelligence there was something lacking . . . What was it that was lacking? Here he could not quite nail it down for me. Above all, there was something "negative" in their thinking: it canceled the possibility of any infectious enthusiasm unless it be calculated and measured beforehand. Greenberg might here have been covertly defending his own tremendous enthusiasm for the new painting. Even so, I would say now in retrospect, that if one had to choose between going overboard on a new movement or not being capable of any spontaneous and previously unsanctioned enthusiasm altogether, the former might be preferable. At least, as an art critic, Greenberg was capable of a generosity of spirit in welcoming what was new.

Yet it was the word "negative" that caught and fixed my attention, and more so as time went on. It was not a question of Rahv and Phillips as individual personalities. It was something that had to do with modern intellectuals generally. What was it that was "negative"—or

139

nihilistic, if you prefer the more philosophical word—about modern intellectuals as a class? What is it that makes them truants? Memory is full of surprises; and suddenly overcome by my memory of that particular warning from him, I have to acknowledge Clement Greenberg as one of those who planted the seed of this book in me.

Clem was speaking to me as an older brother, but in no way that was either pompous or objectionable; and even though I did not fully understand what he was driving at at the time, I felt a wave of gratitude toward him for it. I happened also to admire him for his deliberate concern with his own personal integrity, his efforts to establish a kind of moral code for himself, however corny and quaint this seemed to some people in the circle.

Yet despite this affection and admiration, I too began to be troubled by some of his critical attitudes—especially when I went back to the Club and talked with the painters.

III.

For one thing, they were not nearly so dogmatic. The artist does what he can, and is grateful to any favor of luck or inspiration that can make a particular style at the moment compelling and convincing to him. Greenberg was insisting that abstraction was the only really valid way for painting now to go, that it was the historically inevitable style for our time, and that any attempts at representative painting were historically outmoded and bound to be mere pastiche. The artists were grateful to him for his support but not quite sure of the ideology that came with it. Franz Kline shrugged at the big abstractions about historical necessity. Painting was painting, and the painter confronting his canvas faces the same age-old problems. *"You work from nature, away from nature, back to nature."* He was now on a certain swing of the circle and doing abstractions; but who was to say that the circle might not come around again and he would be doing representative painting?

Kline was not a verbal or glib character. His talk was usually the smallest of small talk; so that when the occasional bursts of generalization came, they could carry a kind of simple and earthy eloquence. He was also a very physical man, short, stocky, and powerful; and his stubby fingers, when they sketched an occasional gesture in conversation, seemed to be testing the sensuous feel of what he was saying.

He couldn't escape being a painter even when he talked. In comparison, De Kooning was the more intellectual, though this last word has to be taken with some qualification. He had the more complex, restless, and darting mind, and he dabbled a little in ideas. But the intellectual excursion was always held in rein by the painterly intuition, which the ideas after all were to feed. He could take in an idea only as a visual image.

Both men, De Kooning and Kline, struck me as absolutely steeped in tradition. Their talk moved back and forth between the present and the past, as if there were no break between, and whatever they themselves might be fumbling toward in their art must find its place alongside the work of the past. Nor did they squint at the old masters merely to extract their "formal" values. That way of looking at pictures became the fashion after the Abstract Expressionists had broken through. I remember a class in painting in the 1950s where the instructor—himself a painter of talent and taste, but now an evangelist in the cause of abstract art—had hung upside down a large black-and-white print of El Greco's "Burial of Count Orgaz." By looking at it that way, disregarding the human and representative content, we were to learn what the painting was really about: namely, the distribution of masses and the patterns of light and shade. I looked dutifully, and think I extracted the lesson intended; but as the print continued to hang there upside down week after week, I began insensibly to have the uneasy feeling of all those noble gentry of El Greco's brush now hanging with their heels to heaven. Painting was really about painting. What would El Greco have thought of that? I began to think that perhaps we had turned him on his head.

But De Kooning came at the work of the old masters with the wonderful directness and energy of a child. There was one show in particular that he had found overwhelming. At the outbreak of the War the paintings in the various Austrian galleries had been collected together and placed in secret hiding so that they might be spared the destruction of bombing. When the War was over, some enlightened official had the bright idea that, since they were all gathered together, they might be sent on tour before they went back to their separate locations; and so it was that the collection came to the Metropolitan Museum, an absolutely gorgeous display mainly of the great seventeenth-century masters that the House of Hapsburg had collected in the days of its power and affluence. De Kooning lost himself in this show with the delight and absorption of a child at a toy fair. He had a beautiful naïveté of response, which together with the Dutch accent that he never lost gave a kind of charming spontaneity to his talk. The Dutch masters were plentifully represented in this collection, and with them De Kooning always felt he was coming home; but this time another picture, a Velasquez of a man on horseback, had taken such hold of him that he had immediately decided, "Gee, I'd like to do something like that." And here De Kooning mimicked the post of the rider nonchalantly and arrogantly holding the reins. And in fact he spent several days thereafter doing nothing but sketches of men on horseback. Some of them weren't bad either, he said now; but in the end he had given it up, he simply didn't know enough about horses and horsemen. Notice, however, that it was the arrogant beauty of a man on horseback and not a pattern of light and shadow that had gripped his imagination.

There was another small, but hardly insignificant, aspect of this occasion that has a bearing on the change that was soon to take place in the painters' situation. We had been talking in my apartment (De Kooning lived then little more than a block away in a cold-water flat on Carmine Street), and I offered him a drink. He asked for it neat, and I poured him a shot, from which he took occasional and tiny sips and hardly had finished it at the end of the evening. He was not then a drinker; but only a few years later, when success and affluence had come, he was to have problems with drinking. He could even take a kind of rueful pride in the story of how leaving the Cedar Tavern one night in his cups and rather unsteady on his feet, he had been followed and "jack-rolled" in a doorway ("mugging" had not yet become the common word at this time) and had been relieved of four hundred dollars. That was a very sizable sum of money at the time, and that he carried it around with him in his pocket was taken as a sign that he had really made it. He could even take further satisfaction in the fact that to lose four hundred dollars had not been catastrophic and he could even tell the story as a joke on himself. A few years earlier a loss of that sum would have left him bankrupt.

Just when the change set in I cannot say, but signs of it were beginning to be visible early in the 1950s. Word had got around that the Cedar Tavern, just off Eighth Street on University Place, was the place where the painters hung out, and now the visitors began coming in. Some were the merely curious, who wanted to gawk at anything

142

that might be going on, but some were eager aspirants, hoping to jump on the bandwagon of a successful movement while it was getting under way. It was not exactly the Klondike gold rush on a small scale, but the bar was now noticeably noisier; and some of the regulars began staying away on busy nights, dropping in instead in the afternoon. But the change was not all noise and unpleasantness; occasionally there was some small incident that carried with it the sweet bloom of success. Once the painter Marca-Relli came in with an Italian visitor in tow. The Italian was from Venice, and had insisted on being taken to the bar for the express purpose of meeting De Kooning. After the introduction was made I pointed out the historical significance of the occasion to De Kooning: Venice had once been the center where the pilgrims from northern Europe had come to learn about painting; now the scene had shifted, and a Venetian had come to New York to meet him. De Kooning blinked for a moment, trying to take in the full sweep of the idea, and then his face lit up with a grin: "Gee!"

And now Harold Rosenberg, turned art critic, entered the scene as another champion of the cause. Clement Greenberg had led the way, but Rosenberg now made the more dramatic and splashy impact. They were antithetical personalities, and naturally took up the new art from very different angles. Greenberg was trying to construct a neat formal aesthetic to accommodate what American painters were now doing within the canon of modernist art. Rosenberg was the glittering phrasemaker, who flung himself at the existential struggle of the painter, both with himself and within society, to bring something to life on the canvas; and so coined his own term for the new style, "Action Painting," the implications of which were not purely formalistic. The two critics even chose different painters for their exemplary figures; for Greenberg it was Pollock, and for Rosenberg it was De Kooning; and this rival choice set off a certain tension among their followers. Consequently, Rosenberg and De Kooning became close; and when De Kooning was affluent enough to move out to Springs, Long Island, they were neighbors. As a lawyer, Rosenberg was helpful to the painter in a number of practical and personal ways; but I had my misgivings whether he was a help intellectually. It may not be the best thing in the world for the concrete mind of the painter to drink too deeply of the waters of ideology, especially when dispensed by so subtle a hand as Rosenberg, who had the bewildering habit, even while he dazzled you, of leaving any subject more complicated and puzzling than when he took it up. But I kept these misgivings to myself. I remember one occasion when I found De Kooning in rather vehement but friendly argument with someone—I forget whom—at the Cedar Tavern. I didn't get the thread of the argument, but at the moment I stepped in, De Kooning was sputtering passionately, "Atheism! Atheism!" He stammered momentarily at a loss for words, and then the simple and spontaneous image came: "It's like an empty lot between warehouses where they've just torn down the buildings." At that time a lot of tearing down had been going on around the edge of the Village, and walking east from Fifth Avenue one encountered those desolate gaps; De Kooning had walked that beat often enough, and at the worst hours of the night, and he could find no more vivid image for the emptiness and desolation of non-belief. I remember thinking at the time, "I wonder how long Harold Rosenberg is going to let him have that thought." De Kooning thought more profoundly when left to the visual material of his own images. If ever a man might have profited by being born into a different culture, it was he.

IV.

In the meantime a new threat to Greenberg's position on *Partisan Review* seemed to be in the offing. The magazine had suddenly acquired an angel, Allan Dowling, who had seemingly appeared, as angels do in the Bible, out of nowhere. The financial aspects of the patronage could not have been very large; everything was so much more modest in those days. But in any case these were matters that Rahv and Phillips, as owners of the magazine, kept to themselves, and I did not ask. The magazine would not now be swimming in affluence, but there would be nevertheless a greater sense of ease in meeting the more urgent bills. The editors felt elated at this new prospect, but also just a little worried about the possible pressures this new benefactor might bring to bear upon editorial policies. As it turned out, they did not need to fear. Dowling was a gentleman; he did not want to bring pressures for any drastic change; we were to continue to do what we had been doing, but perhaps a little better now with a small financial boost. There was only one troubling note for William Phillips in this new arrangement: Dowling had let slip that he was not very enthusiastic about the art criticism in the magazine, and this meant that

William would have to be even more nervous about protecting Greenberg's position.

Rahv, on the other hand, was thinking along another tack. With his perpetual quest for hidden motives, he was puzzled at the arrival of this angel. What did this man expect to gain by putting his money into a "little" magazine? The immediate, and Freudian, answer to which Rahv's mind leaped was that this angel might be looking for girls, and thought that a literary circle was a place where they might be found. But this supposition was quickly disproved, for Dowling seemed to be well provided, or as well as he wanted to be, in that direction. The real motive, as it turned out, was not so far-fetched as any of these speculations, and at length even Rahv himself seemed to accept it: Dowling wanted simply the gratification of sharing in an intellectual enterprise and perhaps thereby of having some sense of belonging to an intellectual community, however small. And it was in this latter connection that he was to make his only positive suggestion about a change in the magazine's structure: he would like there to be a board of Advisory Editors which would meet every month or so to discuss matters of general policy.

Rahv chuckled at the naïveté of this very minimal request. What harm could an Advisory Board do? It would be the easiest bone to throw to the patron if that was what was needed to keep him quiet. Everybody knows that Advisory Editors do not want to be bothered, that in fact they never do anything and, consequently, can't make much trouble. Besides, we would put on this Board of Advisors old friends like Lionel Trilling, Sidney Hook, and James Burnham, who would be on our side in case any dissension arose. For a while William Phillips joined his fellow editor in the fun. So long as their scheming was innocent enough, a kind of game they played together, it was easy for Phillips to slip back momentarily into their old camaraderie, and once again they were the comic pair of Jewish businessmen —the partners Potash and Perlmutter, in Edmund Wilson's phrase— chuckling over a deal they had just brought off satisfactorily.

But suddenly there was a menacing note in this new setup. Dowling was a friend of the art expert James Johnson Sweeney and insisted on putting him among the Advisors. Sweeney was then an official in the Guggenheim Museum, very active in the cause of modern art, and a vigorous partisan of abstract art, but his views were different from Greenberg's and it was known that he did not admire the latter's criticism. Here was a new source of possible trouble that William Phillips would have to be on the lookout for if he were to protect his friend Greenberg.

The monthly dinners with the Advisors turned out, in fact, to be pleasant occasions. Ideas were thrown out and discussed, but nothing of a kind seriously to alter the actual course of the magazine. On only one occasion did Sweeney indicate, and then in an indirect but nevertheless cutting way, his dissatisfaction with what Greenberg had been writing on art. But the incident requires a slight preparation:

Allan Dowling had come up with the idea that *Partisan Review* might give an annual prize for literary achievement. What he had in mind was something like what *The Dial*, the great literary magazine of the 1920s, had done in its period. The *Dial* prizes had established a certain standard for avant-garde excellence, and in turn had brought fame to the magazine. Who could forget that *The Dial* prize in 1923 had been awarded to T. S. Eliot for *The Waste Land?* And with this wistful remembrance something was revealed of his motives that should have satisfied even so confirmed a cynic as Rahv. Part of the aspiration that led him to become a patron was that he wanted *Partisan Review* to fill the role that *The Dial* had once played and which, it seemed, had been one of the stirring memories of his youth. Why is it—the reader may have noted that the question keeps recurring through these pages—that in this period immediately after the Second World War the dreams of anything like a flowering of the arts took the form, at least for some people, of a reincarnation of the 1920s? And it would be a minor but not altogether unenlightening bit of research to find out when these dreams began to give way. I think by 1950 it was clear that we were coming to face another world from that of the 1920s. It was not simply that the political configuration of this world had begun to gel into its present grim mold. The earlier decade had been able to cash in on the presence of traditions that no longer seemed available to our period. It was all very well to daydream about a prize for another *Waste Land,* but where was one now to find a poem like it? The question of genius and talent aside, the circumstances that had converged to make Eliot's poem so electrifying a statement of contemporaneity for its period no longer seemed to be potently at work in our world.

The conversation turned from this difficult question of a possible recipient to consideration of the form the award might take. And the mood began to be a little more playful: if there was no one around to give the prize to, one could still dally with the idea of what the prize might be. A great outlay of cash was out of the question, for our patron was not that generous; and besides it would seem inappropriate: the special *cachet* that this prize would carry was that, though small in comparison with other more public grants, it represented the verdict of select and avant-garde taste. One or two casual suggestions were made, and it was then that Sweeney launched his sally.

Now it so happened that in the current issue of the magazine Clement Greenberg had used a slightly more dogmatic tone than usual, and had solemnly pronounced on the historical death of "easel painting." The painters in "The New American Style," he declared, needed large areas to work out their motifs, and this effort, even when done on canvas, carried with it the scope of something like a mural. The easel painting, which always suggested a window open on space, with all the accompanying illusions of perspective, was now a thing of the past, historically obsolete by the evolution of painting. He did not use the Marxist phrase "the dustbin of history"—but the thinking was along that line.

What then, we were discussing, should be the prize if it were ever to be awarded? Sweeney was a hearty Irishman with a booming laugh; and now the laugh erupted: "Give the winner an easel painting." And he continued for some minutes in a rumble of bass chuckles. They must have sounded like a raucous jeer in the ears of William Phillips.

The sarcasm was possibly lost on those present who had not yet absorbed Greenberg's current pronouncement. But William Phillips was not one of these, and across the table I could see him wince.

But any serious trouble from Sweeney never did materialize. He wrote one piece for the magazine; but writing was slow and laborious to him and more was not forthcoming, so that he did not become the alternate and Greenberg remained in sole possession as art critic—at least for as long as he needed to work out and disseminate the views which have now become more or less canonical with the Art Establishment, or an influential portion of it.

For, make no mistake about it, these views have wielded and still wield a potent influence. The reader may think that we have been engaged here in the intramural bickering within a small circle about ideas that might seem quite special and remote; but in fact, if he is a museum-goer, he will have been exposed to these ideas and perhaps already shaped by them. An exhibition of Cezanne, say, is held in one of our museums. Here and there alongside the paintings will be a printed card instructing the viewer what to look for. (And the crowds, more likely than not will usually spend more time milling around these instructions than they do looking at the paintings.) And what is the controlling interpretation behind those little printed instructions? That the significance of Cezanne is his being a forerunner of Cubism. The viewer then looks for the underlying Cubist skeleton and strips off all the flesh of the painting. Or is it a show of Monet that we go to? (I am, of course, thinking of an actual museum and actual shows.) He will be told that the culmination of Monet's art is "The Water Lilies." Why? Because it looks most like a painting of the Abstract Expressionists. The emphasis—or should I say dislocation?—of taste is always in the direction of the formal element of the painting.

It was only natural that Greenberg's ideas should infiltrate the university. Academicians, and especially young academicians, are usually attracted to formalist theories of any kind, for these theories seem to promise some kind of rigor and exactness. They seem to give one something definite and precise to talk about, in comparison with which the realities of the spirit look vague and insubstantial. In time these younger historians of art graduate, become professors in turn, and teach other students; or they find positions in the museums, whence they are able to write illustrated monographs that become the books the public reads for their authoritative instruction.

My own disenchantment with Greenberg's ideas came slowly. I had followed his lead in learning to appreciate the new painters, and on a few occasions he had taken me to see their works. I went with him to see my first Pollocks at a little gallery that Peggy Guggenheim had for a while on Fifty-seventh Street. It was night, the lights had not yet been fixed for the show and the paintings, unhung, stood around the walls. What with the garish light and Miss Guggenheim's nervous fluttering, these were not the best conditions for taking in a new painter. I came away with my first impression of Pollock as a great sprawl of yellow paint. Later on I saw his work under better conditions and began to appreciate it; but even then something of this first impression lasted: Pollock was not a painter in pursuit of strict form.

And then I began to suspect that Greenberg's position was not even internally consistent with itself when he took Pollock as his exemplary master of the moment. Cubism was central to his historical thesis. The Cubists had developed a strict and controlled form, which took the plane of the picture as absolute, and dissolved and resolved all objects into their formal relations within that plane. The internal logic of painting had brought it to this state, and painters could do nothing but follow in this vein—or produce some inauthentic and quaint pastiche of the past. But if so, De Kooning should have been his exemplary figure among the Americans rather than Pollock. The early De Koonings of this period (the 1940s) worked within the Cubist tradition, to which they brought something absolutely original: they made the Cubist forms move and dance, gave something of the free flow of calligraphy, and nevertheless remained essentially within the Cubist idiom. But the impulse in Pollock's painting came from elsewhere; it did not operate within the convention of strict and controlled form; if anything, it was disruptive of form. Pollock is very much in the American grain, like the writers Walt Whitman or William Faulkner, who throw themselves on the vitality of their inspiration, trusting that its sheer vital flow will be sufficient to generate enough form to sustain the work. In Pollock this inspiration is not always sufficient to generate enough form, and the painting sags; when the vitality of his primary impulse carries him along, the effect is stunning. There are good and bad Pollocks, and I do not think critics have been sufficiently discerning between the two. When an artist enters the world as the leader of a movement, criticism is likely to become tendentious and insist we either swallow or reject the work as a whole.

And once these initial doubts had crept in, the formalist aesthetic began to look woefully inadequate as an account of the whole sweep of the Modernist movement. Granted that modern art had made extraordinary technical discoveries, and that it had created works of an abstract and formal nature that have a singular power of their own that we do not find anywhere in the past. Still, can this formal aspect do justice to the full range of expression and search in a Picasso, Matisse, or a Miro? Greenberg himself did a monograph on Miro, a copy of which he kindly presented to me with the modest disclaimer that it made no pretense of being exhaustive. It was not. Miro is almost the last artist that one could hope to encapsulate under a formalist aesthetic. With him the inventions of form are always in the service of expression; and the sensibility he expresses is at once poetic and surrealistic. Even within the body of Cubist painting itself the purely formalistic aesthetic resulted in some very one-sided judgments of taste. Greenberg extolled the early works of Cubism, the so-called "Analytic Cubism," to the detriment of the later works in which Picasso and Braque put the Cubist devices to work for their own expressive purposes. No doubt those early works of Analytic Cubism contain some massive and powerful achievements in pure form; but do they really cast into shadow a later work like Picasso's "Three Musicians," so haunting in its suggestiveness, at once somber and mocking?

It was not at all that Greenberg lacked sensitivity here. On the contrary. Philip Rahv's cynical suspicion that Greenberg had taken up art only because there were too many literary critics around and he wanted to avoid the competition, implied that he had only a nominal and casual relation to the subject. I knew different; I knew that Clem had a primary and direct response to visual works of art that most intellectuals, and some art critics, do not enjoy. The two other art experts in our immediate circle were Harold Rosenberg and Meyer Schapiro, and I doubt that they had the capacity for visual immediacy that Greenberg did. I went once to the Museum of Modern Art with Meyer Schapiro, an erudite and brilliant scholar in the history of art, and the experience was exhilarating; but there came a moment when I could not help thinking: if only the man would stop talking for a bit, if only that spellbinding flow of words would cease, and some painting or other would stop him in his tracks and make him go silent. I had the feeling that the work of art was noticed only as the springboard to his discourse, a mere stimulus to set the verbal machinery going. But Clement Greenberg could be stopped in his tracks by the sheer visual impact of a painting, and let it work on him in silence. He had a real and discerning response to the sheer sensuous texture of painting; and he did have taste. He looked long and carefully at pictures; and it is worth noting that in a legal suit about the authenticity of some of Pollock's paintings years after his death, Greenberg's testimony, very much of it from memory, turned out to be precise and authoritative. But with all these qualities, the puzzle really began. What point is there in having taste or the capacity of immediate sensitivity to the sheer visual impact of a work, if in the end the ideological machinery is going to take over and fabricate a position that rides roughshod over these qualities? An ideology is a cruel taskmaster and may

150

require of us the sacrifice of our best perceptions. But the thirst for an ideology is also one of our modern addictions.

Greenberg came on this addiction from an earlier immersion in Marxism. There he had acquired the passion for thinking in terms of "historical inevitability," and now with art he must situate aesthetic values somewhere along the line of an imaginary curve of History. The Marxist terminology had very largely disappeared from his presentation, but the way of thinking, the cast of mind, was the same as he had shown on an earlier occasion at the outbreak of World War II. Greenberg himself had then been an editor of *Partisan Review,* and he teamed with Dwight Macdonald against Rahv and Phillips on the issue of the War. The latter supported the War against Hitler; Greenberg and Macdonald were isolationists on strict Trotskyist and Marxist principles. The War, after all, was a capitalist conflict between Germany on one side, and France and Britain on the other. Let it rage on then, whatever human destruction it brought in its wake; for only out of such chaos and ruin would a truly revolutionary situation arise that would bring in the socialist future. Had not Lenin, the master, thus welcomed the outbreak of the First World War as a prelude to revolution? Greenberg was a Jew and a humanitarian, and he detested the horrors of Hitler as much as anyone. But what did those personal feelings count for when the conceptual apparatus took over and one had then to make one's judgments of value in accordance with the long perspective of historical inevitability?

But if the original impulse had come from Marxism, he was quite willing to be eclectic in grasping at any philosophic props for his theory. Kant's aesthetic, as I have mentioned, was an authority he constantly cited in conversation; but now he would reach out to another quarter of the intellectual compass and seek philosophic support in modern Positivism. No matter that Kant and the Positivists might be uneasy bedfellows to get to lie down peacefully together; each might be used separately to lend their support. Ours was an age of science, Positivism was the scientific philosophy of our time, and one had, above all, to be in tune with the deeper *Zeitgeist* of history. Now, from a strictly Positivistic point of view, what is a painting but a flat surface overspread with certain visual data. No matter the artist and whatever his nominal subject matter, this is what the eye really sees when you get down to the scientific brass tacks. (He seemed at this point to forget that Kant had insisted that our basic transaction with the work of art takes place in the imagination.) The measure of the painter's achievement, then, should be merely how well he arranges the pattern of sense data on the picture plane. Ironically for Greenberg, though he did not know it, at the moment he was seeking support from the Positivists, they themselves were in the process of relinquishing their own doctrine of sense data. We do not see patches of color, but objects in space: chairs, tables, other people. It is not just a green shape, mottled with shadow, that I see now through my window but the old maple tree on my lawn. Indeed, of all our sense organs, the eye is the one most riveted to definite objects in the external world, and it has to be for our survival; if we saw only patches of color, we could hardly get about our daily activities. And it is by the simplest and most natural extension of this power that we see through the plane of the picture the space on which it opens and the objects therein represented.

(Art wearied, reader, of all this cerebration? Take heart, just a few steps further and we shall have done. We would have spared you if we could, but modern art is so overgrown with the liana vines of ideology that we cannot try to hack a clearing through the jungle without getting just a little entangled in the creepers.)

Nor was Kant any better prop for Greenberg's thesis. Sometime later, much later, I read Kant's aesthetic and found Delmore Schwartz's suspicions were right that Greenberg had misused that venerable philosopher. Delmore had been trained in philosophy, and had even gone into graduate study for a while as a step toward a career there, but he soon lost patience with the tedium of academic philosophy. Yet he retained from his immersion in it an amazing intuition about ideas, a sensitive nose, particularly, for when a critic was lapsing into "idea-mongering" or "philosophy-mongering," as he called it —the inauthentic rattling around of big terminology. And he was perpetually spotting this malady in the literary critics of his time, even his beloved idol T. S. Eliot. Even though he knew very little of the subject, he had sniffed out the same thing now in what Greenberg was doing with art.

It was not that Greenberg "got Kant all wrong," as Delmore put it, but that he seemed to have read only the first thirty or forty pages of Kant's work. In those pages Kant does develop a formal theory of beauty—Greenberg was right at least there; but this is only a prelude to the fuller theory. For Kant the beautiful in art is subordinate to the beautiful in nature, and indeed it would be morally pernicious to separate the two. The formalist who looks at a picture merely as a flat plane with a certain pleasing arrangement of shapes and colors would be morally suspect in the eyes of Kant: an aesthete who has cut off the work from any reference to the wider world of man and nature in which it finds itself, and is content to go on chewing the cud of his own private sensations. The experience of nature, on the other hand, leads us beyond our private self, and indeed beyond what our ordinary conceptual mind seems able to grasp. The long line of the mountain folds into the curve of the river, and there just above it, clearing the horizon, the first evening star appears; and as I stand rapt before this vision I am invaded—and without thinking—by the feeling that we and this universe are part of some meaning that we cannot grasp. Here the formal theory of beauty takes a theological direction. If the perception of beauty consists in an accord between the formal properties of the object and the formal conditions of our own perception, might not this be an intimation that we ourselves, as perceivers, are in some ultimate attunement with this cosmos we find beautiful, that we have a place and a meaning within it? It is not a formal argument for God—Kant is too critical for that; he is simply describing the content of an experience, and I think the experience is there for anyone who surrenders to it, however confident an atheist he might be in his other attitudes.

Kant was thus the most unlikely of philosophers for Greenberg to have invoked in support of his own aesthetic. Rational and enlightened as the Kant's century might pride itself on being, it still existed within nature and in relation to God in a way that we can no longer manage, and that the art Greenberg extols would altogether forget. Indeed Kant, were he to return to our midst, would find it a sign of the spiritual poverty of our age that one of our leading critics should offer a view of art so narrow and barren, and that this view should have become quasi-official in some influential quarters.

V.

At the outset of this chapter I said that it was to be a success story, of Clement Greenberg as it turned out as well as of the artists; but that it was to bring about a transformation of the art scene in New York with consequences that were not always benign.

153

The transformation really set in with the 1950s, when the art dealers began to get into the act. There was a new affluence after the War, and potentially a new group of buyers for art. This new class of patrons for the most part had little previous experience of art, and therefore no barrier of traditional taste to overcome. The works they bought may have looked strange and inexplicable to them at first, but they were easily reassured by the dealers that these works were "important," and that if they were not at the moment the "in" thing, they were the coming thing; and that their monetary value would appreciate considerably. Had not the new American School become internationally famous almost overnight, their prices now escalating out of sight? And who was to say the miracle might not be repeated for any new style, however odd and unfamiliar it might look at first sight?

Thus the purchase of new art was a good investment altogether; it secured status for the buyer in several ways: in showing his collection he was also exhibiting himself as a man of culture who kept up with the "in" things; it had cultural chic; but it also represented potentially a mass of constantly growing capital. It was important to buy in early, the earlier the better: a painting acquired for a moderate price now might be worth a small fortune in a relatively short time. The dealers naturally pushed this emphasis upon novelty, the new thing, for its possible speculative purposes. One of them remarked to me in a moment of frankness: "I never ask myself whether a work is good or not, but only if it has historical importance." The word "historical" is worth noting here; in practical terms, he meant simply whether it might start a trend, or a new direction, which in turn would give the work more monetary value in time. Again, the push toward novelty.

This attitude of dealers and buyers began to spread, sometimes for different motives, to the artists themselves. Perhaps Greenberg's ideas led this way. After all, if you are a painter and begin to be preoccupied with historical inevitability, and what style must be pursued at this time, you are tempted to feel that perhaps you may give that line of inevitability a push in your own direction. At any rate, the younger artists now coming up began to think of their own efforts in terms of very large abstract notions about something called "Painting," and the stage of development at which it had arrived. A friend and I (this was in the mid-1950s) visited the studio of an aspiring painter, a young woman who had only been at her art a few years but seemed a coming talent. She had just completed a large painting that was not with-

154

out its merits, and we congratulated her for it. At which she only shook her head ruefully, stared somberly at her own canvas and remarked, "Yes, but does it do anything for *Painting?*" Afterward, my friend and I agreed that her response seemed sadly presumptuous: instead of looking at that individual work in its own terms, she had become her own art historian and was speculating on her possible place in the line of history. She was not alone here; quite run-of-the-mill talents began to be preoccupied with "advancing the medium." In terms of the market place, of course, these lofty concerns could be given a quite commercial twist: the artist preoccupied with where he stood in the evolution of painting became in fact intent on producing some new gimmick that might prove to be the "in" thing. When the constraint of subject matter has gone, the artist has only his medium to exploit, and any new twist of originality may possibly be salable as a coming trend.

We reach a stage where the great experimentation of Modern Art, and indeed the greatness of this art itself, begins to be trivialized. Even the success story of the Abstract Expressionists turns against them: in a short while Abstract Expressionism was to become old hat.

There followed thus a procession of new styles and names on the New York art scene. Op Art, Pop Art, Minimal Art, Conceptual Art, Color-field painting, and the rest. Clement Greenberg may have speculated much about historical inevitability, but as a prophet of actual history he fell far short of the mark. One style did not emerge as the inevitable and necessary way of painting in this time; instead, the *Zeitgeist* was to find its expression in a riotous proliferation of new schools, often tendentious and in conflict with each other. To be sure, some of these styles were in the general direction of abstract art: if you push the process of abstraction far enough, you end with the emptiness of Minimal Art; and with so little now left on the canvas, you have but to take a small step further and declare, with Conceptual Art, that the idea alone will do for a work of art. But the emergence of Pop Art was a raucous return to the actual visible world, often in its most crass and glaring aspects; and representative art generally has reacquired status, and is seriously pursued by many of the younger artists. The eye, it seems, is not to be denied in its thirst for the external world. But even here we notice a touch of the modern gimmick in the case of so-called Photo-realism: the painter does not give himself to the objects in the world around him, but to their pho-

155

tographed image by the camera. In a technical age, man imitates the machine.

As the pursuit of novelty went on, the restraining barriers of taste became less and less visible. The disturbed decade of the 1960s, with its squalid atmosphere of permissiveness, descended upon us, and the spirit of "Anything goes!" was in the air. The notion of good taste itself now appeared suspect: it sounded "elitist," than which in the jargon of the time no attitude could be more damnable. To those who had lived with it in the past, the Museum of Modern Art now seemed to take on a new appearance; the rooms on the ground floor consigned to the newest things became crowded with dull, tasteless, and crude objects that seemed very often to have little claim to the name of art. "The junk rooms," my wife and I came to call them, and we were glad to escape upstairs to the permanent collection and the company of the Modern Masters. Here in the short space of a stair flight the whole question of contemporary art seemed to be posed for one: Had the period of Modern Art really passed, and in the post-Modern period in which we now seemed adrift, what were we to build upon? The museum, of course, was now discharging its function as a documentary historian of the times, of what was now going on, and it was following the excessively democratic spirit of the period. To have exercised the discretion of good taste in what one chose to show would have been "elitist." Besides, how could you really be sure? Had not the great works of the Modern movement seemed shocking and impossible to their contemporaries? At this time the city colleges in New York had adopted a policy of Open Admissions—anyone with a high school diploma was accepted as a student. At City College, which had once been a select and elite institution, professors of English were reduced to teaching remedial reading. I felt that the museum had followed suit and adopted its own policy of Open Admissions.

It was Harold Rosenberg rather than Clement Greenberg who turned out to have the sharper eye for the actual drift of history. Always a neat hand at phrases, Rosenberg was to baptize this restless quest for novelty as "The Tradition of the New." The expression is catchy, but if we stop to think of it for a moment, it becomes paradoxical and puzzling, and raises more questions than it can clarify. To my ears it sounds a little like the Trotskyite phrase, "The Permanent Revolution," about which I had mixed feelings even when I was a Marxist believer. If the revolution is permanent and unceasing, then next week

156

you reverse what you have revolutionized this week. A tradition is supposed to be a revered standard to which you hold fast; but if your tradition is novelty as such, then out of the impulse of sheer change you may abolish that tradition too. Thus, literally and logically taken, the phrase is without meaning; but in the actual situation in which Rosenberg invoked it, the art scene of today, it is altogether pregnant with meaning. It points toward the heart of our dilemma today: toward the ceaseless proliferation of new styles and forms that is now going on, amid which there can be found brilliance and originality but also a bewildering sense of loss, and even the sense that the great tradition of Modern Art itself, with its depth and resonance, may be lost.

Perhaps, then, we may have reached a point where the whole question of Modernism in art may be raised with some deeper understanding. Our century provides us enough of this art so that, looking backward, we may draw some conclusions.

The spirit of experimentation and novelty, of course, is not new; they were the watchwords with which the avant-garde broke in upon the scene in the early years of this century. "Make it new!" Ezra Pound proclaimed in those years when he and T. S. Eliot were leading a revolution in literary taste and in the writing of poetry. But Pound was seeking freshness and originality rather than novelty for novelty's sake, and in his revolt against the petrified tradition of the Georgian poets he harked back to the deeper tradition of Dante and the Provençal poets, as Eliot made the Elizabethans and the seventeenth century live again in his own verse. Eliot was to turn his critical powers on this question in the famous essay "Tradition and the Individual Talent," which was published in 1919 but gathers greater force now in the light of everything that has happened since. Like Pound, but not so vociferously, he applauds the search for the new: if we have to choose between a stale repetition of the past and novelty, we should certainly choose the latter. But we cannot leave the matter at this glaring confrontation of two dismal alternatives. If we are serious, we are not interested in novelty for novelty's sake, for the mere shock of it. The genuinely new work of art must be one in which past and present enter into more intimate union. And that, of course, is Eliot's conclusion: that the really new and original work of art is the most traditional, in the sense that it draws most deeply on the resources of its tradition even while bringing these to a surprising and unexpected expression.

Never did a critic call his shots more accurately. The whole history of our century confirms his conclusion: the great works of the modern masters, in all of the arts, are those which draw most deeply on the resources of the tradition, and which in turn enter the body of tradition and give it a deeper and richer life. The oddities of experiment in style or point of view that claimed our attention at first begin to recede in importance as these works enter the company of older masters.

We may think here, if we will, of a biological metaphor drawn from the example of mutations as they occur in nature. Most mutations are harmful and non-adaptive and quickly disappear. Those that catch hold and survive are those that fit in with the inherent structure of the species, that draw upon the resources of the gene pool even as they may give these potentialities a new direction. Meanwhile the life of the species continues through the transformation; or if the change is more radical, the life of the genus continues in a new species. The past comes to life again in another form in the present. The chemical components of our blood, we are told, are those of sea water, from which our own life originally came.

But nature has its own safeguards against random innovation, its own natural means, so to speak, of passing tradition on from one generation to the next, while in our human society at the present time the institutions that would convey tradition are in a rather shaky condition. Under such circumstances the entry of the avant-garde into the Establishment, and indeed its growing dominance within the Establishment, were events of signal importance.

The process began in the 1950s, and thereafter accelerated quickly. The artists got teaching appointments; and from infiltrating the academy, they began to be the dominant voice within it. From the academy their influence passed to the museums and the staffs of museums. The critics had long since been captured, and the number of dissenting voices became fewer. All this was generally to the good; it was well that artists should have jobs and come to occupy the seats of power; and if their voices were sometimes strident, they nevertheless had something vital to say that the academy needed. But since the modern movement is divided into contending schools and styles, inevitably a certain sectarianism and spirit of the clique crept in. We come then upon the paradox of an avant-garde, supposedly dedicated to "The Tradition of the New," dictatorially enforcing in its students the repetition of a narrow and confining style. Also, a certain inflation of reputations set in: mediocre artists could be railroaded through, and praised immoderately, because they were following in the wake of more powerful talents.

Clique or club? We seem to come back to the image from which we started. But what a far cry now from "the Club" of the 1940s, whose poverty and camaraderie seemed to come out of the *Vie de Bohème* of the nineteenth century! That club which met and danced in its loft has now become invisibly transfigured into a club in a different sense —a privileged circle of power; and most of the older and lesser members have long since dropped by the way and been forgotten. But when the avant-garde becomes the Establishment, one is led to question whether it does not thereby lose its own *raison d'être*. It came into existence, after all, in the previous century in revolt against a tradition that had become too narrow and ossified; but if the force of tradition has become so weak, and standards everywhere more permissive, the rebellion of an avant-garde seems perhaps unnecessary and in any case less heroic than once. No doubt, the avant-garde still borrows the older rhetoric of rebellion, but we begin more and more to notice the irony when a critic, safely ensconced in one of our leading universities, affects to speak in the language of the outcast. And we are also led to ask whether what has happened in politics may not be happening here: that when a revolution takes over, it becomes fat, bureaucratic, and intolerant.

Chapter Seven

Beginnings of Conservative Thought

I.

Lionel Trilling was a graceful man. I was reminded of the fact recently by happening upon an old publicity photograph that shows him bowling. I had never seen him bowl, and did not know that he indulged, but there in this unsuspected setting the familiar and natural grace of the man seems to overflow the picture. For the public at large, of course, this grace showed itself principally in his writing: he wrote possibly the best critical prose of his time—supple, flexible, fluent, yet firm. But the inherent gracefulness of the man came out also in a multitude of small ways. In a casual letter or note, for example, there would always be some distinctive touch of style, though never labored—the personal voice of the man without being affected, overassertive, or strident. He had style in the classic sense—*ars celare artem*—style that seemed to be second nature with the man himself.

This gracefulness was, I think, something of a moral quality, or at least allied to the moral character of the man himself. It is remarkable that in a circle so given to character analysis—or backbiting, if you prefer the blunter term—so little was said against Trilling. There were grumblings, of course, against his ideas, or what those ideas might imply, particularly if you pressed them in a certain direction; and there was the inevitable envy of the prestige he was beginning to enjoy and that would grow greater as time went on; but no rumors of scandal or personal defamation seemed ever to be whispered against him. The Trillings were thoroughly civilized people, and behaved as such: they arrived at parties in time, behaved affably without any touch of being there to carry on some private business or personal vendetta; and they left in time—before the small hours of the morning when too much has been drunk and the gathering that remains becomes loud and bathetic. They acted, in short, as if they had a life of their own to lead and were intent on living it without losing any more of it than they had to on the formless sprawl of an end-of-the-evening.

However, there was nothing tight or boxed in about the man; he gave of himself generously to younger people, and in consequence inspired a deep affection in many of them. At his funeral services in 1975 I was surprised and moved by the number of mourners and the sincerity of their grief: not only had he inspired devotion among a smaller band of followers, but he had touched the lives of many others with whom one might have thought he would make no contact. He was, to use the old-fashioned term, a virtuous man and, moreover, a virtuous man without any touch of the prig. And in the particular environment of New York in which we moved that was indeed an accomplishment.

Confronted with somebody like Trilling, Philip Rahv's "analytic exuberance"—his passion for dissecting character into its lowest possible motives—seemed to stand at bay. But Rahv would not have been Rahv if he did not find something to worry over and grumble about in one of his contributors. And in this case, as the guardian of the magazine's revered idols of Marxism and Modernism, he had good grounds to be uneasy about Trilling's position, or what that position might be if its implications were followed out. For on the subjects both of literature and of politics Trilling seemed headed in a more conservative direction than the magazine could endorse. Yet, despite such growing uneasiness, he remained personally on very cordial terms with Trilling.

The personal animosity came this time from Delmore Schwartz, and the reasons for it throw some light on the tangled state of his psyche at this period. For some time Delmore had felt unhappy teaching at Harvard, particularly because he did not like living in Cambridge. If only he could move to New York, he felt, his personal problems would be easier to handle. (They were, in fact, to become drastically more difficult and his behavior more self-destructive.) Since he needed a job, he made overtures to the English Department at Columbia, and it appeared that he was under serious consideration. But the appointment did not come through, and he was convinced that Lionel Trilling had blocked it. Whether or not there were any objective reasons for this belief, I do not know, but the point was that Delmore himself felt absolutely sure that Trilling was the single one who had stood in his way. Of course, his own paranoid imagination was at work here; and looking back now, I realize that this paranoia was more operative even at this early period than most of his close friends suspected. Delmore could joke at his own paranoid promptings, and this spontaneous and overflowing humor of his gave one to think that perhaps the psychological malady was not really there at all. Indeed, he himself seemed to think his neurosis was not so bad as long as he could make jokes about it: in one sense, he kidded himself into psychosis. To be able to joke about your symptoms may be some sign of health, but it is hardly evidence that the symptoms do not indicate something real. Of course, there may have been some objective basis for his suspicions of Trilling's opposition. "Even a paranoid has enemies," to quote one of Delmore's own aphorisms; and the suspicions of a paranoid may sometimes correspond with reality. I do not know in this case. There would have been reason for Trilling's opposition: Delmore's behavior (which we saw in more casual and bohemian situations) had by this time become sufficiently eccentric that he might have been considered an unstable force in an academic department.

This animosity of Delmore's was all the more surprising because he had begun as an admirer of Trilling in the late 1930s. He had read Trilling's book on Matthew Arnold when it first appeared, and had been greatly impressed with it. Here was no run-of-the-mill professor but a genuine literary intelligence for whom the past of English literature was a living thing; and since for Delmore too that literature was a living whole, Trilling seemed a kindred spirit. The appearance of the book was all the more remarkable coming when it did in a period of debased Marxism with its plebeian emphasis upon "social consciousness" and proletarian literature. Now animosity and rancor overshadowed that earlier admiration; not that he had totally switched and denied Trilling's abilities, but somehow his recognition of them, very real still, was buried under this other feeling. The change showed itself in the jibes he tossed off in conversation. He had once labeled Trilling "the Matthew Arnold of Morningside Heights" (the area of Columbia University), where the irony still had a certain gruff good humor. But now the jibe became grimmer simply by switching the location a few blocks: Trilling, Delmore now declared, was "the Matthew Arnold of Grant's tomb"—one of the dreariest and dullest monuments in all of New York City.

For Philip Rahv, however, there were good impersonal reasons for being uneasy at the direction of Trilling's ideas. *Partisan Review* had been founded as a magazine dedicated to the ideals of radicalism in politics and the avant-garde in art, and it had no editorial intention of abjuring these twin articles of its faith. But here was Trilling calling attention to the value of class distinctions for the writer, speaking sympathetically, even when critically, of the middle class, and bringing forward a less audacious and experimental canon of authors to be admired. Where the intellectuals had been preoccupied with figures like Joyce or Proust, or Dostoevski and Kafka, Trilling urged the case of more conventional novelists like E. M. Forster and Jane Austen. Almost single-handedly, in fact, he had brought the case of E. M. Forster before American readers, and had established Forster's permanent place. All of this was disquieting to the more austerely modernist tastes of the magazine.

One tiny incident seemed to bring all Rahv's uneasiness to a head. He had come into the office one day after running into Harold Rosenberg, who, witty and waspish as ever, had asked where *Partisan Review* was headed when it kept printing somebody like Trilling, who was simply making a case for "bourgeois values." This last phrase of Rosenberg's had been the twist of the knife, and Rahv was now visibly shaken. Like the Catholic lady in Stendhal's novel who enjoys trysts with her lover until one day the word "adultery" crosses her mind and she is overwhelmed at the sinfulness of her act and the awful damnation she is incurring, so at the dread expression "bourgeois values" all Rahv's Marxist pieties were shaken to their depths. Bourgeois values!

What a specter! And to think that he, as an editor, had been helping to promote them!

Yet Trilling had been close to the magazine from its very beginning, and the distinction of his performance, both literary and intellectual, made any contribution of his something to be coveted. What, then, was he up to? Could it be a case of what the Marxists called "boring from within"? Delmore Schwartz suggested an explanation that somewhat relieved Rahv: Trilling, he suggested, was using *Partisan Review* to "protect his left flank." That is, by appearing in a left-wing magazine Trilling could hide from the world how conservative his real message was. Rahv liked this metaphor from military strategy, and he appropriated the phrase so that he came to use it as his own: Trilling, he declared, *needed* to appear in *Partisan Review* in order to protect his left flank. He seemed more satisfied when he gave the explanation this turn since it left the relation of dependence (Trilling upon the magazine for protection) in the proper order.

It was into this muddle that Delmore eventually jumped with both feet by launching a critical attack upon Trilling. Under the personal circumstances involved here, Rahv himself would not have ventured on a frontal assault; he preferred leaving that explicit act to his auxiliary forces. "Philip Rahv doesn't mind someone else going out on a limb for him," Delmore had once said, warning me against some foolish polemical project of my own. But this was one limb on which Delmore himself did not mind going out, for it enabled him to discharge some of his pent-up animosity against Trilling. As for the ideas at issue, however, there was nothing captious in Delmore's attitude: he had very serious objections to Trilling's position, and wished to make those objections known; if by the way he were to have some fun letting off a bit of personal steam, that was not to be taken to compromise the underlying seriousness of his intent. Indeed, these ideas had been long gestating with him, so that the piece, entitled "The Duchess's Red Shoes," did not appear until 1953. While the attack encompasses the whole of Trilling's position, it is directed principally against the latter's essay, "Manners, Morals, and the Novel" (reprinted now in *The Liberal Imagination*).

If the two—Trilling's original essay and Delmore's counterblast—are read together, they make extraordinary reading indeed, both as an illumination of their period and for their permanent interest. The matters they deal with are ones which we are far from clear about now, and they are dealt with here on an intellectual level hard to match today. Trilling's original essay had no directly polemical intent; but in the context I am supplying here, the two pieces take on the appearance of a confrontation, with all its various suggestions of personal drama.

One cannot forget, for example, in reading them together the extraordinary difference in personality of the two antagonists. Indeed, as human types they were almost opposites. Trilling was a successful man, par excellence, where that somewhat unfortunate adjective is not given any of its usual disparaging connotations; he was a success both in the academy and the world without, and, more remarkable still, which so few do, in negotiating both worlds at once. He led a tidy and constructive life, and enjoyed a long and devoted marriage of unassailable stability. Delmore, on the other hand, much as he was haunted and preoccupied with the idea of success, had almost a perverse will not to succeed: if he had friends to break with them; if he had talents, to squander them; and where worldly opportunity presented itself, to step on the toes of those who would open its doors for him. There are the words of Yeats that the human intellect is forced to choose between "perfection of the life or of the work." Trilling—and perhaps this was another instance of his rejection of the extremism of modern writers—seemed to escape this dreadful antinomy by achieving both: he made the most of his talents and of himself as a human being. Delmore, in his pursuit of the one, destroyed both goals at once —and himself in the process. And yet, in this moment of confrontation between the two that we are imagining here, this solitary combat *mano a mano*, who is to say that the fallen and self-destructive angel does not at least hold his own?

To be sure, the attack upon Trilling is marred by a certain snide tone here and there. That much of his animosity Delmore could not keep back. Some few mollifying changes of expression had been suggested as the manuscript passed among us, but they were few, and fewer still were accepted. Wishing, for example, to say that Trilling was ambiguous, if not two-faced, on certain issues, Delmore had observed on his great skill in writing on both sides of any question. This was emended to read that he showed great solicitude in writing on all sides of a question, which would directly convey Trilling's concern always for the qualifying circumstances of any intellectual thesis but somehow leave the original imputation of duplicity still there. Also, certain touches of comedy come on as off-key. By this time Delmore had begun taking to the role of the buffoon, that mask of a later self that Saul Bellow was to record in his *Humboldt*. When in his cups, which was more and more often now, Delmore found it congenial to read Ring Lardner, and the latter's flatness of style began to creep into his own writing. As a result, he does get off some funny things, but their whimsical tone is inappropriate in a serious polemic against an opponent of Trilling's stature. But despite such lapses, Delmore at this time was still in possession of his critical faculties, which were naturally very sharp indeed; and this piece marks, I believe, the last occasion when he was able to bring all his intellectual energies into focus in any piece of prose exposition. Poetry was another matter; he was still to go on to write a few good poems.

The title, "The Duchess's Red Shoes," refers to that incident in Proust when Swann visits the Duchesse de Guermantes to tell her that he cannot go with her and the Duke to Italy because his doctor has told him he is dying and will soon be dead. Swann is a dear friend, and the Guermantes would like to stay and console him, but they are on their way to a dinner party to which they cannot be late. And to make even more poignant the contrast between the social ritual, with all its trivial and external compunctions, and the awful fact of death, the Duke notices as the Duchess is getting into the carriage that she is wearing the wrong shoes and he sends her back to change them.

What does the incident show? For Delmore, it reveals the callousness of the aristocratic and upper classes, involved as they are in their social rituals, to the most elementary human sympathies. And these are the aristocrats whose virtues Trilling seems to be extolling. But was this really Trilling's point? He had recommended that manners are important to the novelist, and that he should be a careful observer of them, because it is through them that human beings reveal themselves, as here the trivial business of changing one's shoes for a party brings out the indifference to the death of others as a universal tendency in all of us, whether we be aristocrats or plebeians. This seems to me much more in line with Proust's actual intention. The virtues and vices in his novel are not distributed according to any political scheme of classes: the lower orders—his cooks, maids, menials, and elevator boys—are just as vicious and mean as his aristocrats. Perhaps without knowing it, Delmore was simply following in the path of Edmund Wilson's interpretation of Proust in *Axel's Castle*. Wilson, writing in the pervasive social-democratic atmosphere of the 1930s, had given a rather egalitarian slant to Proust's treatment of social classes. To be sure, Proust in part is writing about the decay of the aristocratic classes; that decline is a historic fact which he records, but he is not writing a socialist tract *against* those classes.

What was troubling Delmore (and the rest of us at that time) was what would happen if one carried over the argument from literature into life. Trilling writes with such enthusiasm about the virtues of class distinctions and the social manners that go with them as material for the writer that he seems to be recommending that they should be kept as a desirable part of the good society. And it is against these possible antidemocratic implications that Delmore protests in words that sound almost threatening in their solemnity:

> He entertains social views (and social misgivings) which would be in-tolerable if they were presented nakedly, as social criticism of a political program, instead of being united with literary considerations.

And here we come upon such a tangle of questions, so much of their particular period, that we have to take a step backward and look at the controversy of our two antagonists within the context of Trilling's work as a whole in its time.

II.

The Liberal Imagination—to my mind, still the most considerable of Trilling's works—appeared in 1950. The essays that make up the book were elaborated over the previous decade; and it strikes us, when we look back now, as something of a minor miracle that the book could have evolved from the background of that and the preceding decade. Trilling as it turns out, was ahead of his time.

Nowadays one hears much of the phenomenon of "Neo-conservatism," but the public at large does not appear to be quite clear about this new doctrine. Some of the leading Neo-conservatives were once very close to Trilling, admired his mind and his writing, and virtually took him as a master. If their thinking on social matters is more explicit and goes further than his, that does not cancel the fact of a certain derivation from him. Events themselves have moved further; the evidence of the last thirty years makes us much more dubious about socialism and more questioning of the Marxist philosophy that begot it. We can no longer prevent ourselves from asking the questions we once shirked, nor can we postpone judgment while waiting for some miraculous transformation of the socialist societies. They have so obviously settled down into the grim realities they are that only internal revolutions can possibly liberate them. But apart from the limitations of this earlier situation in which he was writing, Trilling's own temperament did not lead him to push his questions further, for at heart he was a dedicated liberal.

In *The Liberal Imagination* the audience he addresses himself to is the liberal, educated middle class—and a good deal of the book's persuasiveness derives from the fact that he includes himself among the readers he would instruct. In 1950 that audience in large part would have been Stalinists and Fellow Travelers at one time, or would have gone through such influences, perhaps even without being aware of them. They would also be in large part members of what is now called "the New Class"—a class of professionals and intellectuals who swing free of the ties of the corporations and of labor. The term did not exist then, but the class itself was in existence (though not so preponderantly as today), for it had emerged into the open with the New Deal; and its views then, as now, were always automatically of the Liberal Left. Trilling did not attack the political beliefs of his audience; he left that task to the more restricted political critics among his colleagues. In this sense, it was true that *Partisan Review* did protect his left flank—or, perhaps more exactly, it waged war on the left flank, where he was content to follow along as a more silent foot soldier. He had another job to do, and he was perhaps the one man in America uniquely qualified to do it: he was concerned with the sensibility, capacities of response, and general intelligence about literature of his liberal audience—which means, of course, their capacities for sensitive and intelligent response to life too. Here he had no particular doctrine to offer but only an attitude of mind, being in this respect a true heir of his master Matthew Arnold, but also with the consequent limitations of Arnold that though you could be sure of the critic's intelligence, you could not always be sure what specific conclusions that intelligence had reached. Trilling was concerned that the liberal democratic mind, as we now know it in America, might be becoming too doctrinaire in its views, too fixed and rigid in its outlook to perceive the complex and ambivalent situations in life on which it would pass peremptory judgment. He had already urged the point in his book on E. M. Forster: that it was necessary not only to know good from evil, but to be flexible enough to perceive the good-and-evil that are always so perplexingly mixed in the actual occasions of life. For this purpose, he suggested, Liberals ought to listen carefully to the great conservatives of tradition; for only by appropriating something of the message of these conservatives, could their own thinking become more concrete and adequate. In all of this he was speaking for himself, and addressing himself at the same time, as a liberal. For, despite his plea that the Conservatives had a case, he himself remained a thoroughgoing liberal to the end: the cast of his mind was the rational, secular, and non-religious one of classical liberalism.

Yet at the heart of this liberalism of his there lurked a troubling question. The great works of modern literature—of Yeats or Eliot, Joyce or Lawrence—which we as cultivated readers admire and extol are not, to put it mildly, in accord with the liberal and democratic mentality to which we give our allegiance as citizens. How are we to account for this discrepancy? For someone like Trilling, whose life revolved around literature, the matter was a very serious one: it pointed to some cleft between the rationality of mind which we profess in our political beliefs and the deeper, more intractable regions of the spirit that these authors would seek to reach. The question never quite left Trilling throughout his life; he returned to it again and again, but I do not believe that he ever quite succeeded in giving a satisfactory answer to it.

At this earlier stage Trilling was fighting a battle against the residues of taste left by the 1930s. In the wake of the Great Depression and the vogue of Marxist or quasi-Marxist thought it fathered, the slogans of "social realism" still lingered, and they could, moreover, be allied with the older Populist yearnings of our American inheritance. But in their actual performance the results of these literary tendencies were dismal: a literature that was dull and bathetic, stereotyped, and shallow in its portrayal of human beings. Why then—and this was only another aspect of his more basic question—should we eschew a literature of depth and complexity, of refinement and subtlety, in the name of the empty slogans of equality? So far as the past was concerned, there could be no doubt of the fact that writers had made rich use of class distinctions, and of the fine observation of manners and character that were possible within those distinctions. The characters they portrayed, who dwelt within their class and station, evidently seemed able to develop a rich personality within those constraints. Well, the rejoinder might run, that might be all very well for the past, but would not do at all for the future we socialists envisaged. The past was aristocratic; it tolerated and even promoted a society of classes; but what our socialist and democratic conscience imagined for the future was *the* Classless Society.

And it was just here that Trilling might seduce us to think the unthinkable thought—or at least unthinkable by most of us at that time: Might it not be that the conditions which led to a more interesting literature also produced a more satisfying life within society itself? If in the literature of the past we observe human personality developing its varied riches within the framework of class distinctions, might it not be that those distinctions permitted, and in their own way even promoted, the well-being of society? Trilling himself did not think this thought, at least not aloud, and at the time probably would have recoiled from it. But his writing could lead one that way, and this was the awful threat, the sin that dared not speak its name, to which Delmore Schwartz could only make a veiled allusion in the quotation above.

Well, thirty years have gone by, from which a good deal was to be learned, and some of us have found ourselves able to think the unthinkable thought after all, and find it not so dire as we had expected. The Classless Society looks more and more like a utopian illusion. The socialist countries develop a class structure of their own, which proceeds inevitably out of the apparatus of the State, and revolves around which group has a stronger grasp of the powers of the bureaucracy. With regard to their human qualities, such classes tend to become grim, faceless, and homogenized. Since we are bound, then, to have classes in any case, why not have them in the more organic, heterogeneous, and variegated fashion of the older free societies? Nor would the requirements of justice be violated in such a society. Indeed, a society that imposed a strict equality upon its citizens would be a thoroughly unjust one, since it would fail to recognize the difference among individuals in talent and character. For a class society to be humanly equitable it is required only that there be some means by which the exceptional individual can rise out of his class if he so desires, or that an entire group may be able, through its own proper efforts, to lift its level as a whole. It is just to get what is one's due, which is not necessarily an equal share.

And so far as literature is concerned, the advantage seems to lie with the older class societies. After sixty years of Soviet rule, it seems clear that if the future is to be Marxist, then the future will be without a literature—at least a literature interesting enough to be comparable with the past. And here literature, or the absence of it, is indeed a good indication of life: a Marxist regime could not produce a literature because it imposes such a reign of regimented boredom and monotony that there is nothing interesting to write about—except, of course, the underground life of the dissenters or of the prison camps, as in the case of Solzhenitsyn.

III.

As a poet, Delmore Schwartz did not give much time to thinking through social problems as such. He found Marxism ready to hand as a framework within which his imagination could operate. Others have done so without the excuse of being poets. How confining that framework really was we see only as we review these old debates among the intellectuals, all of whom during those decades were far less free in their thinking than they imagined. It was when Delmore moved to the areas of his own sensibility that his attack upon Trilling became more telling.

Society and class—we are bound within them indeed. But how much of the human spirit may transcend this framework must always be a concern of the novelist. Trilling had written so persuasively about the novelist's need to deal seriously with manners and social class that, carried away by his own enthusiasm, he wished to embrace even Dostoevski in his prescription:

> The Russian novel, exploring the ultimate possibilities of the human spirit, must start and end in class—every situation in Dostoevski, no matter how spiritual, starts with a point of social pride and a certain number of rubles.

Starts, we may say, but does not end there. And if the reference here is, as it seems to be, to *Crime and Punishment*, then we must doubt whether the hero's crime really starts with his impoverished social position and his need for a certain number of rubles. Those are the incidental facts with which Raskolnikov seeks to "normalize" his crime—to disguise it to himself as a run-of-the-mill murder for the sake of robbery, as if even here in his crime the unconscious of this self-isolated man was struggling to join the ranks of ordinary humanity, even if it be criminal humanity in this case. But the crime in fact is generated by an *idea* that has taken over his own febrile mind as the criminal himself comes later to recognize. Dostoevski understood that we are now in the Age of Ideology, when ideas beget crime and terror. Men kill out of a desperation of mind, and not necessarily because their social condition is desperate. The Nihilists in Dostoevski emerge anywhere along the social scale; Stavrogin, in *The Possessed*, is affluent, but he finds in this affluence itself the temptation to desperate crime.

We are here in a very different world from the novels of Jane Austen. That exquisite writer offers us perhaps the last satisfying picture of a harmonious and self-contained world before the onslaught of the modern imagination takes over. To be sure, it is a very materialistic world; her people speak publicly and bluntly about matters of social position and money in arranging their marriages that most of us now would only dare whisper privately to a few chosen ears. And yet within the conditions of that small and closed world she has produced her own beautiful commentary on human nature. It is well that Trilling should have brought the case of Jane Austen again before the sensibility of American intellectuals. And it would have been well too, had he pushed further, and reminded those intellectuals of the importance of her social realities when one theorizes about society itself. But Jane Austen cannot be comprehended under the same critical formula as Dostoevski, as Trilling in his enthusiasm recommends. Dostoevski is writing about something different. He reaches into regions of the human spirit that are not to be found in Jane Austen. What, then, are Dostoevski's novels about? Delmore had answered:

> [These novels] are of permanent interest to all human beings not because they present the observation of the manners of a given society . . . but because they are about the innermost depths of all human beings.

"The innermost depths of all human beings"! That is a very vague

173

phrase, and here one does indeed wish for something more specific. Since the confrontation of the two, Trilling and Schwartz, seems at this point to converge upon a single author and a particular work, *Crime and Punishment*, it may be worthwhile to pause for a moment to sum this up in its thematic simplicity:

A young student, Raskolnikov, becomes infected with a modern ideology. In this case, oddly enough, it is a British import, Utilitarianism. Odd because the British were the most conservative nation in the nineteenth century in holding fast against the ravages of radical thought. They seem to have launched Utilitarianism without being aware how radical and nihilistic its implications were, simply because it sounded like business and commerce as usual. According to the Utilitarian doctrine, an act is justified if it produces a greater balance of pleasures over pains. Raskolnikov happens to have dealings with an old pawnbroker woman, a miserable specimen of humanity, mean and spiteful to others and unhappy in herself, who might be better off dead than alive and whose death would make a great many of her clients happier. Furthermore the money he would rob her of would pay for his own education, and since he is brilliant and gifted, would enable him to bring his gifts to the service of humankind generally. The balance of pleasures over pains is thus all on the side of the murder. There is required only the will and the daring on his part to assert himself as the exceptional individual who can transcend the ordinary and routine laws of morality for the benefit of himself and mankind. He murders the woman, but that is the beginning of a long nightmare from which he comes to learn more about life than from his flimsy reasonings. He learns, among other things, that his crime has been the product of a *deranged rationality*.

Why deranged? A certain spirit of calculation and objectivity has taken over human thinking. The pawnbroker woman is an object to be dissected into so many units of pain and pleasure, self-inflicted and inflicted upon others. Yet a single image breaks into this thinking. What reader can forget that moment in the novel when Raskolnikov raises the ax over the old woman's head? The gray-streaked head, its greasy hair plaited in a rat's tail held by a broken comb. How loathsome she is! How easily quantifiable into negative units! And yet not; for she too is a human life, a human soul, and the image of his victim at this moment will not leave the murderer. The individual human soul belongs to another order of phenomena than he calculated. He can take a life because in his thinking he had already cut himself off from life. The modern mind, in Dostoevski's view, is threatened by just such a *deranged rationality*—deranged because reason has cut itself off from the deepest instincts of life, as these are embodied in the common feelings of humanity, and ultimately expressed in a religious faith. For Dostoevski that faith was the Christian faith. For others it will be different, but in the end it will be a faith of some kind.

On the subject of faith Trilling is studiously silent. He remained an uncompromising rationalist to the end. It may seem strange to apply the adjective "uncompromising" to a writer who charms us by the luminous and flexible play of his intelligence, so that we are enlightened by that free play whether or not it arrives at any hard-and-fast conclusion. If he could be called doctrinaire about anything, it is in his adherence to Freudianism. Freud is the one fixed pillar of conviction to which he personally held. He had had a "successful" psychoanalysis, which seemed to have come at a crucial period, and evidently remained one of the central and transforming experiences of his life. While in such happy cases a transference usually occurs between patient and doctor, here it had reached beyond the particular analyst to invest with a compelling glow the primal father-figure of psychoanalysis, Freud himself. When Freud's name is invoked by Trilling, it is nearly always bathed in something of a numinous glow.

Trilling's Freud, therefore, is a very selective and idealized Freud: a heroic figure, in his way a great poet who brings myth once again to the attention of modern readers and who urges upon the enlightened liberal mind the unpleasant reminder that it too is bound within the confines of our instinctive life. No doubt, there is a heroic side to Freud in the courage and stubbornness with which he fought to bring his ideas before the world; but admiration for the man should not lead us to overlook the persistently negative and reductive aspects of those ideas. Trilling has written about a threat now stalking our culture in words that are frequently quoted:

> A specter haunts our culture—it is that people will eventually be unable to say, "They fell in love and married," let alone understand the language of *Romeo and Juliet,* but will as a matter of course say, "Their libidinal impulses being reciprocal, they activated their individual erotic drives and integrated them within the same frame of reference."

175

without perceiving, apparently, that these words could very well apply to Freud himself. To be sure, Freud is a stylist and would not put matters quite so crassly, but the deflating and reductive aspects of his systematic thought come to the same thing. But this was a side of Freud that Trilling chose not to see, and when he says:

> The pleasure I have in responding to Freud I find very difficult to distinguish from the pleasure which is involved in responding to a satisfactory work of art.

we are puzzled by what seems an extraordinary confusion of genres until we realize that Trilling is reading another Freud, a poem that he himself has created.

Time has passed, and the situation of Freud and psychoanalysis looks different to us today than in 1950. Trilling belonged to the generation for whom D. H. Lawrence and Freud were a challenge and a revelation. Since then, familiarity has rubbed away the sharp edge of shock. So many people have been through therapy, are under therapy, or are clamoring for therapy that we have to wonder what it is in this civilization that produces such a crying need. The needs seem clearly to lie beyond the purview of the original theory. The psychotherapist, even when he considers himself a Freudian, is usually operating in a domain of human problems quite beyond the confines of his theory. Freud's psychology, we now perceive, with its emphasis upon libido or sexuality as motive force, was tied too closely to the Victorian primness that surrounded the question of sex at the turn of the century. We have had the Sexual Revolution since, and it has brought some very different problems in its wake. Sexual Liberation has turned into the Sexual Nihilism of Venice Beach, California, which in this respect is merely a concentration of attitudes that are dispersed throughout American life. The patient in treatment now is no longer your Victorian aunt who came to the doctor plagued by some nervous tic from the excessive repressiveness of her life; she is more likely to have gone through all the adventures of sex in an atmosphere of "anything goes," and is now confused about the sense of it all. What is it all about? What does it mean? In short, the questions of Nihilism again.

And for such perplexities Freud does not offer a philosophy of life nor even an adequate theory of the human Self. His tripartite map of the soul—ego, id, and superego—is an arid and artificial construction. The ego is so obviously the ego of Utilitarianism calculating pleasures and pains. The id, the unconscious, is a morass of desires, to be drained away like the Zuyder Zee (one of Freud's most famous metaphors); it has little connection with the creative and revelatory unconscious of the Romantics, as Trilling tries to suggest. And the superego is the repressive voice of the parents, never the call of conscience that is able to stir our latent and unconscious energies. In short, a picture of Bourgeois Man according to the model of classical economic theory, but now in disarray and going to ruin, stirred by unruly desires, and his touted morality experienced only as an irksome restraint. What is lacking to the theory is any adequate conception of the unity of the Self.

Trilling was, in my view, the most intelligent man of his generation —or at least the most intelligent I knew. The reader will therefore understand, I hope, why we are trying to follow the workings of that intelligence here in some detail. It was also a very subtle and complex intelligence, far more than the lucid and engaging surface of his prose would lead one to believe on first reading. Delmore Schwartz, in his hostility, found it devious; we could at least agree that it was sometimes labyrinthine. And nowhere is it more labyrinthine than when he is touching on a topic in any way religious, as in his well-known essay on Wordsworth's ode, "Intimations of Immortality." It is only on repeated reading that one becomes aware how uncompromisingly naturalistic and Freudian Trilling's outlook is, and how unwilling he is to entertain any kind of religious experience or belief in its own terms.

The essay also seems to me the only one of Trilling's where I find him deliberately at odds with his subject. When one disagrees with him elsewhere, it is usually a matter of tone, emphasis, fine shading, or for not pushing his point far enough, but never for being at variance with the plain sense of the text he is to expound. He begins, for example, by telling us that Wordsworth's ode is not about immortality at all. This would be news to poor Wordsworth unless he was altogether woolgathering when he gave the poem its title. But if not about immortality, then what is the poem "really" about? It really deals, says Trilling, with "optical" phenomena—the ways in which we look at nature. (The introduction of optics here is a touch of pseudotechnical contrivance in which literary critics so often indulge but from which Trilling himself is usually beautifully free.) True enough, the poem is about the ways in which we see nature; but our vision of nature, for Wordsworth, is different as it is or is not accompanied by the sense of some encompassing Presence within which we and our lives unfold. But this is the kind of idea into which Trilling cannot enter on its own terms; he must somehow incorporate his own aesthetic enjoyment of Wordsworth's poem into some more naturalistic position of his own. Thus Wordsworth's mysticism is to be understood in Freudian fashion as an extension of our infantile narcissism. Our adult sense of oneness with nature—what is usually called the mystical experience—is a carry-over from the stage of early life when the infant cannot distinguish the stimuli of his own body from those of the external environment. When one thinks of the long history of mysticism, and the variety of cultures and human types in which it has been expressed, from Lao-tse to T. S. Eliot and Wittgenstein, this is a vast body of human culture and reflection to drop into the lap, or should we say crib, of infantile narcissism. It is surely a strange civilization we live in where such a view can become intellectually fashionable.

It happens also to be a reductive view which deflates not only Wordsworth's experience but the poetry he made out of it. If you keep the Freudian interpretation in the forefront of your mind, the sense and force of the poetry disappear. Even if you hold the Freudian view on other grounds, it is only when you forget it that you can have any satisfactory enjoyment of the poetry. Wordsworth himself would have preferred the interpretation of Kant, which he probably heard from Coleridge: that in our experience of the sublime and beautiful in nature the unknown depths of the Self seem to respond to some unknown and supersensible depths of nature itself, and to be at one with the latter. In the modern parlance: this is one experience in which at last alienation is overcome. But this may be an experience which the modern intellectual, preferring his alienation, has chosen to abandon.

IV.

All roads lead to literature, especially for a literary review. *Partisan Review* had been conceived under the sign of the avant-garde, and it was dedicated to the tradition of modernist literature. That tradition had now to be guarded all the more zealously since no great new examples of this literature seemed to be springing up in the wake of the War, as we had expected. The more moribund they become, the more tenaciously traditions have to be guarded. It was therefore on this particular point that Trilling's impact would be sensitively felt. And it was here that Delmore's sharpest stroke fell—sharpest because directed at the personal sensibility of the man himself. Trilling, he said, did not really respond to the literature of the moderns toward which he made verbal gestures of admiration:

> He is much more drawn to Forster, James, Howells, and Keats, than to Joyce and Eliot; and he has the most serious misgivings about the extremism, the bias and the methods of all modernist authors.

To put the charge in more blunt form: Trilling was a reincarnation of the Genteel Tradition, for whom modern literature was still too destructive and shocking to be accepted.

I think there is some justice to the accusation. Trilling had been trained in the literature of nineteenth-century England, which for the most part had escaped the deeper convulsions of literature on the Continent; and by temperament he was not attracted to literary experimentation. We all remain tied to our profession; underneath his extraordinary alertness to modern issues, Trilling still retained the sensibility of a professor of English whose field was that of the nineteenth century. We are not yet able to define the term "modern." Perhaps the next century will have some comprehensive grasp of its meaning, which is denied to us who are still floundering in the midst of the thing itself. Yet we are able to recognize the meaning of the word in particular instances, and perhaps this is how we must proceed. Dickens, for example, is a very great writer, but we should not say that he is "modern"—in a sense perfectly recognizable but yet to be determined —whereas Dostoevski is a modern. Flaubert's *Madame Bovary* and Thackeray's *Vanity Fair* are almost contemporary, yet the former belongs to the modernist canon—it is in its way the progenitor of the modern novel—while Thackeray's work, despite his various touches of personal temperament, fits in with the conventional novel. No disparagement is intended by this, and indeed there are resources of expression available to Thackeray that Flaubert, in the purity of his detachment, cannot avail himself of. That detachment, as we shall see shortly, is one of the hallmarks of the modern consciousness.

To bring these comparisons to their sharpest point, we might turn to the genre of religious writing itself. England had one great religious writer in the nineteenth century—Newman—while his contemporary on the Continent is Kierkegaard. Within the Christian fold there could hardly be a greater difference than between these two. Newman is encased in the tradition of the Church, and his quest is to seek out and embed himself in what he comes to believe is the deeper and more authentic stream of that tradition. Kierkegaard attacks the institution of the Danish Church ferociously; he gives us the naked individual facing the extreme and ultimate questions in their anguish and desperation, and does so with a boldness and inventiveness of mind that would have scandalized the Englishman. I am not recommending one of these writers to the exclusion of the other, and there are aspects of Newman which even the most devout Kierkegaardian must now take to heart. The point of the comparison is that Newman is traditional, while Kierkegaard is a "modern"—again in a sense which I think we all perfectly recognize.

Coming as he did from this more conservative British literary background Trilling did approach the moderns somewhat gingerly. Yet he could not rest easy with Delmore's accusation. It was an embarrassing position for him to be put in. He was not given to rapid-fire polemics, and to have answered directly would have dragged him down into an aimless personal squabble. Instead, he would meet the issue more slowly and deliberately. He had been accused of not being really responsive to modern literature, and of taking its name in vain whenever he spoke of it. Very well; it was a serious charge, and he would meet it, and meet it in the most appropriate way in which he as a professor could: he would give a course in the subject! And in the process he would expose himself to this alien element of modern literature. Thus his answer came almost ten years later in an essay, "The Modern Element in Modern Literature," which does not at all refer to Delmore's attack, though I believe the latter was the original propelling force. The essay is in good part an account of his experiences in giving the course, and of what he learned from it, and it is to my mind one of the most stimulating and fertile pieces that Trilling ever wrote.

What is "the modern element in modern literature"? The question may look like one of those remote and mandarin reflections in which our literary critics sometimes like to indulge. In fact, it is one of the most direct and urgent questions we can ask of ourselves at this time. For if we knew what was distinctively "modern" about our literature, we would know what lies at the heart of our own age, what makes us tick, what the human situation really is in which we find ourselves today. It would be enlightening, though too tedious here, to go through the authors one by one whom he selected, his sometimes unexpected inclusions and exclusions (Kafka and Joyce, for example, are excluded, and Gide included), what he makes of each, and how he fits them into his general scheme. We may leave it to some scholarly Ph.D. to give us such a detailed anatomy of Trilling's mind. Here we confine ourselves to the blunt statement of his conclusions from that ten years' search.

What is modern about modern literature? Trilling's answer, as we should expect, falls within the Freudian pattern of his thinking. Modern literature is distinguished by its deliberate search into the unconscious psyche. It attempts not only to lay bare but, in a Dionysian spirit, to celebrate those unconscious forces. Trilling puts this in one of his more striking and memorable phrases:

> Nothing is more characteristic of modern literature than its discovery and canonization of the primal, non-ethical energies.

A second leading characteristic is the rebellion within this literature: the modern writer has taken on himself an "adversary role" against his civilization—a phrase that had become well-known by this time. But if an adversary, what then is he fighting? Writers in the past—satirists from Horace and Juvenal to Pope and Swift—have attacked one or another feature of their society, so that the adversary role as such would not be enough to distinguish the modernity of the modern writer. Trilling therefore specifies by pushing his point further: the modern writer has taken up an adversary role, not merely toward this or that feature of his own society, but toward civilization itself. And, fittingly, he chose as a concluding text for the course and its grand summation Freud's *Civilization and Its Discontents*.

One would not want to quarrel with either of these two points as such, but they seem to me radically incomplete as they stand. Psychologically, for example, the *detachment from feeling*, or the striving toward such detachment, that we find in modern literature is as momentous a fact as the plunge into the unconscious. Consider the case of *Madame Bovary* again. It is in its way the archtypal, the paradigmatic, work of modernism—at least in the novel. Read it again after many years and it becomes more shocking. Here is a work in which detachment and objectivity have been so rigorously and beautifully pursued

181

that the world has become emptied of values altogether. The authorities at the time, shocked by the infidelities of its heroine, sought to censor the book. Today we find such "scandals" commonplace; but the instincts of the censors, without their knowing it, may have really been frightened by something else: the vision of a world stripped of value. The mark of Flaubert is everywhere in subsequent literature. Sometimes this inability to feel takes on an overwhelming pathos of its own, as in Kafka and Beckett. This impulse toward detachment in literature is all the more momentous when we consider that the detachment from feeling is an accompaniment and outcome of the workings of modern society in its ever more intricate and impersonal structures. And, of course, this detachment finds its own ideological expressions. What, after all, was that specter Trilling found haunting modern culture—the deflation of love into libidinal impulses—but one more manifestation of the detachment from feeling?

But we are lacking still in our picture the large overriding pattern within which all the agitations of modernity fit. Whether it be Trilling's Freudian bias or his oversubtlety of mind, he seems to me to have missed the very plain figure in the carpet. I do not know what constitutes the essential modernity of modern literature, but I do know—and I think most students of intellectual history know—what is the large overriding framework within which this literature is written. It is the continuing secularization of our culture and the gradual withdrawal of God that have been going on in the West since the seventeenth century. For Nietzsche, this disappearance of God is the paramount event in Western history, indeed in the history of mankind, beside which all other events like wars and revolutions pale into relative insignificance. Matthew Arnold knew this, at least as a poet. As a critic, he himself had written an early essay "The Modern Element in Modern Literature," from which Trilling deliberately borrowed his own title. There Arnold had spoken as a man of the Enlightenment and extolled the modern element in literature as the free play of reason and intelligence. But as a poet he knew that something deeper was afoot in the modern world:

> The Sea of Faith
> Was once, too, at the full, and round earth's shore . . .
> But now I only hear
> Its melancholy, long, withdrawing roar.

But it is not merely a matter of ebbing faith. The whole intellect of Western man has been changed, if we look at it as mirrored in the progress of philosophy from Descartes to Kant into the varied forms of contemporary Positivism.

Alongside this withdrawal of God, there have been the vast social and political upheavals of modern history in the direction of equality. Unlike the momentary revolts of antiquity or the Middle Ages, the conflicts between rich and poor, nobles and serfs, which were sporadic and relatively local, the modern egalitarian process has been continuous, systematic, and world-wide. These two great movements—the retreat of God and the social revolution—have run parallel to each other, but their courses have been intricately linked in many ways. In a more external and obvious way, the egalitarian revolution had to begin by appropriating, where it could, the property of Church and clergy. But the two are more subtly linked than that; the social revolution has been aided and abetted by technology and the technological organization of modern society, which in turn foster a thoroughly secular outlook. Where these two great historic tendencies will end, what future they may bring to humankind, we cannot now know. But we are not without our anxieties about the outcome, and these too are a part of the distinctively modern element of modern literature.

Writers have responded to these cataclysmic changes differently. Some have been greatly shaken by the death of God, and made heroic efforts to restore or compensate for the loss; some appear to be untouched and to go on as if nothing had happened. But I would not be too sure of this last. If something has departed from this world and we do not notice it, the world is still very different for us from what it was for human beings in the past; and sooner or later we find ourselves making unconscious adjustments. Liberals who had seemed secure and at ease within their own secular mind may be suddenly driven to find substitutes for religion in political causes and crusades, and to carry utopian hankerings into the field of politics. They may even aspire to bring about heaven on earth for the dream of heaven they have lost. Hence that very troubling and paradoxical phenomenon of our time: the Liberals' susceptibility to totalitarianism.

Trilling, of course, was too chaste a mind ever to succumb to that temptation. His intelligence is too cool and cautious, forever balancing and qualifying its own judgments, to betray even for a moment a passing longing for the Absolute. In this he departs from his idol and model, E. M. Forster, at least for one moment in the latter's career. Between the opposites of belief and non-belief there is a middle region where the mind, hanging loose, can permit itself the imagination that religion might be true in some way we cannot conceive. Forster had this moment in India. This imagination that religion might be true—and true in some way which we cannot grasp—might seem a small thing in comparison with the positive faith of the believer or the militant conviction of the non-believer; and yet it can make all the difference in reminding us how narrow and one-sided our rationalism can be. Forster has this imagination in his *Passage to India:* the experience of India is so engulfing that it upsets the neat rationalism of the European mind. He had already rejected the prim and tidy Christianity he had been exposed to in his youth; but there is also a prim tidiness about the enlightened mind of Cambridge and Bloomsbury, which had formed him, that seems inadequate to the extremes of life, the depths and heights, he encounters in India: the dismal and nihilistic echoes of the Marabar caves against the affirmation and joy of the Hindu celebration of the birth of Shiva. Toward the end of the novel, the tough-minded and reasonable Fielding, who is Forster's spokesman throughout for sound common sense, declares: "There is a truth in religion that has not yet been sung." Trilling could not follow Forster that far.

It is to be wondered why a mind as sensitive as Trilling's should never have been visited by this imagination, or closed himself off from it if it ever came. There is the fact that he was educated at Columbia University at a time when John Dewey and F. J. Woodbridge, in their very different ways, had been powerful advocates of Naturalism, and had virtually fixed the Naturalistic view as the orthodoxy of that campus. Trilling had a deep *pietas* toward his university, and considerable sensitivity toward its influences. There is also the fact, which we have already copiously noted, of his adherence to Freud, and the disparagement of religious experience that would inevitably bring with it. But beyond these two influences, there seems to me to be a third, which I advance here only very speculatively and tentatively; and this has to do with his Jewish inheritance and the position of his generation of Jews in American life. He was of that generation whose parents had just made the transition, the great leap, by being assimilated into American life. To them "the old religion" meant earlocks, beards, prayer shawls, dark suits—a whole apparatus of life that would mean their exclusion and self-exile from this new world. Their children, for whom America and its opportunities were to open even more widely, grew up in this atmosphere, absorbed it unconsciously, and grew even further apart from the old allegiances. For the first time in history, at least since the Exile, here in this American democracy the Jew was on his way to becoming an accepted member of the community. To be religious somehow implied a step backward in history, toward ghettos and the pale and the exclusion generally from American life. In this respect, though in other ways they were radically different personalities, Trilling's case seems to me perhaps comparable with that of Walter Lippmann, who eschewed religious attachment lest it exclude him from the American mainstream.

V.

Lionel Trilling died in 1975, a year after Philip Rahv. Funeral services were held in St. Paul's chapel on the campus of Columbia University. Both a rabbi and a minister presided; some psalms were read and there was a brief musical offering. The casket was then borne out and the mourners quietly left the church. All was in perfect taste, and perfectly appropriate to the person whom we mourned. It was as if the grace and modesty of the man himself somehow overflowed into the rites of death that were performed in his name.

Yet I remember being faintly troubled at the time; and as I reflect on those last rites I find myself more and more troubled by the perplexing questions they beget. Was the service religious or not? In some sense it was not completely secular—there was the chapel and there were the psalms. Suppose there had been a completely secular service. Imagine it taking place in one of those funeral parlors—they often dignify themselves by the name of chapels—farther down on Broadway. The mourners—or, more accurately, the invited guests—sit around in folding chairs; a meeting is assembled, there are speakers in eulogy, and the business of the session proceeds apace. Whatever solemn notes may be invoked, it is, after all, a business session of a kind, convened for the purpose of dispatching a corpse in some socially acceptable manner. Even the imagination of such a service seems shocking and inappropriate for a man like Trilling. It was fitting that there should be a chapel and those psalms.

Death is the one part of life where a thoroughly secular attitude seems to hit us as crudely inadequate. Whatever our sophistication, in the death of someone close to us we are thrown back into the same emotions as primitive man. Death thrusts us into the great darkness, the mystery that envelops all that is, and we have to reach back for the language with which men could once address themselves to those matters. Hence the psalms.

But here the nagging question. Suppose we, as moderns, still feel the aesthetic need for this archaic language at such times. How many generations before its use as an aesthetic adornment for a funeral service begins to lose its force, and becomes a routine gesture? And when we are at last fully conscious that it is mere routine, what then? Then we have sunk—or risen, according to some minds—to the purely secular level where we are merely dispatching a corpse, in some socially approved way, into the ground or the crematorium, as the case may be. And if that archaic language does become at last routine, what would be required for its renewal?

These are unpleasant thoughts, and perhaps it is ungracious to raise them in the case of this particular funeral. But Trilling was an exemplary figure—perhaps the best example of the civilized humanist our period had to offer—and he is worthy therefore of the most searching questions we can ask. For in pressing these questions, we place ourselves and our whole culture in question along with him.

Part III

Departure

As my entry into the circle had been both casual and unexpected, so my departure from it was equally casual but altogether expected. There was no scene of dismissal or resignation, I simply departed through mutual agreement. My friendship with Delmore had taken a new and drastic turn, and that was one less tie to hold me to the magazine. The tension between the editors became more open every day, and there were scenes of bickering at our meetings. Delmore's behavior had become more erratic and he provoked several scenes himself. If my memories of my last days with the magazine are faint, perhaps it is just as well.

My last clear memories of active appearance at the magazine office do not go beyond the first part of 1952, and these are fixed in my mind by an unexpected circumstance. In the summer of 1952 I led an International Seminar held at Harvard. The nominal director of the Seminar was Professor William Y. Eliot, but the actual manager of it was the young Henry Kissinger, then a graduate student in the final stages of getting his doctorate. The correspondence about taking the job had been through *Partisan Review*, and I remember writing my letters to Kissinger from the office. Hence I was still at that time (the spring of 1952) going regularly to the office. More than that, I was in fact being hired by the Seminar because of my connection with the magazine. The Cold War was now on in full blast, and the Seminar was designed to give a certain number of chosen foreign intellectuals a more adequate picture of American cultural life. Above all, it was to show them that there could be an opposition to Communism from the Left, that American attitudes were not summed up in McCarthyism, and that there were in fact American intellectuals of the Left who were vigorously anti-Communist. *Partisan Review* was now publicly recognized as the leading magazine expressing this point of view, and I was hired to lead the Seminar as a representative editor. Hence I was at this time clearly identified, both publicly and in my own mind, with the magazine. But I cannot speak very clearly of my ties with it after that summer.

I suppose I should interrupt my narrative here with some appropriate anecdotes of Kissinger, but in drawing it now to a conclusion I cannot stray too far afield. Suffice it to say that I liked Kissinger and became, during that summer, quite friendly with him. I was impressed by his energy and intelligence. He was indefatiguable in the work of the Seminar, spending much time and care in sifting through applications in order to get the best students, and then devoting a great deal of personal attention to the students when they were there. These were young people, mostly in their thirties, who were just beginning their careers as journalists, editors, or professors, in short as intellectual shapers of public opinion, and we were there to do what we could toward shaping *their* opinions. The members of the Seminar came from everywhere, Europe, Asia, and Africa, and were interesting both as individuals and as a group. Kissinger ran the whole show, and from my point of view quite satisfactorily. I remember venturing on a bit of prophecy about him to someone or other at the time: "This young man will go far, he will end by becoming a dean." Which is one case where prophecy was outstripped by reality.

However, one price of eminence is to be the butt of unfavorable stories, and I cannot hurry on without adding one small item of my own to the stock against Kissinger. Years later, when he was Secretary of State, there was some sensational news about a private conversation he was supposed to have had with Admiral Zumwalt, United States Chief of Naval Operations, in London. According to Zumwalt, Kissinger had expressed his conviction that the West was in a state of irreversible decline, particularly in relation to the Communist world, and that as Secretary of State all Kissinger could aim to do was to ease the transition. Kissinger hotly denied Zumwalt's account of the conversation. No Secretary of State can ever admit publicly that his task is to ease his country's way into decline. Simply for the record, I have to report that I had that same conversation, or a very similar one, with Kissinger several times during the summer of 1952. He was not then the architect of Détente, and he did not speak of managing our transition into a subordinate place, but only of our learning to live somehow with the decline. True, he was at that time completing a dissertation on Spengler, and he was saturated with the Spenglerian idea and mood of Western decline, and on occasion would give way to them. Perhaps, in his cups while chatting with Zumwalt he had fallen back into the old mood. On the other hand, as I observed him that summer, Kissinger had an unusual capacity to learn and to change his mind; and from more recent pronouncements, he has evidently learned and changed a good deal since he was Secretary of State.

I enjoyed that summer a good deal; I was glad to be away, and I found I did not miss being at the office. In the past when I was away there had usually been some ties of correspondence, some small chores to be attended to, that served to remind me of my connection, and could awaken enthusiasm even at a distance. But that summer I felt peculiarly disconnected. My ties with the magazine had plainly weakened. I was on the way out.

How does one say good-bye? It is sometimes easier to avoid it, to slip away unnoticed; and in the case of my actual departure, I cannot remember that anything like formal good-byes were said. But to say good-bye in memory, especially to a sizable chunk of one's life in reflection, is a more significant act and demands some proper formality. How do I say farewell to the two persons, Philip Rahv and Delmore Schwartz, who were, in their very different ways, my tutelary spirits during that time? It seems to me I can only say farewell by clinging to their memory a little more closely, and following out their fortunes to the bitter end. And the end, as it turned out, was for both of them, though in very different ways, bitter indeed.

Chapter Eight

The New York
Intellectual II:
The Grip of Orthodoxy

I.

Intellectuals are less disconnected from the social body than they like to imagine. As their attitudes shift, some cultural middlemen will always be around to transmit the tremors of change to society at large. The shift may not be noticeable at once, and may seem an entirely small-scale and private affair; and usually the rate of transmission requires a decade or so to be effective. But follow the zigs and zags of any given intellectual and you may turn out to be reading the fever chart of the next generation.

The fifties prepared the way for the sixties. Usually we think of the latter period as a rupture with what went before, but in hindsight we find more continuity than we thought. The earlier decade was fat, comfortable, and complacent; it was not a time likely to prepare a people for heroism and self-sacrifice, least of all when the call to such virtues came in the form of the very dubious crusade of Vietnam. True, anti-Communism seemed to have become a widespread attitude throughout the country during the 1950s; but precisely as it became more widespread, it ceased to be attractive to some intellectuals. An anti-Communism shared by the *hoi polloi* was vulgar and corny; it could no longer be considered an avant-garde position in politics. It would be more avant-garde to stand above the battle, to disdain this senseless rivalry between the United States and Russia. And this attitude on the part of intellectuals transmitted itself to the youth of the next generation. Youth, when it has intellectual pretensions, fancies what looks like the avant-garde position even though, unknown to them, that position may be shopworn.

In Philip Rahv's case the conversion away from anti-Communism has to be regarded as a drastic reversal in view of the long years he had spent fighting against pro-Soviet Liberals. How did it happen? Curiously enough, the change was going on in him at the very time, in 1952, that he wrote his strongest indictment of the fellow-traveling and Liberal mind as a more or less deliberate refusal to confront reality. That occurred in his piece on the Hiss case, which I've already noted in an earlier chapter but whose point needs further emphasis here. What was extraordinary in the Hiss case, as it struck Rahv, was that a large segment of the American public—particularly on the Liberal side, those whom we might describe as "people of good will"— were simply unwilling to believe that Communism existed as a continuing and organized conspiracy that meant the United States no good, and that this conspiracy had been able to penetrate the American Government. But if we acknowledge this, then in simple logic there is a next step that we might very well take. There is the necessity not only of accepting the evidence of the past but of confronting the threat of the future. If the conspiracy is real and continuing, then we ought to take organized steps to meet it in the future. This simple bit of reasoning might have led Rahv to a much more militantly anti-Communist program, and one that would insist on building up American power since that was the only thing that stood between us and Stalinization—a point which Rahv had insisted on in the years immediately after the War. But Rahv did not take this path. His mind was not logical but intuitive—and sometimes intuitive according to his own devious patterns.

For one thing, the taint of McCarthyism had to be removed. It was necessary to detach the issues in the Hiss case from the McCarthyism of the period—which Rahv did in a companion piece. But this was not enough to satisfy him. Something else was bothering him, and I caught an intimation of it one day in conversation with him.

He talked out his pieces as he was engaged in writing them. They took possession of him; he could write nothing from the top of his mind, not even fairly trivial things, and thus was incapable of the journalistic facility for which he sneered at, but secretly envied, his former colleague on *Partisan Review* Dwight Macdonald. It was as if Rahv's whole being, his body included, conspired in the process of getting out his essays, as he grunted, cajoled, and fulminated them into shape. And in the midst of the birth-throes of the piece on Hiss, I remember his remarking to me one day: "The Liberals now dominate all the cultural channels in this country. If you break completely with this dominant atmosphere, you're a dead duck. James Burnham has committed suicide. And Sidney Hook is practically going the same way." Burnham, by this time, had deliberately and openly changed his whole political philosophy and taken a sharp swing to the Right, so that he expected to be cut off from Liberal channels. But Sidney Hook remained what he had always been, a resolute Social Democrat who insisted on preaching the evils of Russian Communism to the benighted American public, no matter if the underhanded accusation of McCarthyism would be made against him. Yet he too was distinctly *persona non grata* with the Liberals. Rahv was right: the Liberals did make up the dominant climate of opinion in the cultural circles of New York, and to follow Hook's path was suicidal. Rahv was obviously doing a lot of thinking here. He was not one who would deliberately choose suicide for himself.

The decisive turn for him—indeed the liberating turn—was the death of Stalin in 1953. The Russian dictator had stolen the Revolution of 1918, and now by his death he was giving it back again—it was as simple as that. I do not think I exaggerate the simplicity of Rahv's thought here; it was a simplicity that could exist within a mind powerful and complex in other respects, and in this point he is typical of the Marxist intellectual generally and therefore very much worth observing. The Revolution of 1918 had abolished the capitalists and established the collective ownership of the economy, the people now owned the means of production; that was progress, indeed it was the great step forward toward which the whole of history aspired; then had come that wicked man Stalin who imposed his own political dictatorship on top of this new economic structure; that was regress; what was needed was to lop off this regressive top that had been foisted upon the progressive economic foundation, and the death of Stalin (since the dictatorship had been his personal work) would achieve that. How abstractly encapsulated everything was here, how neatly severed were the economic and political spheres! As if a centralized economic control had been established without accompanying political bureaucracy! Under socialism, the slogan runs, the people own the means of production; but the question then becomes, Who owns these so-called owners? They end up in the grip of a political bureaucracy. And this bureaucracy is part and parcel of managing a centrally organized economy: the political and the economic are inextricably intertwined. The Revolution had not produced two separate things—economic advance and political regression—from which you could easily remove the offensive part; it had in fact succeeded in producing one unitary thing, an economic and political dictatorship, and this is exactly what should have been expected but what Marxism had never envisaged.

But these chilling thoughts never descended upon Rahv in the moment of his euphoria at the death of Stalin. His mind was so fixed upon Stalin as the diabolic figure who had corrupted the Revolution that he could not help believing the death of the dictator would now restore that Revolution to the pristine purity of its slogans; and he began to look longingly for any least sign of liberalization in the Soviet regime. His heart leaped up when he beheld the Khrushchev "thaw," but that joy was very short-lived as the Soviet bureaucracy ground on unchanged in its old dictatorial rut. Nevertheless, Rahv plodded piously forward, secure in the grip of his old orthodoxy. From time to time, though, he had doubts that the political order in the Soviet Union was merely a superstructure perched on the economy and therefore easily mended. But even when, in his last years, he spoke of the necessity of a "political revolution" in the Soviet Union, he seems never to have imagined that such a revolution, if it were indeed to bring about liberty, would not so much have to complete as to sweep away the work of the October Revolution.

So Rahv came to turn his back upon the political course he had been following. As the 1950s went on, the targets of his attack gradually shifted and he began to drop sharp words about "anti-Communism" and "anti-Communists" whenever the occasion presented itself. This was rather puzzling behavior at the time, since his political life up to that point had been a long war against Stalinist Communism and against Stalinizing and fellow-traveling Liberals. It was also somewhat distressing that some of these "anti-Communists" whom he now belittled had been his comrades-in-arms during those earlier battles. He turned his back too on the power struggle between the United States and the Soviet Union. He chose to forget his own warning to Dwight Macdonald and Clement Greenberg in 1940 apropos of the War against Hitler that you cannot stand above the battle, and that in effect to sit it out is to choose one side.

In 1958 he was appointed professor at Brandeis University. Personally, he felt an almost grim vindication that he, self-taught waif of the Depression, without degrees and with a radical past, should be so academically acknowledged at last. But it did not increase his affection toward the society that had rewarded him. His attitudes, if anything, became more anti-American than ever. He groused about his students and colleagues at Brandeis. He was like those children of affluence during the 1960s who found their middle-class advantages a further reason for hostility toward American society. Rahv, in fact, was one of the intellectuals of the 1950s who was preparing the way for the radical outbursts of the 1960s; and when these came, he was ready to receive them with open arms. All in all, it was to be a strange turn in the career of a man who had always been an outsider: hitherto, in the 1930s and 1940s, he had fought against the dominant trend, but now in the 1960s he had turned about and was running with the pack.

II.

The best part of him, however, lies in his literary criticism, and we had better turn there now to follow his further journey. It is as a mind involved with literature, rather than as political theorist, that he becomes most interesting.

Yet, even here, one cannot regard him altogether apart from his political context. As a literary critic, Rahv was very much part of his actual world. To attempt to distill out the literary criticism, and regard it as something apart, would not give us a proper idea of his importance. To compare him, for example, simply as a literary critic with someone like Edmund Wilson would be both bizarre and belittling. But if we look at the comparison from another direction, the result may not be so belittling. It may come as a rather shocking paradox at first, but I think the claim might reasonably be defended that in his own particular way, and over a certain period, he probably had a more powerful influence than Wilson. True, his output was very slender in comparison, and he reached only a tiny fraction of the audience Wilson did; but his influence was more strategically located—on young intellectuals who went on to teach or to write about literature themselves and who, though they might not have followed him to the letter and even might have found themselves very much in opposition, nevertheless took from him a certain direction in their own thinking, and thus propagated something of his influence.

Of course, this influence was inseparable from that of *Partisan Review* in its earlier and more vital days, but then we have to remember how much he himself shaped the line of that magazine. In his own view, each of his critical pieces, whatever intrinsic points it might make, was intended to reinforce the general attitude of mind for which the magazine stood and which he thought should be that of all intellectuals in our time. The word "line" may have an ominous ring here, which in the present case we ought to dismiss. Rahv did have a taste for power, and there were those who referred to him as aspiring to be a kind of cultural commissar. But though he relished the feeling of power, he would have been too indolent, had a socialist revolution taken over, to become a successful commissar. That would have required too much of his labor and his time, and drawn him away from what he preferred to do—which was to read books and from time to time comment upon them. That he loved literature was indeed one of his redeeming merits. There is, however, a perfectly legitimate sense in which a critic may seek to define a "line" with regard to any subject or author he is exploring. He wishes, after all, to establish some judgment that, even if it does not claim to be definitive, nevertheless marks out a path along which he wants to lead his readers. And it is because Rahv was so conscious of his public role, I think, that he has the critical virtues he does: his ability, at his best, was to bring together conflicting claims and strike some sort of judicious, sometimes even judicial, balance between them.

Take his well-known essay, "Redskin and Paleface," which I have already mentioned in an earlier chapter. There he explores two opposing tendencies in the American psyche: on the one hand, the drive toward the pursuit of experience, and the rawer the better; on the other, the inhibiting forces that come from our Puritan inheritance and from the sometimes overcultivated drive toward culture itself. It has been objected that Rahv's classifications here are not mutually exclusive, and that in fact a writer like Melville is at once a redskin and a paleface. But this is hardly a refutation; opposing tendencies may be embodied in the same writer, as they are in life, and a good deal of light is in fact thrown upon Melville to see him as torn at certain moments between the life of the primitive and the supercivilized. In any case, Rahv was not seeking (I doubt if any critic should) to establish a rigidly precise set of categories; his mind did not move in the direction of logical abstractions. He was dealing with a rather diffuse question of our American habits and traditions that had been thrashed about by a good many critics; and he was seeking to bring that material into some kind of compact image and place the whole matter in judicious focus. And with these qualifications made, the essay still stands up, as valid as when it first appeared in 1939. Of course, there remains the further question as to what might deepen our American life so that we could get beyond the impasse of these opposites. But that investigation would require from the critic the kind of beliefs and temperament, and indeed a commitment of feeling toward America, that Rahv did not have.

In a similar vein, of striking a just and perceptive balance, is the fine essay, "Attitudes toward Henry James," of 1943. Written during the Henry James boom, the essay seeks to perform a dual function: on the one hand, James had been for years a neglected writer and it was necessary to bring him before the public and establish his claims of greatness, but, on the other hand, one had to avoid the excesses of the more rabid enthusiasts who would elevate James to a position he did not quite fit. And, once again, Rahv strikes the intelligent and judicious balance, and, moreover, with a gracefulness and delicacy of touch somewhat unusual for him. He had a tendency, when not careful, to slip into being heavy-handed; but here some of the polish and civility of James himself had rubbed off on him.

However, when he returned to the same theme almost thirty years later, in "Henry James and His Cult" (1972), he had indeed become

199

heavy-handed and doctrinaire with advancing age and his more intransigent opinions. As his political views became more simplistic, his literary perceptions had become cruder; and in general his later writings show his powers to be declining. The subtleties of the later James now elude him. The instances with which he attacks the later novels seem to me singularly unconvincing and in some cases rather obtuse. He finds it "unlikely," for example, that a woman so sophisticated as Mme. de Vionnet in *The Ambassadors* should fall in love with so inconsequential a young man as Chad Newsome. As if any man on whom a woman bestowed her love had first to present her with a guaranteed certificate of his worth and rank! As if the heartbreak of the whole thing in this particular case were not that an aging woman should love in a handsome, charming, if somewhat empty youth the whole overwhelming fact of her own fading youth! But this was an area of romantic feeling, in life and in literature, in which Rahv was not quite at home. He once remarked to me many years earlier, when he was my mentor in things of the world, that "Women are dopes," referring particularly to their choice of men, and having in mind a certain woman who had just then taken up with a younger man whom Rahv judged to be very inferior to himself. He should have remembered that episode, then, and been better prepared for James's heroine.

The two authors who most deeply engaged him, as man and critic, were the Russians Tolstoi and Dostoevski. On the face of it, the choice of these two as his favored writers, the ones on whom he expended his deepest critical energies, was rather a strange one for him, since both Russians hold that human life, without some central religious conviction at its core, is bankrupt. And on the subject of religion Rahv personally maintained throughout the simple-mindedness of the village atheist. Perhaps the bond of his childhood, the memories of Russian as his earliest language, held him emotionally close to them. Or perhaps it was some dim sense, never acknowledged by his conscious mind, that their religious concerns gave them a depth not available to other writers. In any case, Tolstoi—with his overwhelming simplicity and directness—was his ideal of what a writer should be. Though Rahv was a professed champion of modernism (that, after all, was one of the two key points—the avant-garde in literature and art, and Marxism in politics—in the program with which *Partisan Review* had been launched), nevertheless he was really uncomfortable before some of the complex experimentations of the moderns, and he put up with them only as a matter of principle. With Tolstoi, however, he was at home; and his essay on the Russian master, "The Green Twig and the Black Trunk," is the most beautiful piece of writing he did, and to my mind one of the best short introductions to Tolstoi as a writer.

But even in so fine a study one senses ideological limitations of the critic before his subject. Rahv insists on what he calls Tolstoi's rationalism, and this is accurate so far as it applies to that author's direct and literal—sometimes, indeed, literal-minded—approach to things, and to his rejection of the Russian Orthodox Church. But if we are to paste the label of rationalist on Tolstoi, what then are we to make of his *My Confession,* a work which, incidentally, Rahv prized but which, if anything, is a testimony to the inadequacy of reason? This short sketch, part autobiography and part essay, remains one of the most powerful human and philosophical documents of the nineteenth century, and quite central to our understanding of Tolstoi. And what do we get from it if not the picture of Tolstoi like a caged lion, pacing his cell from corner to corner, shut up in the prison his reason implacably builds around him from which it can provide no exit? And he is quite categorical on the means of deliverance: only through the common and ordinary feelings of humankind, not through reason, is it possible for the individual to grasp the meaning of life and experience a bond with the lives of others: "The more we live by intellect, the less we understand the meaning of life." But Rahv's own intellectual program did not assign any important place to feeling. He found his model here in Lenin, who had once said he could not pat the head of a child affectionately because he might give way to feeling and go soft. Rahv did not intend to go soft, and chose to pat no one on the head.

In the case of Dostoevski, the differences between critic and author, in temperament and point of view, are so marked that one can only believe Rahv was held by the fascination of the opposite. He wrote five essays on Dostoevski, more than on any other writer, and at the end of his life was supposed to be putting together a book on the great Russian. In the early essays he is able to contrive some intellectual scheme—the fable of the Grand Inquisitor, for example, is read as an analogue of Stalin's tyranny—that keeps the mind of the ideologue busy while the sensibility of the critic can go to work. Indeed, it is something of a miracle that, given his own intellectual assumptions, he could nevertheless come up with as many penetrating perceptions as he does. But this makeshift procedure does not work so well as he

201

goes on: he misses the central point of *Crime and Punishment*, which is the hero's absolute dissociation of intellect and ordinary feeling (a point on which Rahv personally had made himself blind). And in the final essays the heavy hand of the Marxist ideologue takes over more and more, and Dostoevski's Christian vision of human brotherhood is looked upon as a kind of anticipation of socialism.

The problem which Dostoevski raises here is the old one of the relation between the reader's beliefs and his capacity for appreciation—a question that T. S. Eliot and I. A. Richards used to debate in the case of Dante. One does not need to be a believer in the Russian Orthodox Church to appreciate Dostoevski, but one does need enough sympathy with the religious attitude to enter into his characters at any sufficient depth. It will not do to speak superficially of his "psychological" interest as if he were presenting us with a clinical collection of abnormal cases. The point about his abnormal cases is that each is, in however grotesque and distorted form, an individual soul seeking salvation.

The same problem presents itself in Rahv's fine essay on Kafka. Here again, the critic seems to have gone out of his way to find an author who is a stumbling block to his own Marxist ideology—unless you are willing to come out with the old stupidity that Kafka is merely describing the horror of life under capitalism. Kafka presents the problem of art and neurosis in an acute form, since the neurotic elements are patent and widespread through his work. Rahv attempts to solve the problem by coming up with a neat turn of phrase: Kafka, more than a neurotic artist, succeeds by becoming "the artist of Neurosis." This is a clever ploy, but it leaves unanswered the question of what neuroses are significant in a work of art and what makes them significant. A writer like Iris Murdoch, for example, can lead us through a whole gallery of neurotics; and much as we may admire the intelligence and skill of their author, we reach a point where her characters begin to bore us: we wish they would take their seamy little neurotic tics out into the garden and bury them. We can hardly speak of neuroses in Kafka on that level. Kafka was a man with a strangely dislocated vision and a vast and unappeased spiritual longing, and it is the conjunction of these qualities that gives the nuclear image of his fables their disturbing power. Dostoevski was both a greater writer and a more completely realized man, and therefore more consciously and explicitly in possession of his own religious motif. And that motif is central to his whole work: his characters hunger for a personal salvation that no secular institution or arrangement of society can bring. And unless we as readers can share that longing to some degree in our own imagination, we do not fully respond to him as a writer.

But there is another and more intimate aspect of Rahv's relationship to Dostoevski that provokes my curiosity. When one has immersed oneself in a writer very long, one sometimes has the uncanny feeling that he as writer is gazing back at you as reader, and this is particularly so with a vision as penetrating and disquieting as Dostoevski's. Poor Delmore Schwartz, for example, who was constantly reading some part or other of *The Brothers Karamazov*, always felt the eye of Dostoevski upon him. Sometimes he would read aloud, with quivering voice, certain passages that expressed his own unsatisfied religious longings; at other times, stung by remembrance of some outrageous behavior of his own, he would shout out with Dostoevski, "What a scoundrel I am!" Did Philip Rahv ever feel that Dostoevskian gaze staring back at him, through the defenses of his critical mind into the depths of his soul? And what would it have found? I think it would have discovered the Nihilist lurking there.

For Rahv was a Nihilist, perhaps the most outspoken in his own peculiar fashion that I have ever known. He had an abysmally low view of people and their motives, and usually found their alleged ideals bogus or unconvincing. He was, however, a Nihilist who could enjoy himself, for he was not insensitive to pleasures. He relished his own creature comforts immensely; and when he was in a good mood, he could exude joviality. But of the deeper satisfactions of life, or what ordinary people take such satisfactions to be, he had found none that he trusted. "People talk so much about love," he snorted at me once. "There is either Christian love or sexual love. Do they mean Christian love? Who's capable of that? And sexual love? That only brings more tensions and anxiety."

These nihilistic diatribes did not get into his writing; there he was taken over by his *persona*, the public role of judicious critic that was his to fulfill. But in his private conversations he let the destructive impulse reign free and unchecked. *Schadenfreude* was one of his favorite words, and he delighted to spot this joy of destruction as it masqueraded in others; but he had a more than generous dose of it himself, as we have already witnessed in the scene of "the confrontation."

The satisfactions in life that meant most to Rahv, I believe, were those of the ego: of fame, rank, prestige. All is vanity, says the nihilist, except my own vanity. But Rahv could find no solace even there, for he knew more than most how slippery and elusive a thing reputation was in the literary marketplace, where the caprice of critics and of fashion reigns.

These dark outpourings were not confined to his black moods, frequent enough in any case, but were the regular run of his conversation even when he seemed cheerful. One occasion comes back sharply to mind, because there was a hearer present less inured to the ways of his pessimism and therefore more sensitive to its utter bleakness; and also because something Rahv said at one moment was to turn out prophetic of the last act of his life that was to mystify friends and foes alike. My wife and I were sitting on a bench in Washington Square, relaxing in the sunshine of a lovely spring day, when Rahv happened by and joined us. He seemed to be in a good mood, visibly enjoying the weather, and very soon in his own forceful way had taken over the conversation. But as he launched himself on the full tide of his eloquence, he struck his usual vein and before long was wreaking a trail of destruction about him right and left. His particular theme this time was the tepidness and lack of conviction in the whole American scene. And suddenly he shot out, with a different and more yearning voice, "I wish I were in Israel. At least, people there believe in something."

This was in the late 1940s, when Israel was struggling for statehood, and the heroism of that struggle had evidently touched some deeper and less cynical part of his being. Presently, having exhausted his topics of lamentation, and perhaps his hearers too, Rahv cheerfully said good-bye and left. My wife, who had seen him only on more formal social occasions and was unprepared for this destructiveness of his casual talk, looked aghast: "He leaves the whole world black after him," as if he had suddenly banished the brightness of the spring day. She shuddered: "How does he live with himself?"

How does he live with himself? Well, he was young, just pushing forty at the time, with enough exuberance and energy to feed his conflicts, and with enough that was going on in the literary scene, however he might sneer at it, to keep mind and hand busy. But her question—how does he live with himself?—kept coming back to me when I tried to imagine him in his later years at Brandeis, where he had gone to teach toward the end of the fifties, alone, visibly aging, and—according to my informants—more somber than ever. His wife had perished in a frightful accident. He remarried, but the marriage was unhappy and very short-lived; and he was left in a loneliness beyond any he had ever known before. How did he live with himself? Given his views of human beings and human life, what solace could he find against loneliness and encroaching death?

I think it is not hard to find an answer to these questions. He did have something to interpose between himself and the void: a simple-minded, complete, and sustaining faith—his Marxism—which had never left him and into which he could now relapse completely. That containing framework was with him in his first reviews in the *New Masses* in the early 1930s, continued unchanged though pushed into the background during the 1940s and 1950s, and then jumped very decidedly into the foreground again in the 1960s. During those intervening years he performed a prodigious labor of self-education, polishing and sharpening his literary perceptions, but he never turned these critical energies of mind upon the dogma of his own Marxism. That would remain as it had always been: a simple and comprehensive explanation of the world, above all *unquestioned*, so that it could have the redeeming stability of religious faith. It even permitted him to be saved such as he was, to put it in the old Quaker fashion: for he could be redeemed and still continue as the person he was, railing in his atrabilious humor at the evils of this world because he had faith in a better one to come.

III.

We come back thus to the political motif again, and in him indeed the personal and the political were never altogether separated. And perhaps they should not and cannot be. What we think human beings are like, what we imagine their moral capacities to be, are surely not questions irrelevant to the kind of social order we would devise for them; and political philosophers from Aristotle to James Madison have insisted on the initial consideration of human nature as a central concern for social theory. The paradox in Rahv was that he had the lowest possible view, indeed a kind of Swiftian pessimism, about human beings, together with a utopian faith in socialism. How do you put the two together? How can they be put together? How can a nihilism about human life be joined with a utopian politics?

The simplicity of his Marxist faith would say that people were bad because society had made them bad: they were petty, mean, and vicious because they lived under a capitalist order. I doubt that Rahv ever swallowed this fairy tale. In all his dissections of the human personalities we knew he never alleged capitalism as an excuse for their failings—he was not so kind to his targets as that. Nevertheless, however come by, these failings seemed to vanish from his perspectives on a socialist regime. Socialism would change human nature, and people would become or be made to become virtuous. But surely such a profound transformation could not come overnight; and during that interregnum between human corruption and its socialist redemption, what would prevent the corrupt elements from taking over the new order and even continuing permanently in the saddle? This problem becomes all the more apposite if we consider, among the more questionable aspects of our questionable human nature, the fierceness of the power drive that can take possession of people whenever given the chance. But on the problem of power Rahv thought only in fits and starts, sometimes in intense spasms, but he never put his thoughts consistently together.

Thus he was much taken by George Orwell's *1984* when it first appeared in the late 1940s, and particularly by the bitter and startling words Orwell put into the mouth of the police chief, O'Brien: *"Power is not a means; it is an end . . . The object of persecution is persecution. The object of torture is torture. The object of power is power."* As Rahv never wrote from the top of his head, so he never read in that fashion either; if a book took hold of him, he carried it explosively and oratorically into his conversation. The effect could be contagious and engaging, though sometimes a little deafening. He read or recited O'Brien's speech at me several times, and then added grimly: "That's the real truth about power, but people don't want to admit it." There was even a certain satisfaction in his tone, as if here for a moment mendacious human nature had let the mask fall and admitted the truth about itself.

But if this be the truth about human nature, then it is very bad news indeed for socialism. The socialist arrangement of society requires at the least an extraordinary concentration of power simply that government may take over the whole of the economy. And given the drive to power for power's sake, what under this setup can keep the impulse to power from running amok? Rahv had never pondered Madison on this point: that a chief aim of government, besides securing what powers it needs in order to operate, is to limit those powers as a safeguard against the possible usurpation of power. It is interesting to notice, by the way, that Madison based his view here on his own pessimism about human nature: "If men were angels, government (viz., with its limitations upon power) would be unnecessary." The best bulwark against the fearful lust for power in some individuals is to maintain plural and competing centers of power, which are hardly possible when the economic and political sectors are under a unified command. But Rahv remained innocent of such theoretical questions, as he remained innocent of political theory generally; indeed, he chose to remain innocent.

"Genius," Nietzsche once remarked, "is a will to stupidity"; and on this feature alone Rahv would certainly qualify. Nietzsche had in view a certain type of mind so intent on its own purposes that it closes the doors on any influence that might deflect it from those purposes. It is understandable that Rahv should never glance at classical political thought—that, after all, belonged to the "bourgeois" world—but it is surprising that he never delved much into Marxist theorizing either. Most of us at one time or another had taken a crack at Marx's *Capital*, and some of us even managed to stumble through that heavy tome, seeking scientific underpinnings for our conviction. But Rahv never turned his mind that way; the simplest formulations were enough to satisfy and hold him fast in his faith. The power of his mind was toward a certain concreteness, and he had not only an ineptness but a positive antipathy for abstract ideas as such. When, for example, his exploration of the Russian writers drew him toward Existentialism, he deliberately sought me out for some conversations on the subject, but I would notice that past a certain point of abstractness his mind would immediately turn off. And he was right in this—right for his own purposes. He had his own antecedent perceptions, and he wanted simply to gather whatever might give them further resonance and depth. But this habit of mind that worked well in his literary criticism did not succeed so well in the area of political philosophy, where the turning away from theoretical issues and qualifications made his thought not more concrete but schematic and abstract.

Yet beneath the crustiness of advancing age, and the doctrinaire rigidity that had set in, something still remained of his literary tact. Toward the end of his life, as the ferment of the sixties was heating up, he wrote a review of T. S. Eliot's *Posthumous Essays*. In view of Rahv's mood in this later period I expected his review to be a programmatic manhandling of its subject: Eliot would come out as a religious reactionary who cultivated an overly precious sense of literary tradition. Instead, the review turns out to be appreciative, finely perceptive, and gracious too. Rahv, despite other forces pulling on him at this period, was still too intelligent not to recognize in Eliot the supreme literary intelligence of the century. He even excuses Eliot for his religious views: "His commitment to orthodox beliefs must have answered an irresistible inner demand of his nature for a discipline to shore him up against chaos . . . In this sense it was no more than anodyne, yet we who have not suffered his pains are seldom in a position to reproach him."

But why limit such charitable tolerance to Eliot? We may not suffer his pains, but we have our own; and for each one of us our own individual pains outweigh anyone else's. So that by this same line of reasoning the right to believe should not be confined aristocratically to the great poet and critic but extended democratically to every man— and we would end thus with a much more reasonable and tolerant view of religion than Rahv was ever intellectually willing to concede. And in such a charitable mood, which he himself advances, we may very well now include Philip Rahv himself. We can humanly and charitably sympathize with the desperation, the struggle against chaos, which led him in advancing age to clutch his Marxist gods more fiercely and rigidly than ever, even if we cannot quite condone his choice of those particular gods, since they are the ones that the present generation will have to do battle with.

And something else, something more human than literary, seemed to have remained for him. As a final act, in his will he left his money to the state of Israel. As a last touch to round off his life, this gesture has puzzled many. For myself, I see it against that afternoon years ago in Washington Square, when in the midst of our conversation he suddenly spoke about Israel, and another voice, more youthful and yearning, sounded through all the cynical postures of the ideologue. I like to think that voice was still there, and at the end it broke through again.

208

Chapter Nine

The Destruction of
a Poet

I.

"We were never more free than under the Occupation." These are the words of Jean-Paul Sartre describing the situation of his generation after the defeat of France in 1940. Cut off for the historical moment from so many of what had been the usual channels of life, and under the perpetual eye of the occupying Germans, the young people were thrown back upon their own resources. Amid the dislocation of normal life, they had to search for themselves. In a sense, they were compelled to be free.

Change the last word in Sartre's statement to "Depression," and you have the truth of the 1930s—at least for some of us. Without jobs and without prospects, the young were not chained immediately to the wheel of career and profession. We could abandon ourselves to the delight of irrelevant studies. Columbia University was then a congregation of odd souls. From behind the woodwork; from drains, cesspools, and middens they crept across 113th Street into halls, libraries, classrooms; and then were sucked slowly back into the subway or the adjacent cafeterias. The coffers of the university were hardly swollen by their presence, for many simply sat in and paid no tuition. A park bench or the halls of learning—they were equally a Depression refuge. Why should you pay more for the one than the other?

If the "American Encounter with Marxism" is ever written up properly, it will have to take account of this peculiar relaxation and bonhomie of the thirties. The economy of the country was in a shambles, and by all Marxist laws we should have been in the throes of a genuinely revolutionary situation. Actually, in the camaraderie of poverty the stigma itself of being poor was lost, and the country was swept into a new feeling of social unity: the spirit of bank holiday and moral holiday, in which one was blessedly released for a time from keeping up with the Joneses. Those who are young can catch a glimpse of it in some of the old thirties movies. The same feeling carried on into the war. The war movies—to ring one more variation on Clausewitz—were simply an extension of the thirties movies by other means. Change the guns and uniforms and you had the same actors, types, and plots, the same populist optimism and good will, the same confidence that right and wrong were always clearly discernible and that the right stood by our side. It was our Marxist decade; yet the irony was that its experience of Marxism was of something remote and distant—either intellectually in the intricacies of theory that didn't mesh with our actual life, or romantically remote in the deeds of socialist heroes in far-off lands. Of course, none of this ever occurred to us then while we were passionately arguing Marxist theory.

Thirty years later the same campus was being torn apart during the violence of the 1960s. The children of middle-class affluence, mouthing Marxist slogans, were demanding "relevant" studies. And the economy? The country was then enjoying an economic prosperity beyond the wildest dreams of our earlier decade. You are puzzled, comrades? It's just the Dialectic—as we used to say back in the 1930s.

I didn't meet Delmore Schwartz at Columbia, but I remember him against that background because if it hadn't been for one of the absurdities of campus life I mightn't have known him at all. Among the varied ranks of the drifters whose actual connection with the university was never discovered, there was a young lady who was going around trying to do what seemed a very unlikely thing at the time—to assemble a salon. Her family had a large and sumptuous apartment—which gave her something of a head start for collecting young intellectuals—in that part of the West Side we then called the Golden Ghetto. She had invited me a few times, but I'd never got around to going. This time her invitation was more insistent. It seems there was a young man coming up from downtown and he and I were simply made to know each other. The word "spiritual" was foreign to our vocabularies in those days, but I think now that such was the nature of the bond she was trying to suggest might come to be between myself and this unknown youth. It didn't sound too appetizing, but the promise of refreshments did—in those days one couldn't turn down that kind of invitation casually. The name "Delmore Schwartz" meant nothing, and in fact sounded a little precious. I imagined another lugubrious bookworm like myself, and was scarcely prepared for the bundle of electricity I did meet.

Dwight Macdonald and Philip Rahv, both of whom knew him well, have given us very different portraits of Delmore, and their difference illustrates some of the subtler difficulties in writing history. For Macdonald, Delmore emerges as kind of hypermanic borscht-circuit comedian, for Rahv as a driveling neurotic droning on montonously about his family traumas to a point where one feels only Rahv's great critical dignity restrains him from expressing open contempt. I don't want to quarrel with either picture. And I certainly wouldn't want to quarrel with Dwight Macdonald's motives, which are those of great affection and generosity. But I suspect his image of Delmore is overshadowed by the later years when the need to play the buffoon became more desperate and the comic performance more raucous and high-strung. As for Philip Rahv's motives, they may now be left between him and his Maker; and if he is only a shade of the man he once was, he can be depended upon to give a good account of himself. But neither picture, Dwight's nor Philip's, catches the Delmore I met that first night.

For one thing, there was the quieter Delmore, exquisitely attentive to the person he met, civil almost to the point of diffidence. He was then quite thin, with an ivory pallor, odd-looking but very attractive. (We're talking about the year 1933–34; I date by the academic system from September to the following June but can't remember the particular month of our meeting.) But of course this was a party, and Delmore couldn't stay bottled up forever. When the eruption came, however, it had nothing of the performance about it. There was something very boyish and absolutely spontaneous in the way he got caught up in the excitement of a situation. There would then come that curious hop, as if he couldn't stand still with glee, his arms flapping against his sides like a chicken's wings. He was awkward but very agile. In a later poem he caricatured his body as "the heavy bear that moves with me." There was nothing bearlike or cumbersome in his movements then. The imitation of Chaplin, for example, which as a standard party piece is usually a bore, was hilarious in Delmore's case, with all its odd, eccentric, and yet agile flutterings altogether inimitable by anyone else—unless perhaps Chaplin the master had seen it and wanted thereafter to graft new variations on his original.

We hardly knew each other before Delmore was beginning to build some anecdote or other about me. It was a habit of his I was to enjoy during all the time I knew him, and to watch him practice on other people, on anybody he liked, in fact. The anecdote might make you a bit ridiculous, but in an endearing way. It singled you out as a special and unique person, somebody whose value was only enhanced by this or that harmless and slightly comic eccentricity. He was quite ingenious at it, but the impulse itself was altogether spontaneous. It was his way of building a world of affection around you and himself. He had a great need for affection, both to give and receive, except that—well, this "except," this deep-seated force, whatever it was, that made him ultimately destructive and suspicious of affection, both given and received, is more or less the burden of my story here.

That evening he was escorting Gertrude Buckman, his high school sweetheart whom he was later to marry. She was very pretty and altogether charming, and I promptly fell in love with each of them, and with both as a couple. It was just as well, for my company was to be inflicted upon them a good deal in the years to come.

The friendship must have formed fast, because by the following summer Delmore and I were eating dinner nearly every evening. I had a temporary job, as a social worker, while still studying at Columbia, and had sublet a flat on West Twenty-third Street; Delmore was finishing his college credits at a summer session at NYU, and had a furnished room farther south in the direction of Washington Square. We met at the Foltis-Fisher cafeteria (the chain is long since deceased) on Twenty-third Street, where I invariably ate the forty-cent dinner.

This dinner stands out in my memory as one of the lesser aesthetic triumphs of the Depression years, an austere anticipation of minimal art. Almost musically conceived, it was built along the lines of a progression from liquid to solid. It began with soup, nameless and unnameable, the source of which in flesh, fish, or vegetable was undetectable; passed on to become stew, which had a thickening of flour and here and there a nodding acquaintance with small shreds of meat; and arrived finally at the quivering but unmistakable solidity of Jello. This chaste progression was flanked on both sides by the chords *diminuendo* of bread and cole slaw, the latter watery and limp in order to preserve the liquid-solid theme. So far as I can remember, the forty-five-cent dinner differed only by the substitution of rolls for bread. But the rolls, of the kind called hard rolls, really lived up to their name and seemed to have been baked in express violation of the biblical warning, "Who of you, if asked for bread, would give me a stone?"

I didn't see a nickel's worth of difference between the two dinners, and we kidded together about this. In later years Delmore transformed the story into a parable of the Depression decade: I was cast in the solemn role of the stern friend warning him against his prodigal ways in spending forty-five cents on dinner.*

It may have been because we ate together so often that eating became the theme of a lot of his anecdotes about me, usually blown up to Gargantuan proportions. I had acquired through necessity the happy talent then, which I sometimes wish I could reacquire now, of being able to disregard my hunger for very long stretches at a time. Consequently when food was put before me, it disappeared. But these anecdotes also belong very much to the period—jokes about eating were part of the camaraderie of hunger in the Depression. Some years later, for example, Delmore had worked up similar anecdotes about Oscar Handlin, the historian, whom he had come to know at Harvard. And once in a Boston restaurant Delmore affected to pit Oscar and me in an eating match, borrowing the tones of a boxing announcer: "The famine of the Ukraine against the potato famine of Ireland."

What did we talk about over those cafeteria meals? Delmore was

---

* Memory suddenly stirs: the forty-five-cent dinner did offer something more—the choice of rice pudding instead of Jello.

studying with Sidney Hook, and I heard a good deal of what was going on in class. Hook, then a young professor, was an incomparable teacher in those days, at least according to Delmore's report; Delmore was extremely critical in these matters, and as it also happened not at all a passive follower of Hook's philosophy. In fact, he rather worried Hook, who had a kindly and paternal regard for him, because he seemed to be flirting with neo-Thomism and Catholicism. There wasn't any real danger in this direction, however. Delmore was simply a devoted reader of T. S. Eliot's *Criterion,* in which at the time Eliot was making friendly nods in the direction of the Catholic philosophers Maritain and Gilson, and some of Eliot's rhetoric had rubbed off on him. Besides, Delmore loved to play the stormy petrel in class and surprise Hook with his sudden and paradoxical sallies.

What was real, beneath Delmore's rhetorical flourishes, was that he was drawn inescapably to the religious position—one has to put it that vaguely. I think this was one of the bonds between us. At best, it has to be put negatively: neither of us seemed to be able to feel ultimately satisfied with a purely naturalistic view of the world. Delmore was much more vocal about these hankerings than I, and more vocal as the years went by. That my background was different from his also attracted him: he used to milk me for my memories of Catholicism, for they helped him with Dante and Joyce. At the same time he used to tease me about my Celtic background: "When your ancestors were painting themselves blue, mine were already people of the Book." And I used to tease back that in that case it was a pity he didn't know more of the Book. In retrospect, these jokes do not seem to me so funny now. Of the Jews who have been my friends, I think Delmore had the least grasp of his own Jewishness—he knew neither how far out nor how deep in he was committed. And yet, perhaps for this reason, he was the most haunted by it, and more haunted as the years went by until it became anguish, and finally a distorted and paranoid anguish.

At the same time we were Marxists—naturally. In our environment then it was taken as a matter of course that any young man of reasonable intelligence and good will would be Marxist. What this might mean for our religious hankerings, or our views on literature, art, and a good many other things, didn't trouble us too much. I don't think we two were particularly flippant intellectually; in fact, we were probably more serious about ideas than most of the people around us. It was simply that "good will" was a basic motive in the American encounter with Marxism; and the more this "good will" prevailed the less strict could be the doctrine one took from Marx. Among the most distinguished intellectual interpretations of Marxism to come out of that period were the two books on Marx by Sidney Hook, and Edmund Wilson's *To the Finland Station*. Hook assimilates Marxism to the philosophy of American pragmatism, and in spirit transforms it into a more militant form of the American progressivism of the earlier part of the century. As for Wilson, it is perfectly in the spirit of those times that he should have conceived and written his work as a lovely historical romance—a romance because it was all so far away from the actual American situation. And when years later, disillusioned with Marxism, he appended a postscript, he quite typically found the residual virtues of the whole movement to be thoroughly American in spirit: a protest against class privilege and a plea for an egalitarian society—ideals which any Jacksonian, untouched by the least tinge of Marxist doctrine, could embrace enthusiastically.

I'm not in the least trying to disparage the Marxism of our generation. On the contrary, it was an important chapter in our national and intellectual history. But if we're to understand Marxism as it is operant in the world today, we shall have to start with very, very different premises from those of that earlier period.

The rich are very different from you and me, said Scott Fitzgerald. Delmore was different because he expected to be rich. The riches did not materialize, but the expectation of them gave him different horizons and hopes from the rest of us. We might enjoy the long intervals of joblessness, but somewhere in the back of our minds after all this blissful truancy was something like becoming a high school teacher, which in fact was rather a coveted job during the Depression. As for teaching in a college, that was something to which we dare not aspire. Delmore could think of forging right ahead doing just what he wanted, which was to write poetry. Paul Goodman also had different horizons, for he had a sister, Alice. Bernard Shaw once remarked that he did not throw himself into the struggle of life, he threw his mother. Paul threw his sister, and Alice Goodman proved to be more reliable than Delmore's inheritance. Delmore's father had been a buccaneer in real estate who made his million promoting and juggling developments, and he was supposed to have left a considerable estate. But when he was no longer there to juggle, all the spinning plates he had kept aloft came crashing down. The estate turned into a lot of paper. Delmore had to make several trips to Chicago about it, but he never could make clear to me, and I doubt whether he himself grasped, the intricate details of his father's paper empire in Gary, Indiana. In any case, the copious flow of money that had been expected dwindled into a mere trickle for Delmore, his mother, and his brother. Still, he had been marked by princely hopes, and I don't think they ever quite left him.

This decline in fortunes brought with it some family migrations—a succession of apartments ending in a very modest one in Washington Heights; and Delmore came to live more often at home. When he felt desperate about working, he would move to a furnished room. When money was running low, he would return home. I helped him move on several occasions, and one in particular has a point in this narrative.

He couldn't sleep in his furnished room because there was too much noise around. After a few days he looked absolutely worn out. He would have to move again. After hunting through the ads, we wound up dragging ourselves along some street in Chelsea. When Delmore moved, he had to have typewriter and books, lots of books, and books are heavy. We collapsed in exhaustion on the stoop of a house that advertised rooms. An old woman, poking at the garbage cans behind the iron fence, looked at us suspiciously. At that moment we must have seemed an odd and bedraggled pair. She was the landlady, it turned out, and an altogether remarkable blend of Jewish *yenta* and French *concierge*. In his fatigue Delmore seemed to slip back a generation, and he and the woman might have been haggling across a pushcart. She wanted to know why he had left his last place, he wanted to know if it was quiet here. "Sure it's quiet here," she said. "What do you want, a tomb?" Delmore told her he had trouble sleeping. Not a wise thing to say, for a sleepless man is a threat to all landladies. "Why can't you sleep?" she asked. Delmore would have given thousands then and in the years after to answer that question. "Look at your friend," she went on, pointing her finger almost in my face.

"He has his troubles too," Delmore interjected in my favor.

"Yeah, but he looks like he sleeps. And look at you—" Delmore did look ghastly, his face almost yellow-green with fatigue. They went on that way for quite a while, the woman implying she wouldn't rent to anybody like him, Delmore staying on the step and saying it wasn't even worth his while to go up and have a look at the room. He ended by taking it. Neither of us could have staggered on much further under the burden of his chattels if he hadn't accepted. But a week later he was out of it. "That woman wouldn't stop talking," he said.

He hadn't then discovered barbiturates and alcohol to help him with his problem. Insomnia hit him early in his life and brutally. Now he fought it bare-handed and toe-to-toe. But it's never a winning battle that way. And even gentle tippling piles up dangerously in the end. The only thing is to give in, let the beast work its havoc even if it casts its blight over the energy and pleasure of the next day. Hope that in the course of nature the rhythm of sleep will come back again. And if it doesn't? But Delmore couldn't be patient; he had to force himself into the next day's efforts, even if exhausted and stupefied from last night's battle. When he later took to sleeping tablets and liquor it wasn't for kicks, but out of grim need. He had tremendous reserves of sheer physical strength. "You're as strong as a horse," William Phillips used to kid him. But in the long run that strength couldn't hold up against the toll that sleeplessness, and worse still, its remedies, took from him.

I'd known him almost two years now and I didn't know whether or not he was talented, for I'd seen nothing of his writing. Would it have made a difference between us if he weren't talented? Our friendship had already been completely formed; yet somehow I always believed, without seeing any direct evidence, that he would be talented. Delmore's disclosure of it to me was in his usual abrupt style of doing things. I was to call on him; but unfortunately I had just quarreled with my girl and the quarrel was still rankling when I arrived. Delmore, however, was exuberant. He had just typed out the first copy of a story and he thrust it immediately into my hands. I tried to beg off until I was in a better mood to read it fairly; but he was like a child who has presented you a gift and is crushed if you do not unwrap it.

The story was "In Dreams Begin Responsibilities." I was in no mood to read anything, but for this particular jolt I was totally unprepared. The friends of youth thrust manuscripts upon one often enough, God knows, and here and there one would encouragingly find glimmerings of talent amid much stumbling and awkwardness. But here was something completely formed and wonderfully perfect. None of us had been brought up with any manners to speak of, or I might have had the poise to find some pat words to carry me over my present ill-humor. That would have seemed gush to us; we were supposed to deliver judgments that pretended to be careful and precise. Whatever halting words came out of me must have sounded grudging and churlish—which was in fact my mood—and I could see Delmore's face fall. It took me a long time afterward to explain my lack of response and reassure him totally about the story.

He was then just twenty-two, and he would never write so good a story again. It's just as well we live without foresight in some matters. The discovery of his talent didn't alter our friendship, but did add something new to it. Genuine talent is so rare a thing that one has to shield it. Henceforth, from time to time, I would have to try to play the protective mother hen, though my efforts must have been clumsy and were sometimes grumblingly received.

Delmore went off to Harvard to do graduate study in philosophy. I went out to Chicago in 1936 on some sort of fellowship, along with Paul Goodman. On vacations and during summers we were together again after our various cross-country movements.

Delmore Schwartz and Paul Goodman were to have a peculiar and violently terminated friendship. I introduced them. Since they were virtually neighbors in Washington Heights, at least whenever Delmore was at home, I brought him up one afternoon to Paul's apartment. Delmore was his usual polite and attentive self when he was meeting someone new. Paul had been having bad luck getting published, but he had a great unpublished reputation among us that I'd told Delmore about, and naturally the latter's appetite was whetted. Delmore showed the deference one might accord a *cher maître* with an acknowledged *oeuvre* behind him. They hit it off on their first meeting, but they were too oddly assorted a pair to remain friends.

Owl-eyed and baby-faced, Paul Goodman seemed to have slid into life out of some corner of a Chagall painting. Dressed in black, with side-curls, he could have walked on stage as the young Talmudist, forever precocious and forever *boychik*. He could be lots of fun, though, and in our first year at Chicago I saw very much of him. Paul was also the most abstract, in the sense of detached, person I ever knew. He could discuss his friends with quiet and devastating remoteness. It wasn't malice necessarily, but simply the Talmudist building ingenious and fanciful commentary. Once he began on Delmore, but promptly cut himself short, sensing I wasn't taking it very well. Delmore had his reservations about Paul, but for different reasons. I think he didn't quite grasp where his relationship with Goodman stood. It was difficult to know if one was at any time really close to Paul Goodman.

Paul had gathered a curious little circle around himself in the apartment he and his sister shared in Washington Heights. Delmore has described it unflatteringly in "The World Is a Wedding," which seems to me a dull story unless you happen to know the people. Or perhaps I find it dull because I knew the people. In any case, I was with Delmore once when the circle was in full session, and he was obviously a fish out of water. When aroused, he was direct and stormy; the style the group had elaborated for itself was understatement, playing it cool. They would have talked from the side of their mouths had that facial gesture not been too tough-guy and heterosexual. Delmore was deadly serious about literature and his own efforts to write; Paul and his friends affected to be serious about nothing. It was one of the defense mechanisms the Depression had triggered—take everything as a laugh.

Paul brought out a batch of poems for Delmore, who promptly buried his face in the sheets, while the party chatter went on all around him. He had often wondered about the eccentricity of Paul's verse, but he chose this foolhardy moment to try to unravel its mystery. Had Paul perhaps been influenced here by Auden? There by the deliberately crabbed effects Allen Tate sometimes sought? Or was the deliberate prosiness at this point an echo of William Carlos Williams? Etc. etc. Delmore's tone was very polite and modest, as of a learner seeking the key to a craft that eluded his ear.

Paul took the questioning very solemnly at first. The fact was that he didn't study contemporary poets particularly, whereas Delmore followed them as intently as a stockbroker watching the ups and downs of the market. The questions really were silly in view of Paul's way of writing his poems. On buses, trains, at indifferent moments in a lecture, he brought out the stubby pencil, lifted the small wad of paper from his pocket, and went on from the last line where he had left off. He didn't so much compose poems as squirt them. Imagine a tube of tooth paste with numerous cuts along the sides; you press and it squirts out in all directions in squiggles, whorls, dribbles. So Paul's poems jetted out, innocent of any metrical calculation, left to their

219

own devices somehow to wriggle through the aural canal into the inner ear.

During Delmore's scholarly inquisition the conversation elsewhere had broken off, the group staring in amazement at anyone so deadly serious about anything. At length, Paul, more owl-eyed than ever, began to titter. The titter spread and they were all laughing. Delmore flushed, but held his temper. Later, though, walking away, he was fuming. He couldn't stand the idea of being laughed at. One of his poems later was to begin, "Do they whisper behind my back?" and goes on: "Do they laugh at me, /Mimicking my gestures?" The poem might have been conceived that night. Ironically enough, in his later decline Delmore was to throw himself more and more into the role of the ridiculous public clown.

But his break with Goodman came not over the norms of poetry but of sexuality.

The Goodman circle divided the world into three types: (1) "heteraceteras" (heterosexuals); (2) the "ambidextrous" (bisexuals); and (3) strange that they had no special word for the two serious and *engagés* homosexuals in their midst whose commitment to their special tastes altered their whole way of life. Your option between these three possibilities was left open, for this was a tolerant circle. But the second represented the *juste moyen* between two unnecessary extremes—the abysmal normality of the first, and the dangerous commitment of the third. They were advance scouts in the Asexual Revolution that has now overtaken us.

What triggered the final quarrel I didn't hear from Delmore, and of course not from Paul; but I happened in on the *coup de grâce*. I dropped in on Delmore one evening just after he had come back from mailing a letter to Paul, a copy of which he insisted on reading to me. It was short and brutal, and concluded with something like: "No doubt, you will go on as you have been doing, corrupting young boys and turning them into fags like yourself." Delmore was shaking as if he had just come through an actual scene of violence. He read the letter to me partly to relieve the guilt which always followed his violent acts. But he also felt that he had written out of principle. It wasn't Gay Liberation he was objecting to but Gay Imperialism.

So Paul Goodman passed out of our life into the long travail of the neglected writer, while Delmore was just about to be launched into the blazing orbit of a career. (Goodman was suddenly, if belatedly, to leap into fame at the end of the 1960s, when he became a guru for the liberated youth of that decade, at a time when Delmore's star had definitely set. In their rise and fall, the paths of the two seemed always to cross.) Delmore left Harvard without taking his degree because he was now a young man in a hurry: he was bursting with *the* book he had to get out so that he could then marry *the* girl. And in the success-story manner of the movies then, this chapter of his life might carry the tag: boy publishes book, boy marries girl.

Appropriately enough, the first story he'd shown me was the first step in his launching. It appeared as the lead piece in the first issue of *Partisan Review* in the fall of 1937, taking precedence over contributors like Wallace Stevens, Edmund Wilson, Lionel Trilling, James Agee. To have arrived in such select company was something, but to be at the head of the list was really to have made it. How to describe our dazzlement on that occasion! For a moment all the jaded pages I have written here from my later experience on the inside fade away and I see the first issue of the magazine with the eyes of excitement and youth that were then ours. Amid the stale and heavy atmosphere of the pious Communism and Stalinized Liberalism of the time, here suddenly was a breath of fresh air—a young and lively voice that quickened all our radical sensibilities again. It would deal with literature and art according to their own high and exacting standards, and yet politically would speak from the Left, but a Left that was purged of the distortions of Orthodox Communism. In our good will, our wish for the best of both worlds, we wanted to believe that Marxism—the true Marxism, that is—was thoroughly compatible with the modern literature and art we loved. Compatible? No, more: implied it. For wasn't it perfectly logical that to be radical in politics also implied that one must be radical in art too? We were young and had a strong will to believe.

Delmore thus seemed to have arrived with the right people. He had been received into the circle of the editors and their immediate friends: he liked them, and found them interesting and exciting. He was no longer the lonely young writer adrift in New York; he was now connected with a group, and the right group for him personally. He was pleased when Philip Rahv especially began to court him at this time. I remember clearly the first time an invitation to lunch arrived. I was with Delmore before he went off to the restaurant, and began to fuss over his appearance. I didn't know Rahv at all, but the title "Editor" rang formidable echoes in my mind: I imagined some impeccable type gazing across the luncheon table at Delmore's casually assembled clothes. When he got back, Delmore was a little nettled at me: "You and your fussing! You should have seen Philip Rahv—" I waited for him to find the words: "He looked like the Paris Commune."

This image of Philip Rahv must remain forever elusive to me. When I knew him later, he had long been reading Henry James and acquired enough polish in the process to have faced down any Chairman of the Board. Yet now and then perhaps, even when Philip was being most suave and magisterial, I fancied I caught a gleam of what Delmore must have meant by "the Paris Commune"—a touch of the unredeemed and renegade roughneck that would never quite leave him. He would have been less charming without that touch.

Delmore and Gertrude were married the following June in a little synagogue in Washington Heights. In a movie this ought to have been the fade-out, and I am sorry that in the actual course of events it should have turned out an anticlimax. There were enough touches of a 1930s movie about the ceremony to have satisfied any director of the time: a memento of New York as a city of neighborhoods, the celebration of neighborhood pieties and sentimentalities by all the assembled relatives with their small bickering and contented clucking. I was the only non-family present: the single outlander from another neighborhood, the Irish friend from Queens—not exactly Jimmy Cagney, alas, but perhaps rating a Frank McHugh for casting. A vanished world, and I see it all now as a single still from an imaginary movie of the time.

It was Delmore himself who dissolved this fade-out by a telegram a few days later asking me to come up to Vermont, where they were honeymooning. On the way up I expected some dreadful clash or marital hysteria must have arisen; but none was visible when I arrived, and Delmore never gave any reason for this sudden summons. Probably he was just lonely in the country, and he was more used to having me instead of Gertrude at his side to dispel his loneliness. Still, it wasn't a good omen for the marriage—and so in fact it later turned out.

Delmore's book was now out and had been enthusiastically received. He had acclaim, and from the people whose judgment he valued. In some cases it was extraordinary acclaim: Allen Tate wrote that

Delmore's was the "only genuine innovation we've had since Pound and Eliot came upon the scene twenty-five years ago." There was even a letter from T. S. Eliot, which he handled like a sacred relic, reading it to me, not letting me touch it, but showing me the signature as if to guarantee its authenticity. He had honors and awards—two Guggenheim Fellowships, and a position at Harvard forthcoming. He had made it, at an early age; and he was on his way, as we imagined, only to something greater.

Yet in the summer of 1939, when I had booked a passage for Europe, he pleaded with me not to go just then. Why at the moment when he was riding high did he feel this need to bind me closer to himself than ever? Did he have some premonitory fear that he might topple from this high perch on which he had been placed? Success had come upon him in such a sudden burst that he still felt insecure with it, as if another puff of fortune might blow it away. It was a tough decision for me to make. Europe had always been at the center of our thought, but actually going there had seemed an impossible dream to the youth of the Depression. People did not hop so easily then between the two continents. I had managed to save up enough from my meager instructor's salary for a modest trip, but just to be there at all was the marvelous thing. But Delmore's plea to remain with him was very strong, and I wavered between loyalty to my friend and the strong desire to see Europe now while it was still there to be seen. Then he played his trump: "If you wait till next year, we can go together," and I stayed with him. There was to be no next year, of course; Hitler took care of that. When I finally did get there later it was amid the ravages of war and under the auspices of the U.S. Government. Delmore was to die without ever seeing the Europe that had once been his obsession.

We had grown up in the shadow of approaching war. Some of us had lived with the conviction that it would come in one form or another from the moment we first heard Hitler ranting over the radio. And after 1940, after the fall of France and the British retreat at Dunkirk, most of the young men I knew were also convinced that America sooner or later would be in the war. The arguments for isolationism might rage throughout the country, but the tide was setting too strongly in the opposite direction. The debate over whether it was "our war" even erupted in the pages of *Partisan Review* and split the editors apart. However the intellectuals might babble, it was to be *our* war soon enough. At that time there was a great deal of talk that it would be a long war—perhaps another Thirty Years' War. That prophecy sounded like doom to the ears of our generation. We had grown up under the fatality of a war to come; and now that it was here, it seemed fated to drag on and take the rest of our life with it.

Yet the next two years (1940–42) were to be the most calm and secure I ever knew Delmore to have. We were now in the easy upland, the shining plateau of success of his life, and it seemed to stretch so evenly and smoothly before him that he didn't have to worry about tumbling down from it. I was teaching philosophy at Brown, and he was in the English Department at Harvard. We were able to see a lot of each other, for Cambridge was just a short commute from Providence. He hadn't quarreled with any colleagues yet; he seemed to like them or at least find them interesting in one way or another, and they appeared to make much of him. His academic chores were light, and teaching was a new and enjoyable experience into which he threw himself with enthusiasm. He took a lot of pride, more than he would admit, in being part of Harvard; and walking in the Yard, he would be amused to invoke some of the old ghosts of its tradition. The small intricacies of academic social life in Cambridge interested and even absorbed him for a while, and he didn't seem to miss too much being away from New York.

The last time I saw him before the war caught me up in its movements and separated us was in the summer of 1942. He and Gertrude had rented a pleasant little house near the Charles River. We sat talking in his study upstairs, with the river sparkling in the near distance, and the mild sun streaming over Delmore's shoulders where he sat near the window. A visitor dropped by, a young man connected with Harvard. The talk was of the war and the draft, and how they were already altering the lives of the people we knew. Delmore was in a jovial mood, and I am glad to fix this phase of our friendship in one final joke. The visitor brought up the sad case of another Harvard teacher who in a burst of patriotism had volunteered for military service and been rejected for a physical defect he had carried with him since childhood but over the years had come to forget: one testicle had never completely descended after birth.

Delmore began to laugh. "My only regret is that I have but one testicle to give to my country." Then he was suddenly choking with laughter, "And they turned it down."

On this merry note we may leave him ready to face Hitler and the Axis.

II.

And perhaps there our friendship should have ended.

It had had its passing rough spots and quarrels, and perhaps the in-fatuation and naïveté of youth hung over it all; but throughout there had been affection, devotion, and lots of fun. In his own peculiar way he was the most magical human being I've known—the adjective does not seem to me excessive. What followed was so different that trying to remember him now is like staring at a photograph torn down the middle, the two parts of which do not match. If I were to pray for the repose of his soul, to which of the two would I pray? I'm not sure I can piece them together now. I've lived so long letting the one part die and be buried within me that it pains me already to turn it up and look at it once again.

And yet in the first year after the war, when we were seeing each other again our friendship was for me as intense and happy as it had ever been.

I have already told in an earlier chapter of my first visit to him at his flat, and the shadows hanging over that meeting that I did not see at the time. I did not want to see them. As we sat around talking al-most till dawn, I felt that for the first time I was really back from the war, and that everything between us was as it had always been. But putting memories together now, I think he was already a changed man. Several things had happened that left their mark upon him, and his embroilment with these matters was one of the causes that had kept him from writing to me. Gertrude and he had divorced. While the marriage hadn't been what would be conventionally described as a happy one, it had nevertheless given a certain center and cohe-siveness to his life. He had never really ceased to love her; and when she was gone, there was the loneliness that Delmore never liked and that the various women on the wing only made more acute afterward. The other blow was the very poor reception of his second book, *Gene-sis*, when it came out in 1943. His first book had launched him; his second, which he expected to solidify his position, nearly undid it. I was away at the time, but a friend who saw much of him during that period thinks to this day that Delmore never really recovered from the fate of that book. I am inclined now to agree. For one thing, Delmore never talked to me about it in the years after 1945. Since he talked about almost everything else under the sun, this particular omission must have been because the experience had been so painful that he had desperately to keep it buried.

And now too he would often talk about Scott Fitzgerald. In the pre-war years Fitzgerald had never been one of his special writers; whenever he made mention of him, it was usually casual and in passing. But Fitzgerald was the symbolic figure of early success that had then deserted the writer, and as such he had taken possession of Delmore's imagination. Fitzgerald's saying that "in American lives there are no second acts," ran as a refrain of despair through Delmore's conversation. The identification with Fitzgerald had pushed into another area—drinking, as a necessity to stoke the moral and physical engine. In the last summer I spent with him before the war we would sometimes of an evening take a long stroll down to Harvard Square, and if there was nothing else doing, end at—yes, a drugstore fountain drinking ice cream sodas. We children of the Depression tended to have modest habits. Now, on this first night of our meeting again, we were talking together at a bar—that was something new between us. I had learned to do a little drinking during the war, but that was on occasions; Delmore had been driven to drinking under the whip of more necessitous demons.

I didn't notice these things at the time; or, rather, did not put them together, for I was too glad at being back with my friend. There was also the particular exhilaration of those years. We were free from the war, the future lay open before us, and for the time being we were content simply to exist in this blissful limbo. An extraordinary sense of security and power pervaded the nation, for we had come through the war intact and strong. We didn't even have to worry about the ugly specter of the atomic bomb; we were the only ones who had it, and of course we would never misuse it.

It was against that background of euphoria that we were taking up the old friendship. When I joined the staff of *Partisan Review* in the fall of 1945, we were even more closely bound, for we were now part of the same family. To be sure, a rather special and peculiar family—and like every family, with its own particular tensions. My wife was away for two months, and I was now eating dinner regularly with Delmore, just like old times. But it was not quite like old times, for something new had been added. "There must be something wrong with them," Philip Rahv grumbled, "they eat together every night." William Phillips defended us with the obvious: "Why not? It's boring to eat alone." But common sense, as I found out, wasn't always taken at its face value in this milieu I had entered. In the old days there had been a careless privacy to our friendship; now there might always be someone looking over your shoulder for possible motives. Freud was very much in the air, to be used for whatever purposes suited the moment.

We didn't always eat alone. Delmore was keeping company with Elizabeth Pollet, and from time to time the three of us would have dinner together. I liked Elizabeth, and thought she was good for Delmore; and since he was being reluctantly forced toward the idea of a new marriage as the only protection against his gnawing loneliness, I hoped his choice would light on her. Meanwhile, though, he was enjoying things as they were, and he could let the matter drift.

But in a few months he would have to return to Cambridge, and he dreaded the idea. This was another grave change from three months earlier. Once he had felt secure and at ease at Harvard, but now it loomed before him as a place of exile from New York. He had quarreled with some influential people there and he felt isolated from the other faculty. Teaching had once been an enthusiasm, or at worst he had taken it matter-of-factly in his stride. Now it seemed a lifeless chore. In his depressed moods, he would simply come to class, tell the students to read, and sit there in silence. He tried to keep the thought out of his mind—departure was still months away; but then two months, one, and finally a matter of days.

And then he was gone; and with the return to Cambridge begins a series of incidents—small at first, but ominously mounting in intensity —that foreshadow his decline.

He had hardly been back when I got a telegram that his furnace was broken and would I please come up. I didn't know anything about furnaces, but I could sit with him in the cold until the repair man came. Thereafter the requests were without excuses, and he didn't need any, for it was fun to be there with him. He had the top half of a large house, and there was plenty of room. Over the years he had had many visitors, either staying with him or passing through: Auden, Robert Lowell and his then wife Jean Stafford, Dwight Macdonald, and others. But when the guests, the anecdotes, and the gaiety were gone, solitude became more crushing. Then he wired me to come up, or dashed off to New York. His life was becoming a shuttle between New York and Cambridge.

Months later I got a letter from him denouncing me and declaring our friendship over. It came absolutely out of the blue; there had been no quarrel, and the letter itself was too vague as to any particulars beyond my "monstrous character"—the details of that too unspecified. I was distraught, and went off to William Phillips for consolation and wisdom, as we often did in such situations. I know now that William already grasped more of Delmore's grave state than I could imagine, but out of sensitivity to me kept his tongue in check. A few minutes after I was back home from William's, the bell rang, and there was Delmore unexpectedly arrived from Cambridge grinning at me. I was too astounded to mention the letter, and he said nothing. Now I deliberately watched and waited through our conversation, but he never mentioned it. He appeared to have forgotten it entirely. His erratic behavior had now reached a new stage; it was no longer sequential. What he might do in a momentary fit of rage had no relation to what preceded it and disappeared from his mind after the doing.

He had more or less decided by this time that he wanted to marry Elizabeth; but he had hung back too long, and she had found another man. My bell rang one morning, and there was Elizabeth, frightened and gasping for breath, stammering that Delmore had arrived unexpectedly, and was at her apartment. He was violent, delivering all kinds of threats, and he would have kept her from leaving except that she had crawled down the fire escape. (He had not struck her, only raved madly. Up to now Delmore had never gone in for physical violence; to let himself go in emotional violence seemed to be enough. Saul Bellow, in his novel about Delmore, represents the hero as beating his wife. Since Bellow is generally scrupulous about the important facts, I have no doubt he is accurate here, and that in his later and crazier state Delmore lapsed into this kind of violence too.) I rushed over to Elizabeth's flat, and he quieted down when I came in. We spent the afternoon together, and I put him on the plane back to Boston, telling him I'd come up as soon as I could. He was quietly drunk by this time. It's one of the few times I can remember when I abetted him in his drinking.

He resigned himself to the loss of Elizabeth but was drinking more. When he next came to New York, it was to deliver a lecture at Columbia. There seemed a possibility he might get a job there, and he wanted desperately to leave Cambridge. He arrived several days early, but had no lecture ready and was generally in bad shape. I got a typewriter into his hotel room, and volunteered to sit and type at his dictation. He would start a few sentences, flounder, go blank. I would prod him: Do you mean this? Can you say that? And he would flounder on a few paces more, and then the process would be repeated. Somehow we finished it, but I never found out how it went over with its audience.

This incident sticks out so strongly in my mind because Delmore used once to have a tremendous facility. He could bat out a review or an essay, once its main lines were fixed in his mind, at a sitting. Now that the facility was gone, he grew panicky. The thought of failing powers was beginning to be with him constantly. He would quote the lines from Chekhov—*Uncle Vanya*, is it?—where the aging character claps his head, and exclaims: "My God, I'm forgetting simple words. Am I losing my mind?" The years of barbiturates and alcohol must be taking their toll. His final breakdown, besides its emotional roots, may have had a physiological basis in sheer brain damage.

He didn't get the job at Columbia (for which he came to blame the influence of Lionel Trilling); but he left Harvard anyway. His return to New York, however, did not save him; instead it was the beginning of a descent into the maelstrom, in which I was nearly drowned with him.

In the normal course of things the very close friendships of youth are bound to change. The two people grow up, they enter different ways of life, and they too become different in the process. The friendship may remain, but it has to alter. History does not record what Damon and Pythias became to each other in later life. But certainly their friendship would have been severely taxed if they had been on the staff of *Partisan Review* together. I'm not referring at the moment to the individual personalities of the editors, but to the atmosphere of the whole circle. There were a great number of talented people in the offing—contributors, ex-contributors, anti-contributors, or people generally on the fringe where this and other circles overlapped for the different groups were not then hermetically sealed off from one another. Bring a number of talented people together in a close area, and the neurotic tremors begin vibrating. Nobody seems to have devised a way of building an intellectual and literary circle without adding immeasurably to the usual stock of nastiness, bitchery, and backbiting that are the lot of human nature. Perhaps that is the price humanity has to pay for the centers that generate ideas. Other cultures seem to take these unpleasant facts in their stride and at least maintain the formal gestures of civility. Americans, who have less of a tradition of the salon or literary circle, fling themselves at the business with greater innocence—and violence. It was not exactly an atmosphere to bring Delmore further peace.

As the influence of Marx diminished in the late forties, the figure of Freud loomed larger. We were perhaps the first generation in America to take Freud and psychoanalysis seriously. The twenties, so far as I can gather from my reading, took him along with D. H. Lawrence as an invitation to "throw off your inhibitions." We, on the contrary, faced the matter of psychoanalysis with intellectual solemnity. If you could dig up the money at all, you had a moral and an intellectual duty to face yourself in psychoanalysis, and you were shirking if you didn't.

Naturally then, the question of art and neurosis began to occupy our minds, and it bloomed as a theme in the pages of the magazine. Insensibly, a certain disposition crept in to consider neurosis as a privileged and special condition, almost a gift that the artist had to nurse and yet keep under control if he were to produce. If I feel less intellectually benign toward neurosis nowadays, it is partly because of what happened to Delmore. Neurosis, as it takes over a personality, may become just plain ugly and destructive. Period. If the theme of art and neurosis were to be taken up afresh, perhaps Delmore's case might be a good one with which to reopen the question.

Freud was a disaster for Delmore. It has often been pointed out that one danger of Freudian therapy, particularly in the wrong hands, is that it can turn the patient's attention away from his current life problems and fix it on the years of his childhood. Delmore's self-absorption was such that his mind was already excessively riveted on the "family romance" of his own childhood; and he needed no encouragement that way. He had picked up the collected works of Freud at a Cambridge bookshop, and as he pored relentlessly over the pages, he was absorbed more and more into his own diagnosis of his childhood. In the process he also built up an elaborate conceptual armor—adorned, to be sure, with all the twists and turns of his fabulous wit—through which it became harder to break. When he did finally get to an analyst, he treated the latter as an adjunct to the construction he was building. Once he came away from a session and crowed to William and me that he had spent the whole fifty minutes arguing theory with the doctor and the latter finally conceded Delmore was right. Afterward, William commented sadly: "Delmore is crazy. He pays money to teach the analyst his business."

Meanwhile Elizabeth had reappeared. She was still in love with Delmore, but feared his violence and avoided seeing him. I became an emissary between them; I would assure her that Delmore was getting better, that he was now less stormy and violent, while with him I would urge caution and restraint. Delmore was making efforts, but I wasn't convinced he could hold his calm. One afternoon we were sitting in Washington Square when he suddenly leaped to his feet and started berating me: "We live in the world of Hitler and Stalin, and you tell me to be gentle!" His chest was heaving, his nostrils quivering, almost as if he were physically choking in his frustration. He was struggling hard, fighting off the need for some kind of release into physical violence. If in later years, as Saul Bellow recounts, he did become physically violent, it was simply that these present barriers against it gave way.

Nevertheless, he kept to my restraining advice with regard to Elizabeth, and shortly they were together again. I felt I wasn't so needed, and might withdraw a little. By this time I was a pretty feeble reed myself, and in no way fitted to be a pillar of strength for anybody. But this peaceful withdrawal was not to be. I've recently met Elizabeth again after all these years, and I am glad our friendship remains: "Delmore asked too much of you," was her brief summary of that period. Yet it was not the "too much," but the kind of thing asked that I couldn't give anymore. We began to quarrel. We had quarreled enough in the past, God knows, but the quarrels quickly joined were as quickly blown over. But now the quarrels left a bitter taste.

Delmore had become the play-actor of his own neurosis, he had begun to melodramatize his own evil. *The Brothers Karamazov* was one of his favorite books, and he used to say of Dostoevski, "Just think, he himself was all three brothers at once." And Delmore, I believe, had come to aspire after being all three himself: Alyosha, the spiritual; Mitya, the violent; Ivan, the intellectual and destructive one. But the family doesn't stop there. Old Karamazov, the father who begot them, the self-dramatizing buffoon, is in his own way all three sons at once. And Delmore, in his abusing and self-abusive tirades, began to resemble him at times more than any of the three younger and grander figures.

The tawdry details of our final break-up don't matter at this late date. The ending of a personal relationship is rarely a grand exit in the style of opera; usually it's a squalid anticlimax disfiguring everything that may have been splendid in the friendship. This one took place under the implacable heat of a New York summer, Dostoevski unspoken but in the air, and madness lurking in ambush. Delmore's self-destructiveness could not help being destructive of me. I remember his eyes, always so expressive, gloating now in self-recrimination for his own evil, as he called it, and sucking me into it with him. I couldn't take it any more, and walked out. And so walked away from a relationship that had been a good part of my life.

The decade of the 1940s—with its particular promises and hopes, illusory or otherwise—had already passed away; and now our friendship was down the drain after it.

III.

And so we were no longer friends.

We said hello when we met, exchanged brief and civil chitchat, attended some last editorial meetings together. It may seem silly, in view of our past friendship, to have kept our relations on so external a footing; and there were times when our conversations would go on for a little longer while, and I was tempted to continue; but I was afraid Delmore might swarm all over me in his possessiveness, and I drew back. As soon as our friendship was over, it became a foregone conclusion that I would leave *Partisan Review*—the interest and energy I had to give had also waned for other reasons. I don't know exactly the last issue my name appeared on the masthead, and I haven't looked back to check.

Delmore and Elizabeth, now married, had moved to the country somewhere in New Jersey. Judging from a few of his later poems and from Elizabeth's remarks, I think he found there for a short while as much happiness as he could expect. But he was also tortured, obsessed more and more by the fear that he was losing his mind. The consumption of pills and liquor continued. Elizabeth was now living in fear of him, and she finally fled. Delmore went wild, publicly now, had a run-in with the police, was taken to Bellevue but quickly released. There is no record of it, but I have a hunch he may have ended by explaining Freudian theory to the psychiatrist there.

Eventually they were divorced; and Delmore, now left on his own, reappeared in the city. I ran into him a few times in the Village—I was now walking through different streets there than formerly. We greeted each other—a wave of the hand, hello, and that was all. He was looking seedier now. I heard vague reports of how he had become a barroom raconteur at the White Horse tavern, willing to tell stories to anyone who would stand him a drink; how he was living from pillar to post, from one cheap hotel room to another, or from one to another apartment of anonymous girls who took him in as a stray. But nothing definite from anyone who was seeing him regularly or knew him from the past.

Then one day I ran into William Phillips and heard from him the alarming news that Delmore had crossed the line of sanity and was hearing voices. For a moment there flashed before my mind the image of Delmore once again caught up in the buffoonery of his illness, dramatizing his symptoms in mockery of himself and others, but somehow surviving indestructible underneath it all. No, William said, this was real; and as we were walking, he pointed toward the steeple of the Empire State Building: "Delmore says the voices come from there." You play out a role long enough and desperately enough, you tell yourself it isn't for real, you are only playing, you believe yourself telling yourself you are only playing, and there comes the moment when you have already crossed the invisible line and the role takes you over.

A few years later came the sudden news of his death—alone, of a heart attack, in a cheap hotel room. My first feeling was one of relief that he was at last released from his torment.

Now that he is dead, the legend of the *poète maudit*—the doomed and sacrificial poet—has already claimed him. And before we submit to the distortions that current sentimentalities are likely to inject into this kind of legend, we had better attempt a cooler glimpse at the work he has left. It may, surprisingly enough, provide some very strong imperatives to revise our stock notions of the alienation of poetry and the poet today.

Delmore had a beautiful lyrical talent, and so long as he continued to write anything at all, this gift never left him altogether. It's too early to say what in our period, if anything, will be lasting; but my own judgment, perhaps partial, is that some of his lyrics will survive. But the great triumphs of modern poetry were nearly all in the lyric, and he wanted to help restore verse as a narrative medium. He admired Hardy's *Dynasts*, for example, before it became fashionable among some academic critical circles. But where Hardy had dealt with the fate of nations and empires, and the broad sweep of history, Delmore chose a very personal subject matter as the material for his own major narrative effort.

This work is *Genesis*, and the abstract design of it does not look too unpromising. It tells the story of the growing up of a Jewish boy (Delmore himself), of how his forebears came to this country, the strife of the parents and how it is inflicted as a trauma upon the boy. The narrative would be carried by the prose, but a rather cadenced and rhythmic prose that wouldn't be too glaring a contrast to its verse accompaniment. The latter would take the form of a poetic comment and explication of the narrative in the manner of a Greek chorus. Not bad as an idea, though the material is conventional: another version of the archtypal Making of an American. But the execution of the design fails badly. When I first read *Genesis* I was away from Delmore during the war, and I was disappointed by it, as most of his readers were; but such was my faith in his powers that I imagined it a temporary stop and regrouping of forces, the working out of material that he had to assimilate and come to terms with, before he went on to the next stage. I have just reread it, with a greater effort at objectivity, and I am depressed at how unsatisfactory it is. The subject matter is so intensely self-centered that it could have been better expressed in a lyric, and so small in its actual narrative content that it might have been done in a short story. The prose sections that carry the narrative have some lovely touches but are generally so drawn out that they become flat and monotonous. The accompanying verse commentary becomes too sententious and self-conscious, and the actual texture of the verse heavy and lumpy. How could Delmore, so acutely perceptive as he then was, not have grasped one simple and central fact about this work, which in itself would be enough to cancel any other virtues: that it dragged and was dull? The only answer seems to be that he was hypnotized by the personal subject matter—the history of his own childhood—that he became trapped in his narcissism and could not detach himself enough to judge the work as a piece of writing.

In fiction, he produced two stories that stand out amid all the writing of this kind in his period; and considering the vast volume of stories written during our time, this is no small accomplishment. One is the near-perfect story, "In Dreams Begin Responsibilities," which—significantly enough—uses a kind of surrogate lyrical form to express his inveterate family material. The other story, however, shows even more strikingly the specific powers of the fiction writer in bringing into compact focus a wealth of social and human observation. The story is "America! America!" and it says more in its few pages about the saga of the Jewish lower-middle class in American life than most of the genre novels we have had on this theme. Here again, the material is gossipy, familial, local, but the powerful poetic impulse of the author transmutes it into something universal. When this poetic impulse leaves him, his stories, to my mind, go flat. I know that people whose judgment I respect have spoken well of his later stories, but I think they are willing to settle for less from this author, with his extraordinary gifts, than I am. In these later stories he falls off into the self-complacency of the raconteur retailing anecdotes. The flatness of style, originally deliberate, becomes monotonous because it is a dodge —an evasion of the requirement that an author imaginatively project his characters before us. The raconteur assumes we all know the people he's gossiping about, and imagination in consequence becomes indolent.

For literary criticism he had great brilliance and potential, and I believe, had he given himself to it, would have become one of the foremost critics of our time. His early pieces give very alert and sensitive readings of Hardy, Auden, Tate, and others. He was starting from Eliot as a base, but his young man's mind was swarming with ideas, and he was working toward a position and point of view of his own. But the patience and concentration needed for this were denied him— for a number of reasons, partly because his energies were dispersed into other writing, principally perhaps because of his own psychological disturbances. A few of his essays, as I knew personally, were produced under such stress that it's a wonder he could get them out as coherently as he did. Moreover, he tended to look on his own literary criticism as a *parergon*, an effort incidental to his main business of poetry. He once joked to me about the laboriousness with which Philip

Rahv carved out his essays: "You've got to remember that English is still a foreign language for Philip." But Delmore's facility hasn't served him well. Rahv's essays stand up, rounded off and complete in their own terms; Delmore's provide us brilliant flashes.

When you add it all up, what have you? Certainly, not something at all negligible. To have written anything, however fragmentary, which stands out among the productions of one's time, and which may even lay some claim to permanence, is a higher achievement than to turn out a body of work fully formed but glittering only for the moment. But just as certainly, his achievement is a failure—and a failure all the more in relation to the power of the original gifts. For Delmore was not merely one of the many talented persons who go astray; nowadays talented people swarm all over the literary landscape; he happened to have major gifts, and in saying this, I weigh my words. And in the light of those gifts we have to judge his literary career as a human failure. It is that human failure that currently invokes the facile image of the *poète maudit*—the poet exiled and accursed by the tribe.

Delmore's case is thus assimilated to the suicides of Sylvia Plath and John Berryman (who, as it happens, dedicated his *Dream Songs* "to the sacred memory of Delmore Schwartz"). They are sacrificial victims —whether to the cruel Muse or to that usual scapegoat, Society, is not often clear. A. Alvarez, speaking of Sylvia Plath, actually says that her death was not suicide but murder—in this case, implying she was slain by Poetry itself, a rather strange attribution of an actual crime to an abstraction. Dwight Macdonald attributes the cause of Delmore's downfall to society, but in a peculiarly vague way. He compares Delmore's situation with Poe's a century earlier, and he cites an eloquent paragraph from Baudelaire about the solitude and isolation of Poe in nineteenth-century America. With all due respect to Macdonald, the comparison with Poe is downright foolish. Delmore had recognition, grants, sinecures; and in his last years he was given a position at a university when he was in a condition where anyone else would normally have been considered unemployable—the exception being made because of his eminence as a poet. In somewhat the same vein as Dwight Macdonald runs the blurb on the back of Delmore's *Selected Poems*, and its language is worth noting: "Delmore Schwartz acted out in his life . . . the alienation of the poet from our society." One has to ask just exactly what it would mean to "act out the alienation of the poet from society." I can only imagine a poet living alone and unknown, far from the center of things, whose manuscripts are discovered after his death. Delmore, however, had to be at the turbulent center of things, involved in a literary review where all the jangling wires of human intercourse got crossed; whereas the gentler "alienation" of a Wallace Stevens, who worked in an insurance office, or of William Carlos Williams, who served as a small-town doctor, might have left him more peace and in the end more time for his poetry.

(Apropos of the alienation of Wallace Stevens, Delmore used to tell the story of Stevens's remark after he had delivered a lecture on poetry at Harvard: "I wonder what the boys in the office would think of that." The point seems to be that there was such a disparity between Harvard and "the boys in the office" that Stevens must have suffered from a sense of alienation. On the other hand, there is a later story that Stevens was in fact such a poor insurance executive that the company tolerated him in his high office only because he was a great poet!)

And Delmore himself in a sense has already rejected these glib interpretations beforehand: in a lecture in 1956 when he delivered a blast against Allen Ginsberg and the Beat poets for their facile howl of alienation—an alienation which, as is quite inevitable in the course of modern society, had immediately become the *in* thing.

"I cultivate my hysteria," said Baudelaire, the spiritual father of the *poètes maudits*. It was a dangerous and foolish thing to say. You don't cultivate your neurosis, it cultivates you—as the parasite cultivates and saps its parent host. With some significant modern artists neurosis has perhaps shaped their vision, but in doing so has also cramped and warped it. Baudelaire's own work suffered: the *nostalgie de la boue* makes the aspirations toward the spiritual life that much more unreal, distant and tenuous, and theatrical. When Tolstoi inveighs against Baudelaire as a Parisian decadent, a precious and artificial aesthete, he is of course overemphatic, as is his manner; yet he has a point to which we shall have to pay attention more and more. But however matters may lie in the perennial question of art and neurosis, the overwhelming lesson in Delmore's case is that the sickness impeded and ultimately destroyed the talent.

Macdonald does make a concession: "granting that . . . psychological difficulties were also important." In the post-Freud era this "granting" and "also" are really precious. The troubles of Delmore and John Berryman (whom I knew fairly well in an earlier period), and from my reading I would say of Sylvia Plath too, were so obviously deep-seated in the personality that neither of those abstract specters, Society or Poetry, can be invoked as culprits. Berryman, when I knew him, was a meticulous enough person to have worked as a clerk or junior executive; he would have ended as an alcoholic nonetheless. And if Delmore had had another occupation, he would have experienced comparable difficulties to those he had.

One can construct the scenario of explanation for him that one wants. The materials for it are abundant and obvious enough. The violent split between father and mother; the father whom he admired as a hero and a pleasant companion, only to hear him constantly vilified when he was back with his mother; and the constant closeness of his relation to the mother, who did everything she could to prolong his narcissism, exaggerate his ego with praise, and yet in her clever and poisonous way insinuate in the child, then the boy, and then the young man, that the love and trust of anybody was not to be believed.

But I offer no explanation. Before the human heart our explanations seem to fall short. Despite his absorption in Freud, Delmore would have liked the final word about himself to be spoken from the region that Dostoevski inhabits. Here I simply report a conversation we had one afternoon in 1941 when I had come in from Providence to visit him over the weekend. Occasionally he liked to hear whatever I might be doing in class, partly to keep friendly tabs on me, partly to pick up something he might put to use somewhere in his own writing. I had been teaching Leibniz and somehow got into the problem of Predestination and Free Will. Students, however secular-minded they may pretend to be, are always attracted by the logical niceties of this question. Egged on by them, and also out of my own curiosity, I had researched the question back through the medievals to the drastic passage in Paul, Romans IX, where he speaks of the Potter who, for reasons of his own, shapes some to be vessels of grace, and others to be "vessels of wrath." The last phrase caught Delmore's attention: he begged me to go on, and eventually flung himself passionately into the discussion.

The point not to be forgotten—as well as the thorn in the side for all later philosophic commentators—is that these vessels of wrath retain their freedom throughout. They were created to *be* "vessels of wrath," but all along the way of that "to be" they conspire to make themselves such, their own will thus sealing their damnation. In their wrath they will themselves wrathfully; they cannot help willing in this way, but this "cannot help" is in turn the act of their own will affirming itself desperately and defiantly.

The conversation evidently made a deep impression upon Delmore. When I visited again on the following weekend he had written a sonnet about it, one of those informal bits he wrote from time to time, both as an exercise in versification and to document some thought or experience he felt worth preserving for future use. "Yes," he said quietly, "I'm such a vessel of wrath." It was he who made the personal application; I hadn't even thought of it until he spoke now.

I did see him and speak with him one last time, and I have kept this now to the end. It was in a Village restaurant. I had gone there with a friend of former days from the Midwest who was passing through New York and wanted to see something of the city. He was the least bohemian type imaginable—clean-cut, solid, thoroughly in the American grain; but I thought a little whiff of the Village would amuse him. As it turned out, we got a little more than bargained for.

When we sat down, I saw Delmore across the room with a girl whom I didn't know. There came the ritual of the nod and the wave of the hand, but somehow this didn't seem enough now. Time had passed (this was around 1961) and the memories of emotional violence had receded; some more friendly gesture seemed called for. I went over to his table, said hello, and we talked rather pleasantly for a minute or two. He didn't bother to introduce the girl. When they had finished dinner and were on the way out, I invited him and the girl to sit down with us for a brandy. For a while his conversation was normal and quiet, but then there burst forth a Delmore I'd never heard, not even in his most agitated moments. He started to rant and rave. I'd always been able to follow the acute zigs and zags of his talk without any effort, but this time I found him incoherent, and his voice raucous and harsh in a way I'd never heard it. He meant to be friendly, he wasn't ranting at me but *toward* me—toward me and against the world, as if he would pull me in with himself in some vast conspiracy against it. Every so often the tones of our past friendship would emerge, waver haltingly for a moment, and then be quickly swallowed back into the wrathful and incoherent bellow. I did what I could by way of flattery and cajolery to make him feel better, but there was no moderating his torrent. The girl kept plucking his arm to leave, and at length he yielded.

Our waiter came running over: "I guess you'll want another brandy after that." Delmore's voice—yells, grunts, groans—had filled the place, and the waiter had stood listening across the room, wondering what was taking place. Feeling shaken and drained, I gulped the fresh brandy. The effect was to relax me suddenly, and I burst into tears. I was embarrassing my friend, I knew, but he waited patiently for me to subside. When he spoke, his voice was kindly but matter-of-fact: "Don't take on so. There's nothing to be done. He's beyond salvaging." The voice of reason submitting to inexorable fact. There crossed my mind the ancient story of the father weeping for a dead child. A Stoic philosopher, passing by, tells the father: "Why do you weep? It is irrational. Your weeping will not bring him back to life." The father replies, "That is why I weep, because it cannot bring him back." I looked across the table at the straightforward and uncomplicated face that had spoken, and thought: Yes, that is why I weep, because he cannot be salvaged.

Appendix

I add this editorial piece not for its intrinsic merits but for whatever value it may have as historical documentation. The reader will find the circumstances surrounding it discussed in Chapter Four.

Younger friends to whom I have shown the editorial have expressed amazement that things seem to be at the same pass now as thirty-five years ago. And it is their vividness of response on this point that has led me to reprint the piece here.

THE "LIBERAL" FIFTH COLUMN*
An Editorial

"It is time that the United States
awoke to the truth that nothing is
gained for us vis-a-vis Russia by
'getting tough'."
          Editorial, *The New Republic*

THE NEW REPUBLIC proclaimed this oracular "truth" on April 22, 1946.
Several weeks earlier the German Social Democrats in the Allied zones
voted 7 to 1 against fusion with the Communists; the fusion was later
forced in the Russian zone without any vote. Two weeks after the editorial
appeared, the French people had administered a smashing defeat to the
Communist Party by rejecting the proposed Constitution. The French referendum cannot be interpreted as a swing to the right, since many Socialists
had voted no, against their own party leadership. Moreover the vote called
out the 30 per cent absentees from the last election, who, had they been
Rightists, could have voted for the parties of the Right at that time. The
French people wanted democracy and their nose was keen enough to smell
out the totalitarian odor of the Constitution; their referendum cannot be
twisted to show any other meanings. Both French and German votes indicate that there are millions on the Continent with genuine democratic longings—even though many (for example, the French absentees) are not yet
expressed completely by any party. If these democratic longings do not
exist in Europe, we can write off European civilization right now; if they do
exist, they will certainly not grow stronger by being fed the bread and
water of a feeble American foreign policy. As long as American policy is
weak and halting, the peoples of Europe will persist in believing that the
United States intends to withdraw altogether from Europe, and they will
gravitate helplessly—and under the threat of terror—into the Russian orbit.

* *Partisan Review*, Summer, 1946.

Meanwhile in New York a journal which calls itself "liberal" is advocating a policy to sell out these millions into Stalinist slavery. When *The New Republic* published this editorial, it was actually helping to herd Social Democrats into concentration camps in Germany; helping to shoot democrats, of every shade and color, in Germany, Poland, Rumania, Bulgaria, Hungary, Austria; helping to strengthen the French Communist Party's reign of terror over public opinion—a terror which will wax or wane with the position of Russia in western Europe.

These are not metaphors of political rhetoric, but a literal description of the consequences that follow from the political behavior of *The New Republic*'s editors. The juxtaposition of their editorial statement with political reality could scarcely be more pointed, and the direction in which it points has now become unmistakable: that we have in our midst a powerfully vocal lobby willing to override all concerns of international democracy and decency in the interests of a foreign power. The foci of this infection are the newspaper *PM*, and the liberal weeklies *The Nation* and *The New Republic*. Insofar as the advantage of this foreign power becomes an exclusive end in itself, this lobby functions, as we shall show, as a virtual Fifth Column. Whether those who march always know where they are going, whether they are confused about their purposes or really taken in by sham purposes, they are not any the less a Fifth Column. Political positions are weighed by objective consequences and not by subjective intentions. This is a wellworn truism by now, but it seems it has to be dinned afresh into these "liberal" ears. But when intentions fall out so persistently and shrewdly in one pattern, may we not also conclude that they have a pretty shrewd glimpse of the objective direction?

How has this Fifth Column arisen? and in what forms does it exert its pressures? To answer these questions we must look briefly at its genesis: the process step by step by which the Column has been recruited in our midst during one year of peace.

II

The European War had hardly ended in May 1945, when the rumblings in the Communist Party were announcing preparations for a new line and a new ideological offensive. These had to remain, for a while, preparations only: the war had not yet become entirely imperialist again, as in 1939-41, for Russia had still to play its part in the Japanese War, having in fact to hasten into Manchuria ahead of schedule lest the United States finish the war before Stalin had won it for us. The explosion of the atomic bomb was the dramatic end of the war. The two events were also a simultaneous political explosion which blew the war honeymoon to bits, ushering in the new groupings in world politics and opinion.

Humanity had good reason to be afraid now that the atomic bomb had arrived. But in the first rush of journalistic panic it was not always easy to distinguish those afflicted with fear and trembling from those who were merely glad of an occasion to don the robes of prophecy and pontification. The "liberals" seized upon the occasion to launch a new campaign of war hysteria. War in 90 days! *The New Republic* screamed on the first page of one of its issues—which appeared, by the way, more than 90 days ago. The "liberals" fell all over themselves to violate elementary logic: the bomb was no secret, therefore the secret should be given immediately to Russia; or to violate common sense: the secret itself would explode—as if the secret were a ticking infernal machine, and human hands, with definite political purposes, were not required to make a bomb and set it off. *But behind all these antics the essential point of the "liberal" attack was simply that the United States had the bomb and Russia did not.* Here was the first clear-cut indication that a new standard of judgment for all political and social questions had been found: the potential advantage or disadvantage to Soviet Russia. The "liberal" distrust of the United States was as unbounded as their confidence in Russia: in American hands the atomic bomb constituted a threat to the peace of the world, but of course, if Russia had possession of it, the world could rest secure. The millions of Stalin's political victims, if they could speak from the grave, might have a wry comment to make upon this.

The Fifth Column developed steadily through the period of the first meeting of Prime Ministers in London. Molotov wrecked that conference on a legal technicality, which brought an enormous advantage to Russia. The longer Europe remains unsettled by treaty, the longer it remains prey to the occupying Red Army and the Soviet secret police. Stalin can be counted upon to continue this delaying tactic as long as he can get away with it. (The Russian evasiveness when Byrnes recently offered a Security Pact, which would take the Red Army out of certain parts of Europe, was another illustration of this tactic.) Molotov also began to fiddle another tune to which our "liberals" were soon jigging. He accused the United States of playing "atomic power politics," although up to that point Byrnes—considerably to Bevin's disgust—had been giving a remarkable imitation of a diplomatic Caspar Milquetoast. But this did not bother the "liberals." They were showing that they could dance just as eagerly as the Communist Party to the official tunes of Russian propaganda—and with just as much disregard of the facts, too.

When the UN Security Council met at London, Russia pulled another tactic out of its bag of tricks which has since been worked by the "liberals" for all it is worth. To forestall inquiry into Russian operations in Europe—at that time in Manchuria too—Vishinsky launched a prompt attack upon British actions in Greece and Indonesia. This is Stalin's game of international chess. When a piece in an advanced attacking position is threatened, he relieves by attacking elsewhere, maintaining thus a continuing but shifting pressure. Again the "liberals" showed they knew how to take the cue. It was their signal to launch an all-out campaign to hate Britain. Some of *PM*'s cartoons on the theme of Perfidious Albion became a match for those of the Hearst-McCormick press, when these latter were conducting their anti-British campaign in the interest of isolationism and Hitler. It used to be considered a liberal principle to attack imperialism wherever it showed its head. But now if Russian imperialism is attacked, the "liberals" rise as one man to shout: "what about Britain?"

This dazzling piece of "liberal" logic may be summed up as: *Two wrongs make a right—and it is always Russia's right.*

The dizzy corruption of logic and morals was to reach new depths in the handling of the Iran case by the "liberal" press. The same day that the *New York Times* carried the first reports of the continued presence of Soviet troops in Iran, I. F. Stone produced in *PM* a masterpiece of journalistic insinuation. Stone turned what purported to be an account of the Iranian situation into a minute description of his own confusions as a reporter in getting the news. Before he had finished, he had managed to convey the impression that the illegal presence of the Red Army in Iran was just a concoction of rumor and innuendo, and probably of British origin at that! Stone does not impress us as one of the innocents; he is a clever enough reporter to know what he is about, and the fact that he has subsequently hewed persistently and bitterly to the anti-British line, shows very well what he is about.

All of *PM*'s staff were promptly mobilized for the defense of the Socialist Fatherland. Max Lerner, who had already played so many comic roles in his career hitherto that one more could not matter, rushed before the footlights in the role of the Ambassador of Iran: he knew better than Hussein Ala what the situation and policy of Iran should be. *PM* transformed the question into a struggle between Britain and Russia for Iranian oil, and the onus of guilt was shifted, as one would expect, to perfidious Britain. "We have become tools," I. F. Stone wrote, "in the hands of the British who are intent on maintaining a status quo that would deny Russia additional oil and an outlet to the Mediterranean." What folly for the United States to take Britain's side in this criminal struggle to deny Russia the oil of Iran! From this hackneyed anti-British perspective, the facts that Russia had broken a treaty and that her troops were in a foreign country against that country's will, disappeared from the canvas beneath the deft coloring of *PM's* apologists.

History was making strange bedfellows when Nicholas Murray Butler and Henry Wallace raised their voices together in support of a new found common friend, Joseph Stalin. Butler, old and ailing, had reached the ripe, overripe, fruit of wisdom, to see that Russia had a right to foreign oil. (In official publications Soviet scientists have stated that Russia has some 58.7% of the world's oil resources—and most as yet undeveloped!) The doddering capitalist was delighted to think this might be just good oldfashioned "respectable" imperialism after all. The fellow travelers, Wendell Wilkie style, would love to believe that Russia is capitalist at heart, and so no worse, and therefore just as good—by God!—as anybody else. In a speech in the Middle West Henry Wallace pleaded that even if Russia were wrong on every point, we should give in for the sake of world peace. At last, a frank and open appeal for appeasement! The hotheaded patriot who screams "My country, right or wrong!" could hardly be more partisan and unreasoning than Wallace in the interests of Russia.

This from a Secretary of Commerce—who, but for a manoeuvre of party politics, might now be President of the United States. Never during the disastrous period of fellow traveling in the 'thirties were the Russian zealots so highly placed in American life. On the floor of the Senate itself, Claude Pepper, senator from Florida, made the startling and impassioned accusation that in its foreign policy the United States was pushing Britain's imperialist cart and "ganging up" with Britain against Russia. The corruption of language could scarcely go much beyond this. "Ganging up" had suddenly become the expression for an inquiry (which would have had to remain at most an inquiry, since the Russian veto would have prohibited any action) into the illegal occupation of one country by another. Meanwhile the tireless Eleanor Roosevelt continued her tiresome pleas for "cooperation" with Russia in order to insure Russian "security."

Yes indeed, Russia must be secure even if we have to sacrifice the security of all her neighbors. What about Iran's security? The "liberals" were too busy to raise that question. Besides, as everyone knew, certain reactionary groups in Iran were a distinct threat to Russia. A nation of 15 million a threat to a nation of 180 million! When *Izvestia* made this fantastic charge, it was following precisely Hitler's tactic towards a country he had designated for absorption or conquest—and Hitler had never been more preposterous in his claims of imaginary aggression.

Russia may not gobble up Iran, and the Iranian case may subside into a relatively minor incident; in which case you can expect the "liberals" to set up a shrill hue and cry that the matter was a tempest in a teapot, engineered by reactionaries, over a few months' longer occupation by the Red

247

Army—a few months being, as we all know, but a moment in world history. *PM* has already hinted at this high-historical piece of apologetics. Certainly Russia's operations in Europe are *at this time* immensely more important, however rich in oil Iran be and however decisive Middle Eastern politics will shortly be in the total international picture. Stalin's pressure on Iran eliminates the possibility of opposing pressure against Russian operations in Germany, Poland, and the Balkans. Above all he gains time, which is so important for him. The longer he can operate unchecked in Europe, the more democrats he can shoot. Even if forced to pull back entirely from Iran, he has still won a point, since the Council has been unable meanwhile to bring up the other situations. The Russian game of chess again, and so far working beautifully. Thanks in large part to his various Fifth Columns abroad, who consciously or unconsciously, succeed in misleading public opinion.

But whatever happens, the Iranian case cannot be considered a "minor" incident if for no other reason than that it showed beyond any shadow of doubt what Stalin thinks of the UN. When Gromyko walked out of the Council, his gesture epitomized perfectly the essential *rudeness* of Stalin's regime. Russia—with whom its foreign advocates have persistently demanded "cooperation"—showed itself unwilling to cooperate on anything but its own terms. Protected by its veto, Russia knows it has nothing to fear, and indeed everything to gain from the UN. Stalin will continue to use UN as a front organization, while he carries on his own brand of politics behind the scenes. A few more such walkouts and the UN will be revealed to the world for the farce it is.

Even the die-hard "liberal" apologists became a little hard-pressed as the Iran affair dragged on, and were glad to draw a breath of relief when the Russian satellite, Poland, brought up the Spanish question before the Council. A breathing spell at last! Once again they could wrap themselves in the toga of self-righteousness and parade as aggressive champions of democracy all over the world. The "liberals" of *PM, The Nation,* and *The New Republic,* have always required easy whipping boys; this permits an uninterrupted glow of self-righteousness without at the same time exacting the stiff price of intelligence and courage, two qualities they have shown little trace of for the last dozen years. But the very fury of their attack upon Franco is a self-betrayal: they are really for democracy except when and where the interests of the Soviet Union are involved.

Every argument they use to justify intervention in Spain is a valid argument for intervention in Russia. Spain is totalitarian? Beside Stalin's monolithic police state Franco's fascism is a petty and amateur affair. Spain is anti-democratic? Stalin has not only extinguished all traces of democratic liberties among his own people but is engaged in snuffing out these liberties wherever the Red Army has spread. Spain gave aid to Hitler during the war? By the Russo-German Treaty of 1939 Russia gave the indispensable aid, which was the very possibility of launching the war; that treaty was further supplemented by an economic pact under which, during 1939-41, Stalin gave considerable economic aid to Hitler while the latter was fighting the western democracies; and Franco never gave Hitler such outright military aid as the Russian invasion of Poland in 1939. Franco is a menace to world peace? The comparison here becomes laughable when we consider that Spain is a fifth or tenth-rate military power, while Russia maintains the largest standing army in the world, spread at this moment over vast areas outside its own territories; and when we consider too that every recent international tension, which has made the peoples of the world think fearfully of war, has resulted from one or several aggressive manoeuvres on the part of Stalin.

If the "liberals" are uncompromisingly for democracy throughout the world, why not then be for it in Russia too? If they are still in doubt as to the facts about Russia, why not ask the UN for an international commission of inquiry, as in the case of Spain? But the expectation that they will struggle for any such policy is vain. The "liberals" will continue to evade comparisons between Spain and Russia. They will continue to think that Stalin's totalitarianism is somehow different from Franco's, different from Hitler's. Alas yes; the considerable difference is that the former is able to enlist "liberal" support.

III

It is clear from this outline of their recent behavior that the "liberals" are embarked upon nothing less than a policy of *appeasement of Russia*. This may exist as a confusion and a fear in many "liberal" minds, but it is none the less a policy for all that. A policy is simply the effective direction in which one throws all one's available political weight.

We are not surprised to find appeasement repeating itself, and the new instance already shows all the features familiar from the appeasement of Hitler. It involves first, as we have already said, a campaign to hate Britain, conducted with a new subtlety but with infinitely more political viciousness than that of the Bund and America First groups. When Henry Wallace publicly declares: *"We have no more in common with imperialist England than with Communist Russia,"* he is playing exactly the same game as the appeasers who shouted: *"We have no more in common with imperialist England than with National Socialist Germany."* But those appeasers were at least more honest: they did not masquerade as champions of democracy and they did not have the effrontery to label themselves "liberals." By a well-timed coincidence Ralph Ingersoll's *Top Secret*, which portrays the

British as secret villains of World War II, appeared during the Iran case. One step further and Ingersoll himself would have been openly accusing (in effect, he made the accusation at a rally at Madison Square Garden on May 16) the British of working for the defeat of Russia in World War II.

A second feature of this new appeasement is the consistent attack upon the State Department. The discrediting of the State Department very shrewdly paves the way for the kind of attack in *The New Republic,* from which we have quoted at the head of this article. Not the least dishonest aspect of that attack was its pretending to assume that the State Department had in fact already got sufficiently tough against Russia. Instead of trying to needle this timidly conservative Department into a more aggressively democratic policy, the "liberals" are trying to make it stoop lower to the despicable service of pulling Stalin's chestnuts out of the fire for him. Bad as the State Department may be, to treat it as a greater menace to world peace than Stalin's Politburo, to criticize it violently and consistently while Russia is criticized, if at all, only lackadaisically and inconsistently—is a piece of sheer idiocy or sheer knavery.

But perhaps the grossest ingredient in this new dish of appeasement is the constant "liberal" shout of war. They accuse certain groups of talking in a way that can only lead to war, but in fact nobody is beating the drums of war more loudly than they. Nobody else has been staging public rallies (complete with Frank Sinatra, Olivia de Havilland and the indispensable Pepper) for or against the next war; nobody else has been working with quite such political cunning on the veterans—that particular segment of the population which is most disaffected with war and therefore the easiest prey to propaganda for appeasement—transforming mass-meetings, ostensibly for veterans' housing, into rallies to sanction Russian aggressions.

At this point it is hard to believe we are not being confronted with a piece of conscious deception. Obviously the American people does not want, and could not now be mobilized into war. War cannot therefore be a political issue now. To cry it up as such is to conceal the issues which are really now at stake. If Stalin believed that war were an issue now, he would very quickly change from lion to lamb and pull back from his aggressions. *Pravda* bleated towards Nazi Germany during 1939-41 like the gentlest of lambs because Stalin knew Hitler would not have stood for the kind of treatment now being given the Allies. Stalin knows that neither Britain nor America is ready for a new war, and he strikes while the iron is hot, grabbing off as much as he can now while there is no prospect of armed opposition. This is the immediate compulsion behind present Russian aggression. The "liberals" have been so persuaded that Stalin does not have Hitler's economic compulsions to expand that they will continue to believe whatever he does is done only for "security." How far does he have to go before they will believe it is aggression and not security that is at issue? To the Rhine? the Bay of Biscay? perhaps when Stalin starts to cross the English Channel? But beside the economic reason of plunder, there may be political reasons for expansion—a specifically totalitarian dynamic of expansion to survive. The dictatorship has always been rationalized by keeping the Russian masses in a state of mobilized hostility towards the capitalist world outside Russia. But whatever Stalin's ultimate purposes (and for the present we can only speculate about them), there can be no doubt about what he has done. *We do not have to establish a motive to prove a crime when the crime has been publicly committed before the eyes of the world.*

But granted (which we do not believe) that the situation is as hopeless as "liberals" make out, and any consistent criticism of Russia will necessarily lead to war; will appeasement, then, do any better? If war is that inevitable, does it not become a man's duty to cry stinking fish and face up to the inevitability? Was war against Hitler avoided by appeasement? On the contrary, Hitler might have been permanently checked had he been firmly opposed at his very first steps towards aggression. If war between Russia and the United States is not inevitable, then perhaps the only way to avoid it is to stop licking Stalin's boots. After the disastrous record of a whole decade's appeasement of Hitler, surely it is the depth of folly and self-degradation to cast sheep's eyes at appeasement as the way out of war.

IV

But what, then, do the "liberals" really want? Their program is clearly appeasement, but are there any principles, political or human, behind it?

If you are an international revolutionary, you may override the interests of your government for the sake of some principle you regard as higher—international socialism, for example. You may, on the other hand, be a patriot in the specific sense that in a given international situation you think the political values of your government—however imperfect or circumscribed—are worth preserving. You may, finally, persistently override the interests of the government under which you live for the sake of some foreign government from no general principle except that . . . well, you are for that foreign government. The three available political alternatives thus boil down, without needless division into subspecies, to three: you are an international revolutionary, or an American patriot, or—a Russian patriot.

To which category do our "liberals" belong?

International revolutionaries? They have certainly been keeping the secret very well hidden all these years. Have they ever committed themselves even to socialism against capitalism? Well, on the other hand, they have never committed themselves to capitalism against socialism. By being neither fish nor fowl, the "liberals" think to confound their critics, who will not know whether to take them with hook or gun. But taking them as fish *and* fowl, and allowing them moreover to shift their ambiguous biology wherever convenient, we still cannot make them come out right with either logic or principle. If they were socialists, they could not be loyal partisans of the regime which has paralyzed or destroyed every genuine socialist movement in our time. Perhaps they are the most incorrigible of myth addicts as still to believe that Russia is socialist in fact or tendency? Then they put themselves beyond the pale of serious consideration, they lose authority to speak seriously on any issue, since they will obviously be immune to any and all facts whenever convenient for them. When J. A. del Vayo recently stated that "after all, Russia *is* socialist," he demonstrated only that *The Nation*, which is currently paying his expenses for a European tour, might keep a tighter fist on its checkbook. Nobody is going to believe that a man who makes this statement will be able to report on even the most obvious political matters abroad. But if Russia were really socialist "after all" (after what? one wonders; even del Vayo cannot make the statement without some repressed demurrer), and the "liberals" are pro-Russian because they are socialists, then why shouldn't they be unequivocally and openly for Russian expansion? Why stop at their present mealy-mouthed and squirming rationalizations instead of declaring openly they want Stalinism to engulf Iran; the Balkans; Europe to the Rhine; yes, to the Atlantic—and then why stop there? Instead of smirking slyly at their discomfitures, the "liberals" should root openly for the checkmate of Byrnes and Bevin whenever this pair goes into conference against Molotov. 'But you really ask too much of me,' the "liberal" pops up at this point, 'you ask me to be *unequivocal!* We know that Stalinism is "after all" socialism, and we "liberals" are all secretly socialist at heart, and that is why we condone Stalin's socialist imperialism; (Stalin showed us there can be "proletarian millionaires," and why not then "socialist imperialism"?); but we distinguish between condoning and declaring openly for expansion, we are careful only to condone Russian expansion because "after all" Stalinism may not be socialism and how can we be sure we are really socialists?'

No; however you try to cast up the "liberal" accounts, you cannot make them come out right, you can find no consistent principle behind their support of Russia. We are left with the third category (their behavior obviously removes them from the second): the "liberals" can only be described as Russian patriots.

We therefore call them a Fifth Column. We do not mean by this that they are officially designated and paid by this foreign power; nor do we claim to say what the term of their services will be. Their services are probably altogether too spontaneous and "pure." But this does not mitigate their guilt for a campaign of concealment, misrepresentation, and deception in the interest of a foreign power—all the more reprehensible in being without any other discoverable principle than the devotion itself to that power. We are long since familiar with the fact that the Communist Party is a Fifth Column, since it proposes no other end for all its actions but the advantage of the Soviet Union. The "liberals" have become a more potent and dangerous Fifth Column since they succeed in deceiving a good many more people.

It would take a very obtuse intelligence to miss the Stalinist sympathies of *PM*, but the methods of *The Nation* and *The New Republic* are at once more confused and more subtle. *PM* is the plebeian wing of the "liberal" admirers of Russian totalitarianism, and its methods are therefore far cruder and more obvious. But many readers of *The New Republic* and *The Nation* probably miss the subtle internal politics of book reviewing that goes on week by week. When *The New Republic* wished a reviewer for Victor Kravchenko's *I Chose Freedom,** what happy stroke of editorial inspiration led them to select Frederick Schuman? Is it possible they did not know the kind of review they would get? There is a point beyond which the hypothesis of innocence cannot be stretched. Does the editor know anything about his reviewers beforehand or does he hand his books out to any chance comer in the street? Schuman did not disappoint: for vilification and innuendo his review might almost have adorned the pages of *The Daily Worker.* Among other things, he defended Stalin's terror by pointing to gangsters, lynchings, and strikes in the United States; without mentioning, however, that gangsters and lynchings are not the official program of our government as their equivalents are in Russia. As for strikes, perhaps Schuman would prefer the situation (no doubt, "after all, socialist") in Russia, where striking is a capital offense. The "liberal" weeklies will maintain they are conducting their reviews on the principle of freedom of opinion—remarkable that the "freedom" seems to run so consistently one way. Why didn't they allow such "freedom of opinion" in their reviews of Hitler and Mussolini? Schuman himself is scarcely worth noticing, except that his choice as reviewer and his review itself afford a particularly startling whiff of the "liberal" putrescence. Schuman justifies the Russian terror as the necessary price for rapid industrialization; apart from the fact that this argument has been refuted time and again, all evidence pointing to the continual disruption of industry by the political dictatorship—we might analogously justify Hitler for having reduced unemployment and built magnificent roads in Germany, and Mussolini for cleaning Italian cities and making the trains run on time. From the vantagepoint of Mars or of history 500 years from

* Scribner's. $3.50.

now, some scholarly dilettante might draw up a list balancing favorable and unfavorable aspects of Hitler. But for those who had to confront it politically in their lifetime, a pro and con attitude would have been absolutely without political content: Hitler's regime was essentially vicious and had to be opposed politically. This point is capital, and I dwell on it because the "liberals" somehow think they can salve their conscience by various sad remarks from time to time—which prove their "impartiality," no less!—acknowledging that political liberty is not all it should be in Russia. Are they too stupid or too knavish not to understand that an attitude neatly balanced of pros and cons toward a criminal dictatorship is absolutely without political meaning? Or, rather, that it has only one political meaning: sanction of that dictatorship? The ineffable Ingersoll, again, tells us: "We must be neither for nor against Russia, but we must try to understand her." Analogously, we should have been neither for nor against Hitler, but simply have tried to understand him.

If some "liberals" are slightly taken aback at being called a Fifth Column, they should learn from Victor Kravchenko that the Russian employees in the Soviet Embassy at Washington were allowed to read, of American publications, only *The Daily Worker, PM, The Nation,* and *The New Republic.* During the appeasement of Hitler, these "liberal" publications pointed loudly to every praise the Hearst-McCormick press received in Berlin as proof that these publications were virtual Fifth Columns. Is it likely Stalin is any less shrewd than Hitler in knowing who his friends are?

How far, after all, can we go in excusing people as being unconscious of their motives? When Ralph Ingersoll likened (*PM,* May 6) our military and diplomatic position to Nazi Germany's vis-a-vis Russia, perhaps he was not aware that he was very definitely implying that the United States, and not Russia, is most like Hitler. Perhaps not; but to gauge the effect of such an editorial we must take into account the distinct frame of reference established by the newspaper for its day to day reader—the fact, among many, that Ingersoll's statements appeared in a newspaper whose cartoons have already evolved a snarling bullying type of U. S. Army officer as an American counterpart to the familiar caricature of the ramrod monocled Prussian. And Ingersoll himself gave his cartoons a speaking voice when he declared (at Madison Square Garden, May 16) that the American military were even now engineering a war against Russia—precisely as if we had here a German High Command operating *as a political force* behind the back of the people. We are not writing this editorial from Kansas or Texas, where we have only the printed words of *The Nation* or *The New Republic* before us, but from New York City, where our frame of reference is also further established by the conversations in which we occasionally engage these people. In conversation certain "liberals" become more open or more unwary (it is hard to say which), and when pushed to the point of the alternative, "You must choose between the United States or Russia," they will occasionally break down and admit: "Well, then I choose Russia." Here the Fifth Column confesses itself, but do not expect such frankness from a "liberal" unless you have pushed him to it.

Yet what do "liberals" really stand to gain from their present frenetic support of Russia except their own political death? A world-wide victory of Stalin would mean their immediate extinction. On the other hand they would fall as the first victims of a terror of the Right as American public opinion becomes solidly mobilized against Russian aggressions. Such a mass movement in America would be condemned to fall into reactionary hands by the "liberals" themselves because they have failed to provide their own leadership. In a situation of impending or existing hostility between America and Russia, the Communists will be dealt with for what they are, outright foreign agents; but reactionaries, never remarkable for niceties of discrimination, have always been a little color-blind to the difference between pink and red friends of Russia, and the reaction, when it comes, would thus clamp a tight lid on all political liberties and perhaps even bring a ruthless suppression of civil liberties. If certain "liberals" insist on digging their own graves, that might seem to be their private affair; but we hope they are not past pleading with that they are dragging down in their own ruin everyone else who genuinely desires the values that have been an essential part of traditional liberalism.

Of course, Stalin may go too far, and the "liberals" will be forced to pull in their horns. At the moment, they are already giving signs of pulling back: Stalin has already gone so far that they are hard put for rationalizations to defend him. These days *PM* can defend Russia only by keeping silent, and switching the spotlight to the threat from German rearmament due to the evil laxness of . . . the British. But do not be deceived, reader. Stalin has only to pull back a little, make a few beneficent remarks about peace and the UN, and his American well-wishers will be on the bandwagon again, shouting what a fine fellow he is, and how slanderous, criminal, and endangering to international relations were such criticisms of him as this.

V

The "liberals" will not lack for other evasions meanwhile. Their fecundity for rationalizations has already shown itself bottomless. No doubt they will accuse the views of this editorial as expressing an attitude of hatred towards Russia or Stalin (they do not bother to distinguish)—and probably a "pathological" hatred too, if you please. (Lately they have taken to using a debased and comic version of Freud for what they imagine is an avantgarde weapon of vilification.) But it is they who really hate the Russians, since they do everything within their power to further Stalin's oppression of this people. And is it so pathological to hate a criminal dictator? Was it pathological to hate Hitler? Then it was also pathological for Locke to hate the Stuarts, Voltaire to hate the Bourbons, Beethoven to hate Napoleon, Marx to hate Louis Napoleon, Lenin to hate the Tsar. The "liberals" will also have other worn and tattered scarecrows to shake—any opportunism that comes to hand, anything indeed to avoid the issue of democracy against totalitarianism. Unlike the "liberals," we have no secret and ambivalent longings to "escape from freedom," which we mask under one rationalization or another; and having no totalitarian commitments anywhere in the world, we insist that no compromise be made with totalitarianism.

Until they take at least this minimum position, the "liberals" are obviously usurping a name which they have despoiled of every vestige of its original meaning. The word "liberal" now retains nothing but a denotative value, and that is why we have persisted in keeping it in quotation marks throughout. Whether or not the "liberals" here spoken of will ever earn the removal of quotation marks from their "liberalism," they have already made themselves a long past to live down.

Index

259

Pollock, Jackson, 135, 136, 143,
148–49
Pop Art, 155
Pop culture, 72
Pope, Alexander, 181
Populism, 9, 170
Positivists, 151–52, 183
Posthumous Essays (Eliot),
208
Pound, Ezra, 157, 223
Pravda (newspaper), 250
Princeton University, 89
Proust, Marcel, 164, 167, 168
Provençal poets, 157
Psychoanalysis, 38, 135, 175,
176, 230
Puccini, Giacomo, 133

Rahv, Philip, 1–4, 6, 7, 9, 10,
12–13, 54–55, 63–64, 69,
162, 164–65, 191, 194–208,
211, 221–22, 227, 235–36
"analytic exuberance" of, 42,
162
anti-Communism of, 194–95
art scene in New York, 133,
146, 151
at Brandeis University, 12,
197, 204–5
compared to Meyer Scha-
piro, 55
conservatism of, 71–72
death of, 1, 185
as embodiment of New York
Intellectual, 69–74
essay on Kafka, 202
Existentialism and, 101, 102,
108, 109, 111, 112, 113,
116, 124–25, 126

first encounter with Barrett,
54–55, 56
hatred of Stalin and Sta-
linism, 76, 78–79
irritation with Rosenberg,
58–59
as a literary critic, 197–205
marriage of, 63–64
Marxism of, 71, 79, 124, 125,
164, 205, 206, 208
personality differences with
Phillips, 36, 39–40, 41, 45,
53
personality of, 29, 38–39, 54
post-War American Liberals
and, 79–81, 82, 83, 84, 91,
92, 94
relationship to Dostoevski,
200–3
relations with Greenberg,
137, 138, 139, 145, 150
Schwartz on, 73
Swiftian pessimism of, 205–6
Rebel, The (Camus), 121–22
"Redskin and Paleface"
(Rahv), 199
Religious writing, 179–80
Revolution of 1870, 84
Richards, I. A., 202
Romantics, 177
Roosevelt, Eleanor, 247
Roosevelt, Franklin D., 77
Rosenberg, Harold, 57–59, 69,
164
as an art critic, 143–44, 150,
156–59
Rosenfeld, Isaac, 112
Ross, Barney, 49
Ross, Harold, 2

Besides a long and distinguished academic career as a professor of philosophy, William Barrett has also been active in the intellectual and literary life of America. He was for many years an editor of *Partisan Review* and then literary critic of *The Atlantic*. He was among the first of a small group of philosophers in this country who, shortly after World War II, introduced European Existentialism to America.

Among his other books are *Irrational Man* and *The Illusion of Technique*.

MAR 1982

0